Theoretically nuanced and empirically rich, this new study by sociologist Dr. Cerasela Voiculescu offers a unique and fresh insight on how power, in neoliberal times, is impacting on different Roma communities in Romania. Based on field observations, community work and academic reflection over nearly fifteen years, the project deftly deconstructs "the Roma" as both political projection and as non-static actors with strength, agency and their own power in challenging and disrupting gadzhe (non-Roma) institutions and the state. This is a remarkable book that strikes new ground in both Romani studies and critical accounts of neoliberalism and power.

Colin Clark, Professor of Sociology and Social Policy, University of the West of Scotland, UK

Against the omnipresent liberal governmentalist language of THE Roma, exclusion, ethnicity, and human rights, Cerasela Voiculescu combines Eric Wolf and Michel Foucault in a comparativist historical ethnography of relational power and counter power within and around the evolving social landscapes of two Roma communities in Romania. The result is theoretically astute and empirically insightful.

Don Kalb, Professor of Sociology and Social Anthropology, Central European University, Hungary

European Social Integration and the Roma combines rich historical ethnography and theoretical insights on power to study the production of Roma as a problematic population requiring specific intervention by state and transnational actors. Voiculescu shows that Roma populations are diverse and produced by complex relations to power over time. The homogenising picture of poor Roma requiring specific types of intervention to assist their 'integration' is critiqued by this complex and engaging work that will raise a number of questions on how 'Roma' are produced as 'problems' requiring intervention.

Prem Kumar Rajaram, Academic Director of CEU's Roma Graduate Preparation Program (RGPP) and Associate Professor in the Department of Sociology and Social Anthropology at Central European University, Hungary

In Cera's nuanced and deeply engaged study she has created a powerful framework for understanding the position of Roma in Europe. She ranges across history, anthropology, politics and sociology to produce a profound critique of space and power. The book is a major contribution to the field.

Dr Angus Bancroft, Senior Lecturer, Sociology, University of Edinburgh, UK

This book is a Foucauldian analysis of power in the interpersonal relations between Romanian local state officials and Roma. It is based on extensive and illuminating interviews with Roma and local officials, and fieldwork observation in municipal and social service offices, and through concise and clear theoretical discussions, links the data from these to the extensive literature which attempts a systematization of Foucauldian theory.

Thomas Acton (2017): 'European social integration and the Roma: questioning neo-liberal governmentality', *Ethnic and Racial Studies*, DOI: 10.1080/01419870.2017.1341993

The book is highly recommended to social and political researchers and theorists as it makes available crucial academic and civic contributions by deconstructing the subalternity of one of the most racialised population in Europe, critically questioning neoliberal governmentality, and raising timely, fundamental questions in relation to knowledge, the political subject, the governance of politically unrepresented populations and transnational neoliberalism.

Cosmin Radu (2017): '*European Social Integration and the Roma: Questioning Neoliberal Governmentality*', *Critical Sociology*, DOI: 10.1177/0896920517744162

This book represents a sophisticated discussion of the relations of power on micro- and macro levels that define Roma–non-Roma relations historically and today. Voiculescu's book represents a counter-account to the neoliberal politics of identification, integration and inclusion of 'vulnerable groups', and instead presents the highly diverse Roma populations as agents of power in their own right. I recommend this book to all interested in Roma issues.

Research Professor Ada I. Engebrigtsen, NOVA/OsloMet – Oslo Metropolotitan University, (former Oslo and Akershus University College of Applied Sciences), Norway

European Social Integration and the Roma

In the field of political sociology and European studies, there has long been a discussion on transnational neoliberal development and ethnic groups' self-governance. Notwithstanding, there has been limited exploration in relation to modes of knowledge production associated with neoliberal governance of the Other (e.g. ethnic and indigenous groups), which capture its idiosyncratic modes of political expression and empowerment.

Drawing on Michel Foucault's political philosophy, this book discusses European social integration as transnational neoliberal governmentality and challenges its epistemologically constituted subaltern subject. Neoliberalism is questioned in relation to its programs of securitisation of poverty and authoritarian models of self-governance associated with instrumentality of the market. In this context, the book's rich political historical ethnography develops a new framework for the study of social power. Furthermore, inspired by Jacques Ranciere's radical philosophy, *European Social Integration and the Roma* proposes a new mode of knowledge production about populations excessively subjected to neoliberal governmentality, heralding the epistemological decolonisation of the neoliberal subject.

Presenting an insightful new prospect in critical sociology as well as the conceptualisation of power and the application of theories of governmentality, this book will appeal to scholars interested in the areas of political sociology and anthropology, international relations, social and political theory/philosophy and post-development studies.

Cerasela Voiculescu is an experienced researcher interested in critical social and political philosophy/theory with specific reference to social and political power, neoliberalism, knowledge, governmentality and European studies.

Routledge Advances in Sociology

For a full list of titles in this series, please visit www.routledge.com

183 **Origins of Inequality in Human Societies**
Bernd Baldus

184 **Confronting the Challenges of Urbanization in China**
Insights from social science perspectives
Edited by Zai Liang, Steven F. Messner, Youqin Huang and Cheng Chen

185 **Social Policy and Planning for the 21st Century**
In search of the next great social transformation
Donald G. Reid

186 **Popular Music and Retro Culture in the Digital Era**
Jean Hogarty

187 **Muslim Americans**
Debating the notions of American and Un-American
Nahid Kabir

188 **Human Sciences and Human Interests**
Integrating the social, economic, and evolutionary sciences
Mikael Klintman

189 **Algorithmic Cultures**
Essays on meaning, performance and new technology
Edited by Robert Seyfert and Jonathan Roberge

190 **Becoming Anorexic**
A sociological study
Muriel Darmon

191 **European Social Integration and the Roma**
Questioning Neoliberal Governmentality
Cerasela Voiculescu

European Social Integration and the Roma

Questioning Neoliberal Governmentality

Cerasela Voiculescu

LONDON AND NEW YORK

First published in paperback 2019

First published 2017
by Routledge
2 Park Square, Milton Park, Abingdon, Oxon OX14 4RN

and by Routledge
711 Third Avenue, New York, NY 10017

Routledge is an imprint of the Taylor & Francis Group, an informa business

© 2017, 2019 Cerasela Voiculescu

The right of Cerasela Voiculescu to be identified as author of this work has been asserted by her in accordance with sections 77 and 78 of the Copyright, Designs and Patents Act 1988.

All rights reserved. No part of this book may be reprinted or reproduced or utilised in any form or by any electronic, mechanical, or other means, now known or hereafter invented, including photocopying and recording, or in any information storage or retrieval system, without permission in writing from the publishers.

Trademark notice: Product or corporate names may be trademarks or registered trademarks, and are used only for identification and explanation without intent to infringe.

British Library Cataloguing-in-Publication Data
A catalogue record for this book is available from the British Library

Library of Congress Cataloging-in-Publication Data
Names: Voiculescu, Cerasela, author.
Title: European social integration and the Roma : questioning neoliberal governmentality / Cerasela Voiculescu.
Description: Milton Park, Abingdon, Oxon : New York, NY : Routledge, 2017. | Series: Routledge advances in sociology ; 191 | "Simultaneously published in the USA and Canada by Routledge"—Title page verso. | Includes bibliographical references and index.
Identifiers: LCCN 2016022171 | ISBN 9781138898141 (hardback) | ISBN 9781315708737 (ebook)
Subjects: LCSH: Romanies—Europe—Politics and government. | Romanies—Europe—Social conditions. | Social integration—Europe. | Neoliberalism—Europe. | Power (Social sciences)—Europe. | Transnationalism—Political aspects—Europe. | Europe—Ethnic relations—Political aspects. | Europe—Politics and government—1989–
Classification: LCC DX145 .V64 2017 | DDC 305.8914/9704—dc23
LC record available at https://lccn.loc.gov/2016022171

ISBN: 978-1-138-89814-1 (hbk)
ISBN: 978-1-138-60876-4 (pbk)
ISBN: 978-1-315-70873-7 (ebk)

Typeset in Times New Roman
by Apex CoVantage, LLC

Politics is not the exercise of power. It is the political relationship that makes it possible to conceive the subject of politics (...).
                                                                Jacques Ranciere

What is questioned is the way in which knowledge circulates and functions, its relations to power.
                                                                Michel Foucault

The relation between answer and question is essentially a power relation, hence political: relation of despotic master and slave up in arms.
It is never the answer, but the question that sets the building on fire.
Let this door be a flame.
                                                                Edmond Jabes

*To Roma
and all those populations struggling for political recognition and liberty.*

Contents

List of figures xi

PART I
Book discussion and introduction 1

1 European transnational government for the Other 3

2 Transnational neoliberal governmentality: the moral
  economic order of neoliberalism and its subject 9

3 European social integration as neoliberal governmentality:
  epistemological colonisation of the subject 22

4 Why study power? Questioning the regime of subjection
  and submission of political subjectivity 29

5 Historical entanglements of power: from socialism to
  post-socialism in Romania 48

PART II
**A historical political ethnography of social power
among the Roma** 65

6 On the move within movement from socialism to
  post-socialism: Roma interactions with smooth
  vs. striated spaces of economy 67

7 Transformations of the state and Roma leadership:
  self-governance, state capture and Roma brokers 92

8 Mapping power relations through political fields:
  patronage politics, political patronage and Romani politics 113

9 Street level bureaucracy, documenting identity and
subjection of Roma to neopatrimonial state power 132

10 Self-governance and the political subject: Romani
Pentecostalism vs. semiological state apparatus of capture 149

PART III
The return to the political: epistemological decolonisation
of the subject and historical geographies of power 165

11 Sedentary vs. mobile interaction with spaces of power 167

12 Historical geographies of power: a theoretical and
methodological framework for the study of social power 171

13 The return to the political-thesis 177

Index 185

Figures

4.1a, b	Kalderash, their houses and courtyards	34
4.2a, b	Romanianised Roma in their district	36
4.3	Romanianised Roma district background	41
4.4	Kalderash man on the first half of the street, close to the main road	43
4.5	Kalderash's houses on the first half of the street, closer to the main road	44
4.6	Farmer with his child driving a cart in the Kalderash's district in Liveni	45
4.7	Kalderash women watering the garden in their courtyard	46
4.8	Farmer smoking outside his small house situated in between two impressive Kalderash's houses	46
6.1	Kalderash man in Alexandri demolishing the farmer's old house in the courtyard of his new property in order to build a house for his son	82
10.1	Kalderash's prayer inside the Pentecostal church	151

Part I
Book discussion and introduction

1 European transnational government for the Other

In the way Said (2003) expressed concerns about the Orient as an alter-ego of Western societies projecting their own cultural norms and rules of identification onto the epistemologically construed external Other, the Roma are politically imagined as the 'internal Other' (Balibar 2009) of the European model or Europeanness. Yet, Balibar (2009) considers that Roma need to be socially integrated, but social integration is a neoliberal problematisation in itself, and his statement confirms, once more, that Marxist realist analysis can, unfortunately, overlap discourses of power such as neoliberalism. They are seamlessly portrayed as an unrevealed subject[1] (e.g. 'who are the Roma ?')[2], under continuous scrutiny, inquiry and assessment of its peripherality, as part of a dialectical politics of appropriation and re-subjectification[3] of a boundary subject, strengthening the political imaginary of a European core identity. This brings similitudes to Black People in America and Jews in Europe (Kalmar & Penslar 2005), "subjected to a kind of internal Orientalism" (Wilson III 1981: 63), a Western colonising knowledge of the Other entangled with governmental practices, which aimed at exorcising the idiosyncrasies of an imagined non-Westerner or non-European which grounded their existence and expansion.

"Vocabulary, imaginary, rhetoric" (Said 2003: 41) of the West's Orientalism placed subjects of knowledge in a continuum of "scrutiny, study, judgment, discipline, or [and] governing" (p. 41). Notwithstanding, Orientalism is much more than a political doctrine of the West. It is an apparatus of knowing, colonising cultural identities and territorialising alternatively construed political subjectivities, employed by architectures of power – transnational polities – which reify and project their geopolitical needs of government (e.g. neoliberalisation of Eastern Europe) onto subjects of governance (e.g. the Roma in Europe). The Roma were construed, in Balibar's terms, as the internal Orientals or Orientalised subjects of a purified idealised Europe and "neoliberal conception of European governance" (Balibar 2009: xi), which still conforms to modern architectural models of apprehension and incorporation of the socially disobedient Other. Furthermore, he argues that the expansion of Europe and the EU triggered divisive mechanisms of categorisation and governance in relation to the Roma and Eastern Europe, which by default were projected as the reversed Other. The latter were mainly construed in relation to an antithetical ideology – socialism and its reminiscences – threatening the security of the Western model of economic and social development. EU enlargement brought these distinctions and dialectical antagonisms at the forefront of political and economic integration of the neighbouring antipode, which commanded processes of translation, epistemological and cultural appropriation. As he further suggests, within the political imaginaries of the already constituted EU, the Roma were projected as 'stateless people' and, therefore, disentangled from previous or current regimes of citizenship structured by Eastern European modern states in order to be appropriated as a signifier of processes of accommodation of Eastern Europe within larger frameworks of governance produced by a neoliberal Europe. In my terms, Roma were subjected to a *dislocated spatialisation of governance*, which diffused their subjection from the nation state policies towards transnational neoliberal governmental power discussed in this introduction.

In substance, EU enlargement implied a sort of pre-accession neoliberal 'normalisation' of Eastern European states, which had to undergo reformatory transitions promoted by big international actors such as the World Bank (WB), the European Union (EU), the United Nation Development Program (UNDP) and the Organization for Security and Cooperation in Europe (OSCE), which raised concerns about a population not yet developed or socially integrated, implicitly not subjected to its legislative structures and ideological contents.

> More recently, the processes of EU accession have been an important impetus focusing international attention on Roma issues from Central and Eastern Europe (...) Roma issues emerge under political criteria for accession as part of the subchapter on "human rights and the protection of minorities" that was adopted at 1993 European Copenhagen European Council.
>
> (WB 2000: 38)

Prior to 1990, "'European' institutions paid little attention to Roma/Gypsies" (Kovats 2001: 1), but after the fall of the iron curtain, when the former socialist states joined transnational polities such as the Council of Europe and OSCE, Western European states and associated large polities became increasingly interested in securitising Eastern European Roma migration (WB 2000), which was portrayed as a threat to 'the stability' of the European economic area. As already suggested, the Roma themselves were the signifier of Eastern European poverty and de-regulation, whose status had to be supervised constantly, and the OSCE was the first to pay attention to issues of securitisation of Eastern European populations. The High Commissioner of National Minorities (HCNM) (1993) report underlined both the intrinsic and extrinsic scope of its policies and prioritisation of their instrumental character aimed at migration prevention through a process of state allegiance enhancement involving higher standards of living "for the sake of such improvements, but also for the reduction in pressures on international migration" (p. 10). These programs were designed to provide "an enduring sense of belonging" (p. 10), social and economic, to migrants from Southern-Eastern Europe to Western Europe, who "unable to reintegrate at home may be likely to consider the international migration again" (p. 11). The implication of this programmatic deliberate governance of the Other as the migrant populations to the West was the localisation of the implementation of development and social integration programs in the home countries and ideological abode in the political and economic government of Western Europe:

> Every effort should be made to support such returned migrants, particularly in the context of more comprehensive programs for improving literacy, job training, and economic opportunity for Roma in their own countries.
> (HCNM 1993: 11)

Furthermore, under the requests for enlargement of the economic area, the EU started to "monitor candidates on minority protection" (Gugliemo & Waters 2005: 771) and frame its migration prevention policies as social integration of the Roma and populations generally considered 'poor' and 'vulnerable'. Yet, once the European inclusion of the Eastern European states was achieved, the EU internalised the problematic of governance and strengthened the focus on social integration and minority rights. Thus, "underlying concerns about Romani migration have not disappeared" (Kovats 2001: 2), but they have rather been incorporated into new strategies of securitisation of Roma migration as human and social development. Hence, it can be implied that the social integration of the Roma and the Europeanisation of its contents expanded progressively as a European discursive practice and bureaucratic machinery, but, in practical terms, continued as a transnational apparatus of governance of Eastern European migration. In other words, securitisation of mobility was politically translated into the language of human development and social integration, which mainly represented the Eastern European Roma as a European 'problem' that needed further assessment and supervision. New mechanisms of knowledge production and technologies of institutional governance, mainly extraneous to Romani civil society and nation states, became engines for transnational securitisation policies. Although the problematic of governance had become European, the population subjected to it has not been yet Europeanised. It was rather placed in a liminal position from where it was expected to acquire and realise the commitments of the so-called European social integration. Generally, the Europeanisation of the problematic of government for the Roma brought a dialectical command and technical passage between the freedom of movement and technologies of securitisation of migration in the format of human development and guided or 'good governance', largely employed by all transnational organisations for development.

> Security is directly linked to development: there is no development in chronically insecure environments (...). Security is key to regional stability, poverty reduction and conflict prevention (EC 2003: 7) (...) The concept of security is increasingly understood not just in terms of security of the state, but also embraces the broad notion of human security, which involves the ability to live in freedom, peace and safety. Security must be both as a national interest and as part of individual rights. Security systems reforms is an integral component of *good governance* [my emphasis].
> (p. 8)

In this case, security is tied to human development and governance, but also to further EU enlargement and, therefore, to migration prevention strategies, which discursively construed by transnational actors in development (EC 2003; WB 2000, 2005) need to be implemented by sending states. Thus, the migration of the Roma to Western countries remains a primary concern for regional EU stability and a target of securitisation apparatuses.

> However, the current situation of Roma living in poor conditions in enlargement countries has had consequences in terms of the increased number of Roma temporarily migrating to EU member states under visa-free regime and even applying for asylum. This can have a negative impact on visa liberalisation, which is one of the greatest achievements towards the integration of the Western Balkans into EU.
>
> (EC 2012: 17)

In this regard, the transition has been made from a 'human rights' perspective to that of 'governance', which "became an integral part of the [EU] Poverty Reduction Strategy" (EC 2003: 5). 'Governance' or 'good governance' was conceived by both WB (1992) and EC (2003, 2006) as a more comprehensive and less authoritarian concept in its definition, but a more controlled, pervasive and effective mechanism in its actions and leverage. It generally aims to organise the conduct of particular people and states, including the migration of Eastern European Roma to Western Europe.

> Sound management of migration is also a factor in ensuring overall a good governance (. . .). By promoting good governance the EU is addressing one of the important roots of migration.
>
> (EC 2003: 12)

> There was a broad understanding about the need for a new and strong partnership of all key actors in this field. Moreover, it became evident that only a targeted culturally sensitive approach, which aimed at inclusion of Roma into mainstream society, could lead to progress.
>
> (EC 2010: 4)

Furthermore 'marginalisation' was conceptually connected to poverty, and the social integration of populations such as the Roma became "instrumental in reducing poverty" (EC 2003: 5). In other words, programs of human development and social integration of 'the vulnerable' as mechanisms of securitisation of migration became entangled with the concept of governance of the Eastern European Roma. Yet, the whole responsibility for the undertaking was left in the hands of the EU member states and the site for the exercise of 'good governance' was confined to their jurisdiction (EC 2012). Overall, these institutional efforts for 'good governance' and social integration of the Roma have been expanded and incorporated into a matrix of transnational neoliberal governmental power

European transnational government 7

practically enacted by main transnational polities and organisations which deal with worldwide 'development' and governance of the Other (Escobar 2012).

> Furthermore, cooperation takes place in the framework of international organisations, such as the Council of Europe, the United Nations and their Agencies, the Organisation for Security and Cooperation in Europe, or the World Bank, as well as in multilateral initiatives, such as the Decade for Roma inclusion 2005–2015, or more informal networks focused on Roma issues.
> (EC 2010: 28)

All these transnational actors devise programs of social integration which, considered to be beneficial to the targeted population, are part of a broader neoliberal economic instrumental rationality which is expected to be incorporated into the new EU state apparatuses of governance. Decreasing welfare through the integration of the Roma into the official labour markets is aimed to be beneficial primarily to the Eastern European states, which can reduce their costs and adjust their economies to the national and global markets.

> According to a recent research by the World Bank, for instance, full Roma integration in the labour market could bring economic benefits estimated to be around € 0.5 billion annually for some countries. Great *participation of Roma in the labour market* would improve *economic productivity, reduce government payments* [my emphasis] for social assistance and increase revenue from income taxes. According to the same World Bank study, *the tax benefits* [my emphasis] of Roma integration in the labour market are estimated to be around € 175 million annually per country (EC 2011: 3). Studies demonstrate that the exclusion of Roma entails important economic consequences in terms of direct costs for public budgets as well in terms of indirect costs losses in productivity.
> (EC 2010: 3)

In other terms, the social integration of populations considered to be living at the edge of the newly 'liberalised' economies becomes "both a moral and economic imperative" (EC 2012: 5) that needs to be endorsed by the nation states. The latter "have the primary responsibility and competences to change the situation of marginalised populations" (EC 2012: 5) by engaging with the transnational governmental power's legal and technical or semiological apparatuses.[4] Thus, the social inclusion of the reversed Other to these political and economic commitments advocated by transnational organisations for development is part of a process of global economic 'liberalisation' and integration. Furthermore, this transnational governmental power and its enactments are mainly upheld by and in need for technical knowledge apparatuses and mechanisms of identification of the targeted populations.

> [C]ountries need to look carefully at their statistical instruments (for example, censuses and household surveys) and administrative data to assess how

8 *Book discussion and introduction*

> they can better capture information on Roma and other minorities that will be useful from a policy perspective. (. . .) More information on international practices, particularly in addressing the privacy issue on ethnic identification, is needed.
>
> (WB 2000: 39)

> In order to get useful data in the long term, the Commission will also foster cooperation between national statistical offices and Eurostat so as to be able to identify methods to map the EU's least developed micro-regions, where the most marginalised groups live, and in particular Roma, as a first step.
>
> (EC 2011: 13)

The quotes show how technical knowledge about the Roma and their conditions of existence is an essential component of governance, in a continuous process of regional expansion and diversification of its mechanisms of production, which are mainly yielded by transnational organisations and polities in collaboration with states, experts and also scholars in the field. Following this brief analysis, European social integration, the program of governance questioned in the framework of this book, can be seen as a reflection of these particular articulations between global-national social, economic forms of governance and technical knowledge production they are associated with, or in other terms as a transnational neoliberal discourse or neoliberal governmentality. The latter is further inquired into conceptually and theoretically in the next section, in relation to liberalism vs. neoliberalism, Foucault's discussion on government, knowledge and neoliberal subject of governance, issues of sovereignty, world development and human securitisation.

2 Transnational neoliberal governmentality
The moral economic order of neoliberalism and its subject

In the early 1990s, the reconfiguration of the social, economic and political space of Eastern Europe brought to the forefront the problematic of development, which has been progressively defined and tied to technologies of human securitisation, and ideologies of economic progress focused both on delocalised forms of governance and state-led ones. Human development, as an approach, was more attentive to the enhancement of the individual capabilities and realisation of human rights, an approach mainly promoted by the UNDP. On the other hand, an economic developmental perspective exploited the sovereign power as a form of conducting an Eastern European *ataxic democracy*[5] (see Ranciere 2010) which emerged outside of a legal framework ordered by global neoliberal governmental power.

> In Eastern Europe, the lack of a legal system conducive to private sector development is a severe impediment to privatization and new investment (WB 1992: 4) (. . .). Even in societies that are highly market-oriented, only governments can provide two sorts of public goods: rules to make markets work efficiently and corrective interventions where there are market failures (McLean 1987: 19–21). With respect to rules, without the institutions and supportive framework of the state to create and enforce the rules, *to establish law and order* [my emphasis], and to ensure property rights, production and investment will be deterred and development hindered.
> (Eggertson 1990, in WB 1992: 6)

The foundation of law was associated with order as the main first target in the process of the institutionalisation of the market. At a first stage the latter aimed at reforming the state and establishing the rule of law as mechanisms of ordering the social and apparatuses for the market appearance, command and corrective adaptations to a continuously reformed economic environment mainly portrayed as the Eastern European transition to a market economy.

Without assuming the responsibility of direct intervention and ownership of the reform, the main transnational exponents of neoliberalism endorsed the role of policing the emergent 'void'[6], in Ranciere's (2010) terms, which, nonetheless, equalled governmental action at a distance as a dislocated spatialised intercession.

10 *Book discussion and introduction*

> The World Bank is assisting countries to review, update, and simplify their legal systems. Such reforms of legal systems will improve the capacity of government to regulate the economy efficiently and to reach administrative decisions on the basis of a dear set of new and relevant laws therefore the cost, of committing capital or labour.
>
> (WB 1992: 35)

> [However] [f]irst, as an external agency, the Bank cannot substitute for the political commitment that governments must bring to reforms in this area. Outsiders can assist and advise, but unless governments are committed to reform, changes that are brought about will not be sustainable. Full ownership of reforms is as important in this area as it is with economic policy reforms.
>
> (WB 1992: 50)

The WB's statement also implies that the ownership of the economic reform was shared, even if not assumed. It also reveals that neoliberal governmental power, in its incipient stages of expansions, when both its material and discursive devices were not yet sown in local governmental technologies, appropriates sovereign power as executive apparatus of its ruling, which has the role of establishing a new order, filling the new vacuum with its global Master signifier-neoliberalism (see Zizek 1993).

> In the former Soviet Union and Central and Eastern Europe it was the state's long-term failure to deliver on its promises that led, finally to its overthrow. But the collapse of central planning has created problems of its own. In the resulting vacuum, *citizens are sometimes deprived of basic public goods such as law and order* [my emphasis].
>
> (WB 1998: 16)

Hence, paradoxically, in seeking to implement an order that was dissolved with the falling of Eastern European states, transnational neoliberalism, with the force of deterritorialisation and re-territorialisation[7] into sovereignty, reinforced the state as an apparatus of command for its discursive enactments and local interventionism. On the other hand, it delocalised and projected its ideological command as a de-responsibilised extraneous authority, which was portrayed as the outsider in the process of Eastern European national neoliberalisation. After the incipient stage of the neoliberalisation of Eastern Europe in the late 1990s, transferred capitalism to the states of the East placed at its centre *capital as axiomatic apparatus of subjectification*[8] *of labour power*, for which the nation state became its main model of realisation (Deleuze & Guattari 2005). The interventionist character of neoliberalism changed its delivery when WB set a new agenda for the reformation of the state and its complementary functionalities in relation to the institutionalisation of the market. More exactly, in the 1997 report, WB advocated a transition from a quantitative to a qualitative state intercession, which should

Transnational neoliberal governmentality 11

not interfere with the market functioning and development, but rather facilitate its "institutional foundations" (WB 1998: 17) and amplify its supervision functions. Social and economic development should no longer be confined to the sovereign exercise of power, but brought under the realm of expertise and expert knowledge.

> Good advisers and technical experts would formulate good policies, which good governments would then implement for the good of society. State-led intervention emphasized market failures and accorded the state a central role in correcting them.
>
> (WB 1998: 15)

The statement implies that the role of the state in ensuring social, economic order and expansion has to be partially delegated to experts – including social scientists – who would promote a certain moral engagement with the government of economy and society. The latter would be able to exorcise the ataxic democracy, 'the vacuum', for a new economic and social order to be addressed by the market in the name of the market. Complementary expertise would bring state 'closer to people' by including their voices into governance, implicitly legitimising the use of sovereign neoliberal power in the government of the social.

> Governments are more effective when they listen to businesses and citizens and work in partnership with them in deciding and implementing policy. Where governments lack mechanisms to listen, they are not responsive to people's interests, especially those of minorities and the poor (. . .) And even the best-intentioned government is unlikely to meet collective needs efficiently if it does not know what many of those needs are.
>
> (WB 1998: 25)

> The Bank spreads best practice in this area by encouraging participatory processes (. . .). In some cases, intermediaries are identified through which the Bank can work. It may mean working with local NGOs, or it may mean searching for especially skilled local sociologists, development managers, anthropologists, or consultants for aspects of project work.
>
> (WB 1992: 57)

Following these, states would increase their governmental powers and 'effectiveness' by the use of expert knowledge, revealing particularities of the economy and the governed through its individualisation mechanisms in order to translate them into 'collective needs' through technologies of totalisation. Additionally, since the early 1990s social scientists (e.g. sociologists and anthropologists) have been encouraged to participate in the reconstruction of Eastern Europe and contribute to the governance and policing of the social, mastered by the constitution of the market and business sectors and their associated needs. Thus, the so called 'marginalised' and 'poor' would become, in Foucault's terms, subject to neoliberal

12 *Book discussion and introduction*

governmental power through processes of epistemological individualisation and totalisation (Foucault 2002a) informed by expert knowledge, indicated by the WB as reflective or shared governance. Hence, it can be implied that these apparently contradictory epistemological devices of assessing the object of governance (e.g. individualisation and totalisation) aimed at releasing 'effectiveness' in conducting the poor's conduct. The 'conduct of conduct' is here a direct reference to Foucault's definition of government of the self and others or what he calls governmentality, which has at its core the strong relation between governance, knowledge/social sciences and power (Foucault 1991a). It is a complex entanglement between knowledge and governance, generally discussed by Foucault (1991a) as governmentality, which has as its source a primary political examination of the government in relation to sovereignty made by Machiavelli in 'The Prince', which became the subject of controversial political inquiries in the nineteenth century. Foucault (1991a) reveals how Machiavelli's work was not only contentious but also 'theorematic', in Deleuze and Guattari's terms (2005), a reasoning for the enhancement of state power addressed by royal sciences/sciences of the sovereign. The main problem discussed in 'The Prince' was the maintenance of sovereignty or the strengthening of the feeble relation between the territory and the Prince, an object of continuous dispute and conquest. Generally, Machiavelli's work emphasised the external character of the relation between the Prince and territory, which is acquired by conquest or inheritance and is kept under jurisdiction of the Prince artificially without the engagement of the subjects. The principality is constantly exposed to external dangers by other sovereigns seeking conquest and internally from its subjects not yet owing allegiance to the Prince and unwilling to support his rule. In order to increase his power, the Prince has to strengthen the relation between his sovereign ruling, territory and the people by making it more omniscient and reflective, productive of command through a circulatory epistemological movement (e.g. upwards and downwards). This seamless articulation between the sovereign, his territory and people became the object of the art of government through upward mobility from the subjects to the Prince and downward mobility from the Prince to the subjects. On one hand, the upward mobility indicated a pedagogy of the Prince, engaging in learning about himself ruling and his ruled subjects or the way they can be governed. On the other hand, the downward epistemological mobility followed the patriarchal pattern of family-economy for which the father was responsible with both the pastoral care, knowledge of the members' needs and direct ruling. The latter was defined as 'police' and developed within mercantilist forms of the state and economy as a science of the state, aiming at increasing the sovereign's wealth and power. Compared to the juridical theory of the sovereign, which was concentrated on singularity and exclusiveness of the sovereign power in relation to his subjects, the art of government exposed a continuous multiplicity of forms of governance which were integral to the society and the state (Foucault 2002b: 204):

> [T]he people who govern, and the practice of government, are multifarious since many people govern – the father of a family, the superior in a convent, the teacher, the master in relation to the child or disciple – so that there are

many governments in relation to which the Prince governing his state is only one particular mode (Foucault 2009: 49) (. . .) the government of oneself [self-mastery], which falls under morality; the art of properly governing a family, which is part of economy; and finally, the "science of governing well" the state, which belongs to politics.

(p. 132)

These alternative technologies of power and techniques of government became progressively incorporated into the epistemological state apparatus, dealing with the knowledge production concerning its objects of governance, which has been developed in time through a 'reflective' relation with its subjects since the early beginnings of capitalism. Furthermore, the eighteenth century, which brought economic, demographic expansion, reconfigured the problematic of government and its new subject, population, "as the correlate of power and the object of knowledge" (Foucault 2009: 110). The modulation of the problematic of government or art of government imputed a refinement of modalities of knowing the Other/the population. The latter became more than the subject of sovereign power. It was construed as a "technical-political object of management and government" (Foucault 2009: 98), continuously transformed by expertise and revisable techniques of producing expert knowledge. Population was no longer an assemblage of subjects of judicial power of the sovereign, but an epistemologically constructed quantifiable artefact construed by the human sciences of the nineteenth century. It aimed at grasping its differences, commonalities and events, a demography, as part of a regime of truth, construed through upward and downward epistemological movements, configuring the objects of study. Therefore, 'to govern' or 'government' is distinguished by Foucault (2009) from ruling and sovereign power as a plurality of forms of management, conduct and modalities of knowing, which are coextensive with both society and state. It is considered to involve multivarious epistemological movements from subjects (e.g. self, population) to authorities of government (e.g. self-mastery through knowing oneself, state governance through knowledge of a population), which do not always originate or coincide with state institutions, but reflect existing forms of governing the social.

Nevertheless, these already existing multiple modes of conduct, alternative to state governance (e.g. family governance, religion), or techniques of 'management of possibilities' of action (Foucault 2002c: 341) are subject to incorporation into larger domains of government and subjectification and assembled into a major mentality of governance. The latter can generally be shaped as a 'problem-space' (Burchell 1996: 26) enclosed by fields of expertise, which 'materialise government' and intervention in the existing reality of the social (Van Baar 2011: 38). This technology of government is currently and extensively embodied in states, civil society, but also transnationally within polities such as the WB, UNDP and EU, aiming at reconfiguring articulations of economy and society and constituting new domains of subjectification once controlled only by the state. Notwithstanding, in the early 1990s, WB (1992) placed an emphasis on the role of the state in establishing the so called 'rule of law' as an infrastructural device for economic development and democratisation in Eastern Europe, aligned through a judicial immersion into the reconfiguration of economy towards the axiomatics of the market.

> With respect to rules, without the institutions and supportive framework of the state to create and enforce the rules, *to establish law and order* [my emphasis], and to ensure property rights, production and investment will be deterred and development hindered.
> (Eggertson 1990, in WB 1992: 6)

In this case, the practice of government incorporates practices of domination asserted by the state, authorising legislative devices to uphold law and order, which are constitutive to neoliberal government. Similarly, in relation to the reformation of Eastern European economy, European Commission reiterates the emphasis on development, poverty eradication and, additionally, the exercise of power as governance.

> Governance refers to the rules, processes, and behaviour by which interests are articulated, resources are managed, and power is exercised in society (EC 2003: 3–4). Governance has become an essential ingredient of development co-operation and is now an integral part of the Poverty Reduction Strategy process.
> (p. 5)

Furthermore, UN and UNDP, promoters of human rights as components of human development, highlighting development as a medium for their fulfilment, expanded accountability from the state to non-state actors such as national and transnational civil society and financial institutions and corporations. This process, informed by expertise, suggests a relation of government, which is constantly alienated to extraneous institutions and technologies of governance.

> Information and statistics are powerful tools for creating a culture of accountability and for realizing human rights. Activists, lawyers, statisticians and development specialists need to work together with communities. The goal: to generate information and evidence that can break down barriers of disbelief and mobilize changes in policy and behavior.
> (UNDP 2000: 10)

This transnationally guided process associated with new technologies of government based on expertise – transnational governmentality – has also put pressure on nation states to governmentalise, in other words, to absorb, to embody the expert knowledge(s) produced by social sciences into new, designed apparatuses of establishing beliefs and truths conducting the management of the social, economic practice and behaviour.

> Data are helping some governments make better policies. Data are enhancing public understanding of constraints and trade-offs and creating social consensus on national priorities and performance expectations.
> (UNDP 2000: 10)

All these relations and directions of government that expanded transnationally, gravitating around the axiomatic power of the market and upheld by expert knowledge production, can be considered an assemblage of technologies of neoliberal governmental power, or in other terms, can be called transnational neoliberal governmentalities. The problem of neoliberal governmentality is a contemporary conceptualisation discussed by Foucault (2008) and liberal scholars in contradistinction to that of early liberalism of the eighteenth century and reason of the state of the late eighteenth century, which advanced 'police' as a form of government and knowledge of the state aimed at strengthening administrative monarchal power and wealth. In Foucault's (2008) terms, liberal government placed the market at its core as a site of veridiction and truth making, conducting governmental practices, for which the state had a supervisory function only. Furthermore, early liberalism was considered to establish the naturalism of the market – *laissez-faire* – which "is here both a limitation of the exercise of political sovereignty *vis-a-vis* the government of commercial exchanges, and a positive justification of market freedom" (Burchell 1996: 22). At the same time, governmental action was seen as external in relation to the subject of governance "whose activity must remain forever untouchable by government" (Gordon 1991: 43) and not yet constitutive of society. After WWII, a different form of liberal governmentality emerged, the welfare state, which concentrated on governing society through society (e.g. social support for citizens, civic and social organisations upholding the local social initiatives) and constituted society as a realm of governance. The latter meant that society was governed at a distance through social programs and later on through models of self-government or techniques of the self, which were advanced and expanded throughout society by neoliberal governmental technologies of power (Burchell 1996; Rose 1996) ruled by the principle of the market. In this context, Foucault (2008) discusses neoliberal governmentality as an entanglement or fusion between government of self, others and the market:

> *Government must accompany the market economy from start to finish* [my emphasis].The market economy does not take something away from government. Rather, it indicates, it constitutes the general index in which one must place the rule for defining all governmental action. *One must govern for the market, rather than because of the market* [my emphasis]. To that extent you can see that the relationship defined by eighteenth century liberalism is completely reversed.
>
> (Foucault 2008: 121)

This portrayal suggests that neoliberalism brings in a specific model of government which, diffused throughout society (e.g. enterprise), is applied widely to individual and institutional management techniques. Throughout his discussion, Foucault (2008) indirectly implies that these may act on their own, without central command. Notwithstanding, he indicates market as the main principle of governance and indirectly as an instrumental rationality – 'for the market'– which can be viewed, in Deleuze and Guattari's terms (2005), as an axiomatic apparatus of power, which rules over all the other mechanisms of managing the social. This suggests, in my terms, an *apparatus of commandment incorporated into practices of government* informed by epistemological devices and diffused widely to both social and political bodies worldwide. Contiguously to this line of thought, Foucault (2008) speaks about neoliberal governmentality as 'positive liberalism' or 'intervening liberalism', differentiating itself from eighteenth century liberalism, which assumes naturalism of the market. In this case, neoliberal interventionism indicates a new problematic of government through which society is configured and managed according to market principles, which nonetheless does not have to rectify the damaging consequences the market brings in relation to society. The latter as forms of adjustment were technologies of governance previously incorporated into welfare state governmentality.

Generally, neoliberalism enhances the intercessation and arbitration of the social by expanding and configuring new modes of subjectification through which the instrumental rationality of the market can be tacitly realised. In this context, the subject of neoliberalism is distinctly conceived from that of eighteenth-nineteenth century liberalism. The latter was mainly envisaged as a subject of rights, a citizen, but continuously disciplined institutionally by the institutional infrastructure of capitalism (e.g. schools, prisons, hospitals) (Foucault 1991b). On the other hand, the neoliberal subject is an instantiation of the entrepreneurial field extended and expanded into the fabrics of the social by its institutional exponents (e.g. WB, OSCE, UNDP, EU). In other terms, neoliberalism brought a transition from the liberal conceptualisation of the subject as autonomous to the "neo-liberal homo economicus [who] is manipulable man, man who is perpetually responsive to modifications in his environment" (Gordon 1991: 43), but also to a responsibilised subjectivity (Rose 1996) – the entrepreneur – engendered by a discursive space ruled by the axiomatics of the market, performing control over and supervision of the social.

> Neoliberalism should not therefore be identified with laissez-faire, but rather with permanent vigilance, activity, and intervention.
>
> (Foucault 2008: 132)

Additionally, Rose (1996) suggests that beyond its responsibilisation and entrepreneurial engagement, neoliberal subject is expected to fulfil a different functionality of the market – consumption, and in general terms become both the producer and consumer-client of an entrepreneurial field inferred from neoliberalism: "consumer of health services, of education, of training, of transport" (Rose 1996: 49). It instructs individuals to "enterprise themselves, to maximize their quality of life through acts of choice" (p. 49), promoting 'pedagogies of the self' upheld by epistemological devices (e.g. media, social sciences, economics), which, from a different viewpoint, produce *subject-entrepreneurs for the market realisation, not political subjectivities*[9] *critically engaged with the public sphere and state governance*. These lines of thought reveal neoliberal government as a source of authorisation of authoritarian depoliticised models of self-conduct commanded by the market by the use of expert knowledge produced by 'experts of subjectivity' (e.g. social and political scientists) which, as Rose suggests, aim at 'civilising'/ responsibilising 'the poor' and 'the marginals' as entrepreneurs of the self. This adviced approach is, in general lines, what Dean (1992) discussed as 'policing the poor', which has always been at the core of liberal government. The latter aimed at "biopolitical objectives of establishing and maintaining national power" (Dean 1992: 227), but also capital augmentation, as far as "wealth is the outcome of wise administration, [and] poverty is a sign of the failure of policies" (Dean 1992: 233).

Policing the 'poor' refers to the way a population becomes an object of knowledge and governance and the way in which 'the poor' as an identification category to be projected onto the "bearers of labour" (Dean 1992: 234) is construed to fit the frugality and demands of capital or market economy. Poverty itself has been construed as an object of the liberal governance, naturalised and conceptualised as an available labour resource ready to be used and governed "making it necessary to the functioning of the economy" (Dean 1992: 235). Notwithstanding, liberal policing was strengthened by being increasingly focused on a slightly different subject of governance – the pauper – the undisciplined embodied labour power, not yet ready to be exercised, governed, not yet integrated into the circuit of capital reproduction and accumulation.

Thus, liberal governance marked the relation between labour and poverty as an object of governance, which needed to be mediated by a management of the pauper's conduct, securing labour surplus and upholding the base for capital accumulation, opposed "to the life-conduct of the independent labourer" (Dean 1992: 238). In this context, capital and market represent moral standards for a socio-economic behaviour, which is subject to policing and constant supervision – including *epistemological supervision* –[10] against a standard of economic performance. Therefore, neoliberal interventionism, for which "[t]he moral element is *order*, that order which liberal society discovers as a vital need" (Procacci 1991: 158), seems to find exoneration in the reciprocal enhancement and entanglement between morality and expert knowledge. As Procacci (1991) argues, neoliberalism appropriates and incorporates poverty into its programs of governance not as a problem of inequality or social justice, but, in my terms, as a conceptual apparatus of correction of the distortions in the economy of the market and labour. This economic moral order of the market is unerringly pronounced in the UNDP main platform of human rights and development:

> Rights make human beings better economic actors (. . .). So economic and social rights are both the incentive for, and the reward of, a strong economy' (UNDP 2000: iii). Human rights are moral claims on the behavior of individual and collective agents, and on the design of social arrangements.
> (p. 25)

The morality of human rights indicates a direction of conduct individuals and communities need to follow in order to become 'better economic actors' (UNDP 2000: 25) and generally entrepreneurs of the self. In other words, neoliberal programs of eradication of poverty do not necessarily aim to liberate the poor, but to incorporate their unclassified potentialities (e.g. transformation of labour power into labour) into a capital commanded economy, which places at its core *enterprise* as a typified behaviour and model of human action. Furthermore, as Procacci (1991) suggests, pauperism has always been associated with 'mobility', 'promiscuity', 'ignorance' and 'insubordination', and both categories of features have been subjected to alterations. The latter were largely diffused as technologies of securitisation of poverty and migration, largely called programs of human development and social integration of the 'marginalised'/'vulnerable' for which "the objective is the elimination not of inequality, but of difference"[11] (Procacci 1991: 160) through an over-expanding moral economic order grafting domains of subjectification (e.g. neoliberal subject as enterprise) for the unclassified.

Therefore, as far as "security is directly linked to development" (EC 2003: 7) and human rights as moral claims to economic development and subsequently to governance, neoliberalism aims at expanding capital's commandment apparatus through the use of governmental power and poverty reduction programs, fed by expert knowledge across peripheries of capitalism (e.g. Eastern Europe, Africa, South-Asia) subject to adjustment. Hence, poverty and 'the poor' are domains of governance, part of the same neoliberal political rationality or moral economic order epistemologically fostered and engendered by the axiomatics of the market and global capital. In other words "[t]he resulting poverty-reduction initiatives emphasise aspects of advanced liberal agendas, rather than reducing poverty and facilitating development as a form of social justice" (Ilcan, Lacey 2011: 7).

> Thus, poverty became an organizing concept and the object of a new problematization. As in the case of any problematisation (Foucault 1986), that of poverty brought into existence new discourses and practices that shaped the reality to which they referred.
>
> (Escobar 2012: 24)

The so-called 'the poor' of the world became subjects of a 'disciplinary neoliberalism', which "combines the structural power of capital with [the] 'capillary power' and 'panopticism'" (Gill 1995: 411) of the capitalist institutions (e.g. work places, schools, cultural institutions). The latter through governmental and epistemological devices formulate and alter the poor's conduct, not yet amenable to the economic moral order of the market and capital. In these terms, human development of 'the poor' or 'the marginalised' "can be seen as part of an emerging and essentially neo/liberal system of global governance (. . .) [part] of a dream of order through the management of non-territorial processes, flows and networks of which the open market is the foundation and ultimate driving force" (Duffield 2002: 1050). Furthermore, "[i]f global poverty eradication is both a moral obligation and global public good" (UNDP 2000: 82), it indirectly engages an apparatus of moral economic ordering and commandment – 'a pro-poor global

Transnational neoliberal governmentality 19

order' – rooted in epistemological and judicial devices policing the social and the conduct of individuals.

> In practice, this means governing substantial minorities (social welfare recipients, illegal immigrants, delinquent parents) [or the Roma] in a way that emphasises the surveillance, detailed administration and sanction.
> (Dean 2007: 127)

Dean (2007) argues that these forms of surveillance and supervision of forms of conduct are the mechanisms of a 'liberal police' aiming to train, discipline and transform individuals into 'autonomous' subjects of neoliberalism – entrepreneurs of the self – through "techniques and agencies located within civil society"[12] (p. 113), which aim to incorporate the subjects into the economic and moral order of the market. In other words, neoliberalism advocates for supervisory and disciplinatory mechanisms as preparatory stages for individuals' economic freedom and human development. This also shows, as Hindess (2001) suggests, that freedom, domination and security are entangled in the neoliberal governmental reason and political rationality and are generally upheld by apparatuses of "knowledge of civil society" (Dean 2007: 113), or in general terms by social sciences including sociology.

In addition, as Valverde (1996) argues, these practices of governance can be classified as authoritarian or even 'despotic', liberal government performing a dialectic and "a persistent coexistence of liberal and illiberal modes of moral/ethical governance" (p. 357). The latter are continuously employed to constitute the disciplined subject of governance, who is expected to deliver the promise of self-enterprise by following an economic moral order or 'good governance', which stands at the core of neoliberal governmentality. Notwithstanding, performing the distinction between the illiberal liberalism and liberal forms of government, and pronouncing their coexistence might avoid revealing the instrumental holistic incorporation of governmental practice into the global economic order of the market and capital's commandment, clearly underlined by transnational neoliberal actors of development such as the WB.

Similarly, Foucault (2008) distinguishes between *despotism, police state and the rule of law*, which can be considered features of neoliberal governmentality. In his view, *despotism* establishes a direct interdependent relation between law and other governmental authorities and "refers any injunction made by the public authorities back to the sovereign's will and to it alone, or, rather, it makes it originate in this will" (p. 169). On the other hand, whereas the *police state* "establishes an administrative continuum that, from the general law to the particular measure, makes the public authorities and the injunctions they give one and the same type of principle" (pp. 168–169), the *rule of law* makes a jurisdictional variation between "laws, which are universally valid general measures and in themselves acts of sovereignty, and, on the other hand, particular decisions of the public authorities" (p. 169). Yet, Foucault's definition of the rule of law seems to be conceptually detached from the economic programmatic aspect of neoliberal government, the moral order of the market and capital's commandment, which seeks instantiation in individuals' actions as entrepreneurial behaviour. Accordingly, the main exponents of neoliberalism, such as the WB, advance the rule of law as an instrument for market realisation and capital expansion.

> The *rule of law* [my emphasis] is a wide – some would say all-embracing – concept (. . .) Some elements of the rule of law are needed to create a sufficient stable setting for economic actors – entrepreneurs, farmers, and workers to assess economic opportunities and risks, to make investments of capital and labor, to transact business with each offer, and to have reasonable assurance or recourse against arbitrary interference or expropriation. This connection of the rule of law with efficient use of resources and productive investment (. . .) is the aspect most important to economic development, and hence to World Bank assistance.
> (WB 1992: 28)

Following WB's definition, the rule of law is the main grounding for the economic development or rule of the market, mainly being subordinated to economic needs, which are pursued by individuals as economic actors-entrepreneurs. This interdependence and entanglement between the *market rationality* and *the rule of law* features a neoliberal moral order of the market and capital's commandment, which continuously polices countries' and individuals' behaviour. A good example in this sense is OSCE's programs of securitisation in the European region, as measures of assisted governance and development in peripheries of capitalism, by the use of mechanisms of liberal policing of the self and the social, which stand at the core of neoliberal governmentality.

> [T]here is room, in this view, for civil policing, i.e., for citizens and non-governmental organizations to play an active role in the policing of their communities. The nexus of self-policing and external policing is regarded as containing the potential for both effective and democratic policing.
> (Merlingen & Ostrauskaite 2005: 346–347)

External policing/intervention/government and self-policing are considered to be part of a process of democratic policing, which most of the time is the basis for the market realisation and capital expansion. Furthermore, as already discussed, securitisation as governance is considered in a neoliberal formula dependent on the rule of law that provides the medium for the subjects of neoliberalism to be governed by *the rule of the market*, "to make investments of capital and labor, to transact business with each offer" (WB 1992: 28). In a Smithian logic, as Dean (2007) suggests, the latter are part of "the 'system of natural liberty' of the market as an instrument of police" (p. 122). *Thus, as discussed above, market and capital can be seen and examined as apparatuses of commandment and moral economic ordering for the Other* (e.g. people, institutions, countries) *and these make neoliberalism indistinguishable from authoritarianism.*

Thereafter, neoliberal governmentality as a concept does not have to exorcise the instrumentality and authoritarianism of the neoliberal project in order to reveal multiplicities of forms of government, knowing the self and others. It should also refer to *a dispositif and ontology of commandment directed by capital and contiguous economic rationalities of the market* which stand at the core of European neoliberal governmentality. The latter embodies and exercises mechanisms of policing those populations, who are not yet subject to neoliberalism, by producing technologies of normalisation of control, dispositifs of "articulation of security as freedom of circulation" (Bigo 2008: 96). In this context, the European Roma are continuously and dialectically constituted as both 'free' EU citizens and controlled subjects of European human securitisation, which is subsumed and translated into a general framework of neoliberal human development and social integration.

3 European social integration as neoliberal governmentality

Epistemological colonisation of the subject

Human securitisation of migration and programs of social integration acted as preparatory stages for the unready subjects of neoliberal government – the Roma, releasing domains of subjectification, mainly issued by the moral economic order of neoliberalism, built around axiomatics of the market and proliferated by worldwide capital's commandment. Implicitly, the Roma population became an epistemologically quantifiable, manipulable artefact construed by expert knowledge, able to register regularities and variations in behaviour. This knowledge production around an object of study has been seamlessly engaged in a process of truth making, reconfiguring the subject of governance.

As Foucault (2002a) discussed, following Nietzsche, knowledge is itself a violent act against things to be known, a "relation of power and violence" (p. 10), which does not necessarily represent the object of knowledge, but is rather a laboratory for truth making and government of the self and others. Similarly, expert knowledge is fundamental to the exercise of neoliberal governmental power disciplining bodies and constituting "subjects in terms of certain norms of civilization, and effect a division between the civilized member of society and those lacking the capacities to exercise their citizenship responsibly" (Rose 1996: 45). The 'responsible' way of performing citizenship, Rose (1996) speaks about, is connected to neoliberal enterprise as a pattern of behaviour and model of self-government. It is mainly informed by "new technologies of expert social government [which] appear to depoliticize and technicise a whole swathe of questions by promising that technical calculations will overrule existing logics of contestation between opposing interests" (p. 50), inducing new stable ethical forms of governance gravitating around axiomatics of the market.

Generally, depoliticisation is involved in the process of constituting the neoliberal subject. Throughout the whole process, expert knowledge production appears as a mechanism of simplification, technicisation of language (e.g. resort to statistics), decontextualisation and epistemological re-embodiment of the object of knowledge into market and capital's regime of signification. The latter eludes alternative lines of subjectification, which might reside in local cultural-political manifestations, and critical engagement with the public sphere and forms of self-government. Furthermore, the architecture of neoliberal forms of self-government requires an epistemological identification and a construction of the subject of governance, its needs, economic and political structure, as far as "an act of knowledge could never give access to the truth [of governmental-mentality] unless it was prepared accompanied, doubled and completed by a certain transformation of the subject" (Foucault 2005: 16). In the following, some of the mechanisms of this epistemological subjectification or constitution of the neoliberal subject, standing at the core of transnational programs of social integration and human development as securitisation, which construe Roma as a subaltern subject to neoliberal governmentality, are revealed.

As far as poverty is considered a failure of the market economy in a neoliberal formula, programs of governing the Roma targeting poverty eradication/social exclusion/marginalisation have been epistemologically construed to match an axiomatic market moral economic order and rationality that transcends the states and local cultural-political engagements of the governed. These concepts were operationalised and embodied in epistemological devices of governing the Other as enterprise.

> Social exclusion can be associated with long-term unemployment, with such group characteristics as ethnic affiliations, or sexual orientation, health status (HIV-AIDS), or with social pathologies (e.g. ex-prisoners or drug abusers). Social exclusion is often a first step to marginalization (. . .). A process of socio-economic degradation resulting from the failure to meet inclusion requirements for participation in different social systems (e.g. labor market, political institutions, educational and health institutions). These systems are usually interlinked, so exclusion from one makes exclusion from others more likely.
>
> (UNDP 2002: 11)

These definitions show how neoliberal social integration takes as object of governance the relation between labour and poverty, indirectly subjecting officially unemployed labour power to market rationalities that aim at its integration into the circuit of capital expansion. According to these, Eastern European Roma, experiencing the lowest rates of employment (UNDP 2002) among the non-Roma people, are profiled by the transnational actors of neoliberal development as the 'poor', 'marginalised', 'vulnerable' or, in other words, the not ready subjects of neoliberal government.

> Increasingly severe poverty among Roma, or "gypsies," in Central and Eastern Europe has been one of the most striking developments since transition from socialism began in 1989. Although Roma have historically been among the poorest people in Europe, the extent of the collapse of their living conditions is unprecedented (. . .). Who are the Roma? The Roma are Europe's largest and most vulnerable minority. Unlike other groups, they have no historical homeland and live in nearly all the countries in Europe and Central Asia.
>
> (WB 2005: xiii)

24 *Book discussion and introduction*

> While Roma are considered to be among the poorest and most marginalized minorities in Central and Eastern Europe, information on their living conditions and the characteristics of their poverty is scarce, fragmented, and often anecdotal. Measurement problems are daunting and include undersampling in censuses and households surveys, (. . .) the reluctance of many Roma to identify as Roma, *and the incredible diversity of Roma groups and subgroups* [my emphasis].
> (WB 2000: vii)

> Roma are both poorer than other population groups and more likely to fall into poverty. (. . .) Despite methodological challenges and issues with data comparability across countries, the overall impression is the same.
> (WB 2000: 10)

The Roma's poverty is profiled as a field of governance associated with a "complex mix of historical, economic, and social factors, including the location of Roma settlements, low educational statements" (WB 2000: wiii), subject to alterations aiming at designing community and self as enterprises, engines for economic development. Whereas the Roma are distinguished from other vulnerable groups who are integrated into the social and economic profile of the market economies, poverty appears as a recent Eastern European occurrence, the result of a transition from a state socialist controlled economy to a capital commanded one, and implicitly to a neoliberal model of marketisation of society. The Roma themselves became the signifier of poverty, engendered by an externally induced transition from socialism to neoliberalism in Eastern Europe, and epistemologically constructed by "growing bodies of qualitative assessments" (WB 2000: 10) made by experts, social and political scientists. The latter attempt to ensure a methodological geographical comparability for the homogenisation of a field of governance and its correlative domains of subjectification to which Roma are expected to acquiesce, as far as problems of identification might challenge the process of personification of poverty through which the targeted population is objectified. The lack of national political representation, or, in WB's terms, historical roots make Roma subject to a dislocated transnational neoliberal governance targeting their depoliticised subjectification. In this sense, *vulnerability* is a category of subjectification for the 'not yet ready' to the neoliberal government, which is extensively incorporated into the programs of human securitisation and social integration fostered by exponents of neoliberal governmental power. Its latest realisation is materialised by the "Decade of Roma Inclusion [which] has been associated with the targeting of policy support for vulnerable groups" (UNDP 2006: 2).

> Seen from this perspective, the concept of *vulnerability* [my emphasis] is closely related to that of 'human security'. This concept was first introduced in the UNDP's Human Development Report of 1994 as an attempt to move from state-centered emphases on national security towards more people-centered approaches (UNDP 2006: 3) (. . .) human security complements state security, supports human rights and strengthens human development

Epistemological colonisation of the subject 25

> (p. 4) (. . .) The concepts of human development and human security are therefore closely linked to vulnerability analysis. People who are facing human security risks, who are in deep poverty, or socially excluded, are vulnerable.
>
> (p. 5)

Vulnerability, as insecurity and lack of assets, appears to be part of the same strategy of neoliberal governance which focuses on development as security. Furthermore, it is concatenated with 'social exclusion', which as a multidimensional concept "is linked among others, with employment, housing, culture and institutional representation" (UNDP 2006: 4) and "stresses the importance of social networks for inclusion" (p. 4). Nevertheless, vulnerability as security risk is still attached to the lack of employment and available labour power, which has not been integrated into the new market economies.

> Since for many Roma the lack of regular job is synonymous with unemployment, high subjective unemployment rates may indicate a combination of greater involvement in the informal sector and a greater willingness to accept the stigma of declaring oneself unemployed.
>
> (UNDP 2006: 41)

The quote shows that whereas formal employment and its high earnings are morally endorsed, informal work, which implies no state taxation and fiscal contribution to the neoliberal state, is morally undervalued and classified as stigma.

> Roma vulnerability today is a reflection not just of the above mentioned, but also a displacement, and a weak education and skill backgrounds that leave them uncompetitive on many labor markets (UNDP 2006: 15). Aspects of Roma culture and living conditions also reinforce stereotypes by limiting communication between Roma and non-Roma, and contributing to a vicious circle of isolation and marginalisation.
>
> (WB 2000: wiii)

Furthermore, the lack of formal education, a component of neoliberal government, appears as an indicator of vulnerability as far as it might deter the access to the formal labour markets or minimise people's competitiveness in the market. Thus, the not yet subject to neoliberal moral order, the ungoverned labour power is subjected to liberal policing or entrepreneurial models of self-government, prompted by liberal state education. The latter is generally portrayed in opposition to local cultures and models of self-government, which might hinder *neoliberal ontogenetic mechanisms of subjectification of labour power by Capital*, as far as "[c]apital is a point of subjectification par excellence" (Deleuze & Guattari 2005: 130). The opposition is entertained by the instrumental rationality of neoliberalism, which aims at reducing state costs by new modes of subjectification (e.g. entrepreneurial behaviour and waged labour), yielded by capital's commandment, cementing the conquest of society by the market.

> The informal sector was found to provide important income generation opportunities, and, in Romania, is a key factor in the relatively low Roma employment rate (UNDP 2002: 2). At the same time, Roma participation in the formal economy is more limited than that of other groups, so relatively large numbers of Roma do not pay the social security taxes needed to fund these benefits. This causes "asymmetrical" Roma participation in social welfare systems: active regarding benefits, limited regarding contributions. This asymmetry can further promote exclusion and ethnic intolerance.
>
> (p. 3)

Following these, state welfare and informal economy, which coexist in a relation of direct proportionality, are able to hinder the functionality of the market, generally strengthened by entrepreneurial modes of government of the self, delivered through expertise and social scientific knowledge production which stand at the core of neoliberal governmentality. Conceptually, the asymmetrical participation of Roma in the welfare system, which is associated with social and ethnic exclusion, authorises a direct relation between formal employment, tax payment and social inclusion into to the neoliberal state structures and modes of government. The latter aim at reconfiguring self and community as forms of enterprise through which market interests are strengthened and preserved, and implicitly engagement with alternative forms of self-government lessened. Overall, the morality of the neoliberal project of social inclusion of the Roma is strongly grounded in a market rationality, which gives the main directions for further epistemological examination and government of the self.

> Quite apart from the moral tragedy of Roma marginalization, Roma unemployment and under-employment represent an enormous drain on CEE economies. Welfare payments upon which a large share of Roma people depend represent an immediate cost to governments, straining budgets and diverting finance away from more productive uses. Finally, poor and excluded Roma do not contribute to growth as they could through their own consumption and investment. Pockets of deprivation in areas where Roma congregate indicate how marginalization can negatively affect investment and growth.
>
> (UNDP 2005: 45)

Formal employment and entrepreneurship among the Roma are continuously emphasised as a source of national welfare and growth. Their exclusion and marginalisation are mainly risks for the neoliberal state and the market, which seek their realisation through individuals' behaviour and economic action, not the other way around: the agential capacity self-materialising its potentialities (e.g. economic and cultural abilities) in a dialectical communication with the marketisation of freedom.

The combination of low levels of employment and low wages among those who are employed translate into economy wide productivity losses of

> hundreds of millions of Euros annually (. . .). This note demonstrates that very low levels of education among the working-age Roma translate into exclusion from the labor market and subsequent economic and fiscal losses.
> (WB 2010: 2)

The process of cost reduction opens up the opportunity for the scientific assessment of the vulnerability of the Roma as insecurity, or in other terms as risk of unemployment and lack of formal education. This economic reasoning commands the reconstitution of their subjectivities as entrepreneurial, self–reliant, responsible, and implicitly not critically engaged with these models of neoliberal subjectification. By disengaging alternative models of welfare and social security, these mechanisms of epistemological realisation of the market profile Roma as the vulnerable, marginalised subjects, who need further epistemological consideration and liberal policing.

> Vulnerability is not about ethnicity or group affiliation: it is a matter of facing certain vulnerability risks (. . .). Most Roma are vulnerable, but not all vulnerable are Roma (. . .) proper policy targeting is only possible on the basis of appropriate vulnerability analysis.
> (UNDP 2006: 6)

In these terms, vulnerability is an epistemological category engaged in the government of the social, subjecting Roma to entrepreneurial models of subjectification, relinquishing alternative models of self-government opposed to the economic morality and order of the market. Implicitly, European governance for the Roma has been dialectically coupled to enterprise and business engagement as two self-reliant intermodes of governing self and individual action, productive of formalisation and capture of the unclassified or ungoverned labour power by capital.

> Businesses – not governments – are the real drivers of employment, and it is business that has the potential to make a significant difference. For these reasons we consider business engagement for integration of Roma into the labour market complementary to governmental and civic society's initiatives.
> (UNDP 2005: 7)

Although entrepreneurial or economic models of action and self-government are portrayed as complementary to the state and civic models of subject constitution, all are part of the same neoliberal governmentality. They place at its centre enterprise as both self and market realisation, devolved from the political and economic body and dispersed throughout the social as *self-reliant and self-mastery small units of market and capital's commandment* working through individuals and institutions. In this case, human securitisation or development is required for this diffused manifestation of the market to appear in the social body and reduce the state costs of labour power ungoverned by capital.

Roma integration should boost growth through heightened productivity, new skills, increased consumption and investment. Lower requirements for welfare spending will free governments to invest in infrastructure and raise productive capacity.

(UNDP 2005: 9)

To sum up, social integration of the Roma, conceptually coupled to their social exclusion, vulnerability and marginalisaton, appears as an encompassing rationality of governance directed by the two world apparatuses of commandment and moral economic ordering – market and capital, which largely define neoliberalism. Hence, the European program for social integration per se, promoted by exponents of neoliberalism, can itself render its power mechanisms and domains of subjectification visible by being conceptualised as neoliberal governmentality. The latter is assisted by social scientific knowledge production, which assesses Roma insecurity as vulnerability, marginalisation and poverty. Additionally, as discussed in the first section, Eastern European Roma have been construed as signifiers of Eastern European poverty and subjected to mechanisms of securitisation of migration to Western Europe, which were politically translated into the language of development and social integration at the countries of origins (see Roma Decade Program). Following this process of constituting the subject, Roma became a European problem, the 'internal Orientals', or in my terms the subaltern subjects of transnational neoliberal government, whose peripherality and identity (e.g. 'who are the Roma?'), adjured by depoliticising entrepreneurial models of self-government, became continuously appraised, supervised and inquired into.

Thereafter, Orientalisation of the Roma, in Said's terminology (1977) or, more exactly, *neoliberal epistemological colonisation of the subject*, in my terms, involved a territorialisation of their subjectivities into the neoliberal discourse, employed by transnational architectures of power which gravitate around the axiomatics of the market and capital's commandment, constantly authorising 'enterprise' as an exclusive form of self-government. In this context, the book aims to question social integration as neoliberal governmentality and, therefore, the epistemological constitution of the Roma as a subaltern subject. An important contribution to this epistemological colonisation of Roma subjects is brought by social sciences, which justify and assess neoliberal models of self-government. They are more specifically involved as expert knowledges in the elaboration of European policies and transnational governmental organisations' reports, discussed in this introduction (see, for example, WB 2002). Therefore, the book proposes a critical sociological mode of knowing the Roma in contradistinction to the one corresponding to social integration as neoliberal governmentality, which can uphold processes of epistemological decolonialisation of the subject of transnational neoliberal government. The following sections discuss the possible reformulation of the current object of study – marginalisation/poverty/vulnerability of the Roma – and transition towards the study of Roma as an unsubjectified or nonclassified subject continuously reconfigured within macro-micro social histories of power.

4 Why study power?

Questioning the regime of subjection and submission of political subjectivity

The question of power is raised and discussed by Foucault (Foucault 1983) himself, who advocates for "the struggle against the forms of subjection – against the submission of [political] subjectivity" (p. 213).

> They [struggles] are an opposition to the effects of power (. . .): struggles against the privileges of knowledge. But they are also an opposition against secrecy, deformation, and mystifying representations imposed on people (. . .). What is questioned is the way in which knowledge circulates and functions, its relations to power. In short, the *régime du savoir*. Finally, all these present struggles revolve around the question: Who are we? They are a refusal of these abstractions (. . .) and also a refusal of a scientific or administrative inquisition which determines who one is.
>
> (p. 212)

This entanglement between social knowledge and power as a relation of government is constitutive of Roma as the subaltern subject to neoliberal models of self-governance, questioned by the study of this book, revealing the importance of a reflective critical immersion into their social histories within self-transforming spaces of power (e.g. economy, state, politics, religion), discussed in the following sections. The latter configure their subjectivities and the repertoire of subjectification and should represent the main epistemological references in their empowerment. Notwithstanding, NGOs and state representatives aim at improving their lives by emphasising the 'option' of their empowerment through 'social integration' within the larger society (Barany 2002). In line with this option, there is also a great amount of academic work still focused on issues of poverty, marginalisation or exclusion of the Roma (e.g. Barany 1995, 2002, 2004; Gabel 2009; Guy 2001; Ladany & Szelenyi 2003, 2006). These contributions adopt, reiterate and reify the general political discourse on Roma, depicted and analysed as a powerless and helpless population. Nevertheless, a new literature questioned the degree of utility of the categories of 'marginalised' and 'vulnerable' used by 'image makers', researchers, politicians and journalists in Romani studies, media productions and policy programs (Clark 2004; Saul, & Tebbutt 2004; Woodcock 2007). For instance, Matras (2004) criticises researchers of Romani studies for "subordinating their findings to a political agenda" (p. 132) and Hancock (2004) calls for critical scrutiny regarding the use of popular culture in Romani studies, which might romanticise Roma existence. On the other hand, as Surdu and Kovats (2015) argue, the ideological construction of Roma ethnicity upholds their exclusion and violence against them, and these, in their turn, reproduce the European institutional need to address social issues through social policy.

As an important contribution to this critical epistemological trend, the ethnographic work of this book aims at showing that Roma do not have any fixed statuses (e.g. powerful, weak, poor, marginal). Their knowledge, actions and discursive practices vary in the course of different micro-power relations they develop with local authorities, political, religious and economic actors, other Roma communities and their local neighbours throughout their social histories. As Foucault (1980) argued, power never exists in a 'substantive sense' and is not a stable ascription, but rather "relations, a more-or-less organized, hierarchical, coordinated cluster of relations" (p. 198). Social power thus emerges from interactions and social relations from past to present, enacted by the Roma and ultimately transforming their lives.

Yet, the Eastern European Roma's histories have been full of interventions by the state and, more recently, supra-state institutions such as the EU. All these 'intrusions' into the Roma's existence were aimed at imposing external categories and classification schemes (Brubacker and Cooper 2000). From enslavement of some Roma to the boyars' courts and monasteries in the late Middle Ages to subsequent processes of peasantisation, proletarianisation and sedentarisation, the Roma have been subjected to various forms of symbolic violence (Bourdieu 1991), mobilising categories of identification aimed at transforming their socio-cultural identities and ways of living.

These days, transnational organisations like the EU, the WB, the UNDP, the OSCE and the Soros Foundation became international partners in the Roma Decade[13], a program initiated in 2005. It claims to be a project for the 'social integration' of the Eastern European Roma, who are considered to be part of the larger category of the 'poor' and 'vulnerable' (FRA et al 2012; WB 2000, 2005), almost 'outsider' groups or 'groups in waiting' to be included into the larger society (Drakakis-Smith 2007). Furthermore, both states and international organisations which promote development and social integration of the Roma in Europe use the rhetoric of sameness and homogenisation for a large variety of Roma groups to devise a stable basis for planning, policy-making and control. In Foucault's terms (Foucault 1984: 86), these programs have "the power of normalization [which] imposes homogeneity", "a system of formal equality" (p. 86), a fertile ground for general norms to be introduced and enforced. Notwithstanding, nowhere in Europe have the Roma been a homogeneous group. As acknowledged by Zamfir and Preda (2002) there are almost 40 groups of Roma in Romania, each claiming different identity and status according to their traditional economic occupations (Badescu et al 2007). Among these, there are the "*rudari* (wood carvers), *aurari* (gold washers), *lingurari* (spoon makers), *caravlahi* (coal miners), *caramidari* (brick makers), *blidari* (bowl makers), and *caldarari* (boilermakers)" (Barany

2004: 257). However, the policy statements regarding governance for the Roma in Europe have created a symbolic division between them and non-Roma, who are considered to be less poor and better educated, and a symbolic homogeneity among a variety of Roma groups generally included in the category of 'the poor' and 'the vulnerable'. These profiles and descriptions imposed by outsiders upon Roma are not devoid of power and symbolic value. They are ways of envisioning the world, "the power to make things with words" (Bourdieu 1989: 23), official discourses which establish the truth and "tend to picture the world as evident" (p. 21). As Rose (1999) warns, "language is not secondary to government; it is constitutive of it" (p. 29). The symbolic categories are part of larger discourses of human development and social integration, which impose themselves as authoritative maps of understanding the social, opaque layers over a much more complex dynamic of power relations enacted at the individual and group level. Furthermore, discourses of development advocate progress as a disjunction between 'developed' and 'under-developed', 'traditional' vs. 'modern', promoting expert knowledge(s) which assume a progressivist vision (Kothari 2005): "the only force capable of destroying archaic superstitions and relations, at whatever social, cultural and political cost" (Escobar 2012: 39).

This modern form of power, able to classify, 'subjugate' local knowledges (Foucault 2003) to expert knowledges, is ultimately in Foucault's words, a relation of governance which, as discussed previously, is clearly emphasised by transnational organisations such as the WB (1992) and the EC (2003) in their programs of human development and social integration. Disqualifying local histories and cultures has been part of a constructionist (e.g. constructing a problem of governance) and de-constructionist (e.g. deconstructing local meanings/forms of self-government) process of depoliticisation, and consequently technicisation of language. The latter is seamlessly employed in governing the social, reconfiguring existing power relations, "thereby shaping expressions of dissent and potentially limiting critical, challenging and emancipatory approaches" (Kothari 2005: 437).

Post-developmental studies (Rapley 2004) showed that programs of development designed by states and transnational organisations decontextualise the social and political aspects of the problem (Iordache 2011) and follow a depoliticising discourse of governance. More specifically, the act of 'depoliticising' was understood as a discursive practice that reduces the complexity of the social, which is divested of conflicts, struggles and hierarchies and composed of equal power relations (Ferguson 1994; Harris 2001; Inglis 1997; Miraftab 2004). For instance, in international programs of development "[p]articipation and empowerment are treated as independent of the structures of oppression" (Miraftab 2004: 242). Furthermore, the governance's perspective on development, made through the lens of social networks or social capital, creates the image of horizontality of social relations (Harris 2001) and silences conflicts, hierarchy and differences of power (e.g. patron-client relations). In practical terms, instead of empowering Roma communities in their material contexts of power relations, these projects can reproduce existing inequalities. Resources could remain in the control of some prominent leaders, who pursue political interests rather than the community's. Moreover, qualitative differences between Roma groups, which can place different demands on governance, are ignored. Thereafter, the research on Roma should distance itself from neoliberal models of subjectification and start from conceptualisations and themes (e.g. power relations), which do not carry the risk of reification of marginality and, implicitly constitution of Roma as the subaltern subjects of neoliberal government. In other words, the historical political ethnography of this book aims at contributing to the deconstruction of the subaltern subject, more specifically categories of identification ('marginalisation', 'poverty', 'vulnerability') employed in neoliberal governance, and the projection of a rigid homogeneous identity onto a diverse Roma population. Additionally, the examination of local level social histories of power is a preliminary stage for any civic project aimed at empowerment (Inglis 1997; Miraftab 2004).

Yet, program for social inclusion as economic rationality of governance both altered and constituted Romani civil society – NGOisation of Romani civil society – which became, in a Gramscian vision, a site for the exercise of the neoliberal hegemony (Trehan & Sigona 2009), not a civil society born from grassroots undertakings. Therefore, without excluding the importance of leadership, the historical political ethnography of the book is mainly a political act of representing the everyday Roma interaction with economic, social and political transformations, voicing and revealing their political subjectivities in the making, within and across spaces of power engaging their local level power relations. In the Eastern European context, these aspects of power capillarity (e.g. local individual practices and relations) were considered by scholars of post-socialism to be crucially important in the understanding of the unintended consequences of post-1989 capitalism (Burawoy & Verdery 1999; Grzymala-Busse & Loung 2002). The transition to the market economy and transformations of the state and political pluralism have produced a general politics of clientelism in which local patrons were linked to central state actors through political favouritism (Burawoy & Verdery 1999; Stoica 2004; Verdery 1996). This context was better understood through its local level dynamics, which revealed the individuals' or groups' participation in these transformations. According to these observations, in the study of the Roma and other populations highly subjected to governmental power, the relational power dynamics become essential in revealing both sides of the coin: the power of large structural transformations and the power released by the relational dynamic created through individuals' and groups' practices. Both forms of power interact and participate in the transformation of individuals' and groups' life trajectories and are accountable for social change and transformation of the Roma communities.

The kernel of the book is a political historical ethnography of the power relations, from socialism to post-socialism, among two Roma groups in Romania, who live in the same geographical area and who experienced different historical life trajectories: Kalderash and Romanianised Roma. The Kalderash[14] are former nomadic Roma, who are portrayed by the locals and the media as the wealthiest Roma. Romanianised Roma[15] are the former seasonal labourers and workers of socialism, who generally experience poverty and are portrayed as the poorest. The ethnographic case study arose out of numerous field research observations I have made as a sociologist involved in community development projects in different Romanian regions[16] (see Voiculescu 2002, 2004). Over the last 14 years of research[17] I have noticed that different Roma groups in Moldovia and Transylvania (e.g. Kalderash and Romanianised Roma, respectively Gabors and HaziCigany[18]) with different life and occupational trajectories (e.g. former nomadic traders, respectively day labourers and workers in socialism), who share the same geographical space, display sharp socio-economic differences. Whereas the former 'nomadic' groups have decent to opulent housing conditions, historically 'settled' groups such as the Romanianised Roma or HaziCigany can best be described as people living in poor conditions. The pictures below illustrate this polarity I noticed throughout the years (Figures 4.1a and b and 4.2a and b).

Yet, it cannot be assumed that the two Roma groups have always had the same status or economic condition. During socialism, the Romanianised Roma were either seasonal labourers or workers in state factories and had access to better living conditions than today. During the same period, the Kalderash resisted proletarianisation, partially accepted territorial sedentarisation and were less affluent than today. The two groups have experienced the political and socio-economic changes from socialism to post-socialism differently. Connected to these field observations some ethnographical questions can be raised: a) Why do these two Roma groups, usually included by the national and international development organisations into the category of 'the poor' or 'the vulnerable' seem to experience strikingly different living conditions? b) How do the power relations and discursive practices, in conjunction with larger transformations from socialism to post-socialism, participate in the differential transformation of the two Roma groups?

Following Inglis's (1997) suggestion that any form of empowerment should start with an analysis of power, the political ethnography of this book is generally an inquiry into the historical aspects of power relations of Roma populations who experience utterly different conditions of living. It generally aims to offer a contribution to the social power studies and empowerment programs for the Roma. The latter, as previously discussed, seem to blur qualitative differences and largely subsume the variety of experience within the Roma population to unreflective categories – 'the poor' and 'the vulnerable'– which reify a construed subaltern status, reproducing the status quo. These identifications blur the qualitative differences between Roma groups with distinct historical paths of social and political organisation (e.g. Kalderash's self-governance and Romanianised Roma subjection to state power) and living conditions (e.g. affluence or poverty). In this context, the book's ethnography shows, among others, that the Kalderash's successful model of self-government, largely ignored by neoliberal programs of development, can provide, in this case, a different direction for empowerment and challenge the existing problematisation of social integration, envisaged for an allegedly homogenous poor Roma population. Furthermore, without being reliant on statistics[19], the exploration of qualitative differences can suggest a new reflective critical research basis for an epistemological reconsideration of object of study and, consequently, of Roma's forms of governance and empowerment.

Figure 4.1a and b Kalderash, their houses and courtyards.

Figure 4.1a and b (Continued)

Generally, throughout the book, I concentrate my attention on relations between individuals and their discursive practices in different spaces of power struggles (e.g. informal economy, politics, state, religion). I pay special attention to the aspect of struggle through which the Roma negotiate their social relations with

Figure 4.2a and b Romanianised Roma in their district.

local, regional, and central government actors. Local and central state representatives, Roma leaders, local and regional politicians and bureaucrats act in different spaces of power struggle and have different degrees of participation in the power dynamics. In the analysis of power relations among the Roma, the difference between centres and margins is blurred (Massey 1999). Furthermore, the Roma are not studied in opposition to the dominant society (Guy 2001; Sibley 1981, 1995). On the contrary, their practices and local level relations are entangled in the on-going history of power dynamics, as far as individual practices, group relations and state discourses of power are sources of transformation. For example, it can be said that the socialist programs of proletarianisation and assimilation were experienced differently by the Roma, either as resistance or compliance. The Kalderash's collaboration with the state representatives during socialism and their resistance to the central state's repression of their nomadic lifestyles are also illustrations of negotiation with programmatic forms of power. Generally, the analysis of social power emphasises local level power[20] relations and Roma as active and full participants in historical processes. In the following section, social power is theoretically discussed in relation to history, neo-Marxist and post-structuralist streams of thought as they prove relevant to the historical political ethnography of this book. The last section concludes with a presentation of the main theoretical and methodological guidelines for the study of social power, which incorporates the analysis of micro-macro power dynamics in the analysis of power relations.

Theoretical and ethnographical considerations for the study of social power

The ethnographic analysis of this book is attentive to local level histories of social power, which can alter and challenge state programs of assimilation, social integration and modernisation. As Foucault (1980) argues, power should not be studied as a stable referential object with clear-cut hierarchies, but as a relation and dynamic through which individuals are both controlled and empowered. Power works and flows through connections and circulates "in the form of a chain" (p. 98), never localised or possessed by individuals. The network-like character of power is not necessarily a trap. The individual can "circulate between its threads" (p. 98) and "has at his disposal a certain power, and for that very reason can also act as the vehicle for transmitting wider power" (p. 72). In addition, Foucault (1980) considers that power and acts of resistance coexist and that "the latter are all the more real and effective because they are formed right at the point where relations of power are exercised" (p. 142). The main concern is with the practical character of power, which starts from its "infinitesimal mechanisms, which have their own history, their own trajectory, their own techniques and tactics" (Foucault 1980: 99), and might differ from the history of the social and political programs coordinated from the centre by the state or big institutional actors.

Foucault's perspective on social power and space has recently become attractive to poststructuralist geographers, who were interested in developing the relational and spatial approach to power. For example, Sharp et al (1999) looked at 'entanglements of power' in which resistance and domination shape each other as its components constitutive of social relations. The metaphor 'entanglements of power' is mainly a critique of Pile and Keith's (1997) theorisation of resistance, which assumes that resistance is dislocated from the space of domination. Domination and resistance are considered two interdependent phenomena, each acting within and upon the space of the other. Notwithstanding, the struggle or negotiation of meanings is experienced differently by different groups, but as Fletcher (2001) and other authors (Gledhill 2000; Guttman 1993; Ortner 1995) remarked, divisions and different reactions to power within groups were rarely examined. Following these observations, the ethnography of this book takes a historical comparative approach to the issue of power and reactions to power for the studied Roma populations engaged with local level power relations, which extend to central politics across spaces of power struggle (e.g. party politics, state, economy and religion).

In connection to this ethnographical approach to power and Foucault's conception of history, Eric Wolf (1999), an important neo-Marxist anthropologist, linked the micro to macro levels of political and historical analysis in a "systematic attempt to write a history of the present as a history of power" (Ghani 1995: 32). Notwithstanding, his interest in ideology differentiates him from Foucault's (1980) conception of power which assumes that practices and ideas are entangled and convergent in discursive practices. The latter, as well as the micro-macro power dynamic approach advised by Wolf (1990, 1999, 2001) constitute the core interest in the study of social power for the studied Roma populations. In addition, Wolf (1999) and Foucault (1980) use a similar historical approach to the understanding of power, which is crucial to the current study. They understand history as contingency, rather than a teleological, progressive narrative in which one event or action causes the other. Contingency approach to history is concentrated on particular events and relations, which are able to produce, at different levels, transformations in individuals' and groups' histories and life trajectories. Particular discursive practices and power relations, located in different spaces of power struggle and manifested locally, can have relevance for the transformation of the Roma's life trajectories.

Furthermore, as emphasised earlier, the historical ethnography of power highlights the space of communication and interaction between macro- and micro-power manifestations. Bourdieu's (1977, 1985, 1989) theorisation of fields and power struggles at the individual level offers this kind of communicative ground between micro- and macro-connections and manifestations of power. In his understanding, power relations between individuals are the reflection of an already constituted social structure. The stability of power relations is produced through the accumulation of resources, which "are not the same thing as power and the exercise of power" (Allen 2004: 30). Notwithstanding, in the context of the book's ethnography, power relations and struggles are not expressions of stable structures of capital, but mechanisms of transformation and change within and across spaces of power. On the other hand, individuals do not necessarily have

Why study power? 39

a fixed socio-economic status and their life trajectories do not necessarily take a business-like route of capital accumulation, as Bourdieu suggests (1984), but they are always transformed through a temporal dynamic of individual and group relations. Additionally, as Vigh (2009) argues, in countries with high levels of economic and political instability (e.g. Africa, Eastern Europe), individuals and groups do not develop coherent strategies, but follow 'tentative mappings' which match an unsettled, fast-transforming socio-economic-political environment. In this context, the historical political ethnography of this book takes consideration of two forms of transformation inspired by Vigh (2009):

a   transformation of spaces of power struggle (e.g. state, politics, economy, religion) from socialism to post-socialism.
b   the interaction of the two Roma groups with the macro-social, economic and political transformations, manifested in local level relations and discursive practices.

It is also worth noting that ethnographic studies on Eastern Europe (Burawoy & Verdery 1999; Verdery 1993, 1996, 2002) confirm Vigh's (2009) elaboration on continuous movement of the social, economic and political environments, which cannot be viewed as stable structures, but rather as processes within which the individuals' practices and relations participate actively in the larger transformations. As Burawoy and Verdery (1999) showed, people of post-1989 Eastern European countries, including Romania, experienced high levels of uncertainty[21] and were, in this way, locally involved in domestications and contestations of the law and institutional practice (Verdery 2002). What was usually understood as structural change and almost linear process from A to B became a continuous process in which the centre no longer dictates a unique direction, but leaves space for micro-power relations to participate significantly in larger transformations (Burawoy & Verdery 1999). In other terms, as far as "power is co-extensive with the social body" (Foucault 1980: 142), power relations cannot be disconnected from other relational manifestations, enacted in different spaces of power struggle. Individuals' economic practices, interactions with the state, political actions and religious practices are all connected through webs of power. Throughout the book's ethnography, I generally follow a Foucauldian relational perspective on power, which goes into the complex analysis of its capillarities, local relations and practices enacted by individuals, groups and institutions. Generally, by looking at individuals' and local groups' practices in interaction with larger transformations of state, economy, politics, the main methodological focus of the research is on the dynamic micro-power (individual/group relations and practices) vs. macro- power (spaces of power struggles). Micro-power is hereby understood as discursive practices and relations between individuals and groups enacted within and across different spaces of power struggle, including state, politics, economy and religion. Thereafter, power relations and discursive practices are the main mediums of transformation, which take the form of power struggles.

The field site

The book is the result of a doctoral field research, a continuation of a field inquiry I made in 2007 for a dissertation I have written for the Central European University. My first visit to Alexandri[22], the field site of my research, took place in 2005 when I participated in a qualitative study on Roma health issues, co-funded by the Roma NGO Romani CRISS. During the autumn-winter of 2009 and the spring-summer of 2010 I lived in Alexandri. While based in Alexandri, I made short research visits to nearby localities including Liveni, where I conducted interviews with leaders and families from different Roma groups. The main research instruments used were semi-structured interviews and participant observation recorded in rich field notes. The collected data comprises 40 recorded interviews, some in the form of oral history, and 100,000-words of field notes of participant observation transcribed electronically. In the following, a general description of Alexandri and the two studied Roma groups is offered.

Alexandri is a suburban place in Eastern Romania, composed of two localities – Alexandri and Regna with an equal number of inhabitants. According to the 2002 census, Alexandri had a population of about 10,225 people, out of which roughly 2,000 were recorded as Roma: Romanianised Roma and Kalderash, almost 1,000 persons in each group. The mayor and deputy mayor described Alexandri as one of the wealthiest communes in the county. It has good road and rail access to two important towns in the region, as well as access to facilities such as gas, running water, electricity and internet. There are four primary and secondary schools, two health clinics, a hospital, a police station, two Orthodox churches, a Pentecostal church, a 'house' for cultural events, a hostel, two large supermarkets, an open-air market, two main pubs and many other small pubs for locals. In the centre of the commune there are several important institutions all located on the main road, which links the locality to the two main towns in the county: the local council, two Orthodox churches, four primary and grammar schools, Hortensia Papadat Bengescu (an inter-war Romanian novelist memorial museum), a police station. One kilometre north from the centre, in the area of the hostel, there are a petrol station and two large stores that sell construction material. These stores and other smaller ones started to appear in the mid-1990s, when Kalderash began to build their large houses. Across the road from the petrol station and the hostel, there are two supermarkets and a pizzeria with a large terrace visited by lorry drivers and affluent Kalderash.

The districts where the Roma live are located in different parts of the village. The Romanianised Roma district is located in a valley that lies between a river and the main road, just behind the hostel and petrol station. It is a crowded area of small dwellings with un-asphalted small alleys. Houses are generally in a poor condition, made of baked clay and with improvised roofs. Yet, some of them look newer and better, resembling the farmers' ones. Asking Romanianised Roma living in the area, one can find out that the better-looking houses were built in the last few years, after the 2005 heavy floods, when the government provided funds to help the victims and recover their belongings.

Why study power? 41

Figure 4.3 Romanianised Roma district background. In the background: the Orthodox Church (left), local council (building on the right) facing the school mostly attended by the Romanianised Roma.

The Kalderash's district is some metres away from the hostel in the part of the village opposite to the river. Their district is located on a large asphalted road going to the East, perpendicular to the main road. Before the 1990s, the Kalderash used to live at the outskirts of the village, in a sort of hamlet close to the forest, with almost no access to piped water facilities and electricity. Their relatively new district used to be a different village, belonging to the commune and inhabited mainly by farmers until the early 1990s. However, in the mid-1990s, many Kalderash families who had been successful in informal commercial businesses[23] succeeded in buying farmers' houses and began building their own multi-storey, large residences, usually called by the Romanianised Roma and farmers 'Gypsy palaces'. For both locals and outsiders, the Kalderash's streets, full of 'palaces' on both sides, are impressive. They are well-known by people living in the region, with journalists and even foreign tourists attracted by the conspicuous architecture. However, not all Kalderash used the 'palace' model in construction of their houses. Some of those who live on the first half of the street, closer to the main road have smaller houses, usually crowded around smaller courtyards. The Kalderash families with smaller houses and more crowded gardens are usually portrayed by the locals as poorer Kalderash. Walking along the street, one notices that the aspect of the houses changes: from smaller, modest residences to more and more conspicuous 'palaces'. The biggest 'palaces' populate the upper part of the street. Their owners were the first Kalderash who settled in the area.

The wealthiest Kalderash families moved in first, in the mid-1990s when some farmers' owners were attracted by the good prices offered. In addition, following the example of the richer families, poorer Kalderash still living in their old district in the late 1990s, with almost no access to facilities, associated as groups and bought the unsold Romanian houses which were situated closer to the main road. These movements significantly changed the power geography and the appearance of the area.

Today, in the new Kalderash's district there are three important institutions: an Orthodox church mainly attended by the few Romanian families who still live in the area, a primary school attended mainly by Kalderash children and the Kalderash's Pentecostal church. Whereas the Orthodox church is located on the main street that crosses the district, the primary school and the Pentecostal church are on a peripheral alleyway running parallel to the main street.

The general aspects of the two Roma districts are quite different. Infrastructure and landscape differ as well. Whereas in the Romanianised Roma's crowded, un-asphalted area, the traffic in the small alleyways consists of old carts pulled by horses, the road in the Kalderash's district is populated by speedy expensive cars (e.g. Mercedes, Audi Q6, Audi Q7).

The historical references to Alexandri draw extensively upon an unpublished monograph written by a local history teacher and documents he provided after an interview conducted at his house in April 2007. As stated in the monograph, the first reference to the place was made on 15 July 1448. The presence of the Romanianised Roma in Alexandri was acknowledged in the fifteenth century, when they were slaves on the local boyars' lands. From 1856 onwards, when Roma slavery was abolished[24], Alexandri became a large regional market town inhabited by different ethnic populations – Roma, Jews, Greeks, Tatars, and Armenians – involved in commercial activities (e.g. store keeping, workshops). Romanianised Roma, now released from slavery, began to work for the local Jews and other merchants. While women worked as housekeepers in Jewish houses, men worked as day-labourers in Jewish or Greek workshops as furriers or knitters, in restaurants, or as brick-makers for Romanian farmers' households. Some other Romanianised Roma families were fiddlers at local parties and weddings. After WWII, they gave up brick-making and during socialism they worked in the socialist state economy as seasonal labourers in regional state farms, as well as workers of the Alexandri's collective farm. Some were employed as unskilled workers at the regional steel-work plant of Granit.

At the beginning of the 1960s, the socialist state began to enforce a program of sedentarisation for nomadic Roma. All nomadic Roma with no proof of residence were considered 'illegal', fined and not allowed to continue travelling. Since the early 1960s, nomadic Kalderash started to come to Alexandri. They were not a unified, compact group of newcomers. Some came from Transylvania, others from Banat, whereas others came from the today's Republic of Moldavia. After settling in Alexandri, the Kalderash received land from the local council to build

Figure 4.4 Kalderash man on the first half of the street, close to the main road. In the background two smaller farmers' houses followed by poorer Kalderash's houses.

houses. However, while settled, most of the Kalderash families continued to travel seasonally and practice their customary economic activities – cauldron-making – until 1989 and even after. Since the 1990s, some Kalderash families started to become successfully involved in semi-informal businesses. They used to purchase

Figure 4.5 Kalderash's houses on the first half of the street, closer to the main road.

old materials and assets from large industrial state plants that were in the process of dismantling old machinery and privatisation and sell them to small new commercial companies. On the other hand, the Romanianised Roma were laid-off from the socialist state farms and factories and began to work informally as day-labourers in agriculture for farmers' households, as well as working as construction workers for the Kalderash's houses. State and local council benefits became their main sources of income. Unlike the Kalderash, the Romanianised Roma speak only Romanian, wear casual clothes and are hardly differentiated from the local Romanian farmers. During my fieldwork, the Romanianised Roma discussed their identity in terms similar to those of the Romanian farmers' subsistence economy and in contrast to the Kalderash's lifestyles. They generally emphasised several characteristics, which, from their viewpoint, bring them closer to a 'Romanian identity': a) during socialism they were settled and employed in state farms and factories; b) they only speak Romanian and have no knowledge of Romani language; c) compared to Kalderash, they spent at least four years in local schools and do not marry their children at a young age (16–18 years old is a common marriage age for the Romanianised Roma). On the other hand, the Kalderash claim to be the 'genuine' Roma and generally despise the Romanianised Roma who, from their viewpoint, are 'poor', and, therefore, not 'real' Roma. Other differences and similarities between these people are reflected in production and consumption. All local farmers own small pieces of agricultural land and livestock and are involved in subsistence agriculture. Neither the Romanianised Roma, nor the Kalderash own these means of production. Whereas the first offer small services to the others in exchange for a little cash, the Kalderash are involved in handicraft production, trading, cauldron-making and businesses with old technology.

In terms of leaders, there are some general differences between the Romanianised Roma and the Kalderash. The Romanianised Roma have never had a specific leadership 'formula'. Nowadays they have both a formal and an informal leader, well-connected to the state structures of governance. The formal Roma leader – Roma expert – at the local council represents both Roma communities. He is a Romanianised Roma appointed by the Roma Party and employed by the government to deal with Roma issues in Alexandri. On the other hand, the Kalderash have a long 'tradition' of leadership. Since they were nomads, they used to be organised in small travelling groups represented by leaders called *bulibasi*, empowered to negotiate interactions with local authorities. The term *bulibasa* is a Romani word similar to *Rom baro* – *Rom* (man), *baro* (big) – translated as 'big man' or 'big boss' (Lee 2005). However, the term and its corresponding institution altered during socialism and both are much contested these days by Kalderash leaders and common Kalderash alike. Generally, for both Roma communities, informal and formal leaders play an important role in connecting the Roma to local authorities and patronage actors (e.g. mayor, deputy mayor).

Figure 4.6 Farmer with his child driving a cart in the Kalderash's district in Liveni. In the background: A farmer driving his motorcycle and a Kalderash woman outside her house.

Figure 4.7 Kalderash women watering the garden in their courtyard.

Figure 4.8 Farmer smoking outside his small house situated in between two impressive Kalderash's houses.

In the following, the historical context of the ethnography is discussed in relation to the main methodological and theoretical tools used for the analysis of historical transformations. The section pays special attention to economic and political processes, more specifically, state surveillance and the local domestication of state control, as well as the post-socialist emergence of the informal economy, patronage and clientelism during Romanian socialism and post-socialism. It examines the element of power manifested in the macro-movement/transformation, from socialism to post-socialism, of what I call spaces of power struggle (e.g. politics, state, economy and religion), micro-level politics and individuals' engagements with these transformations.

5 Historical entanglements of power

From socialism to post-socialism in Romania

Individual experiences are always connected to larger political and economic transformations. Investigating power relations in the Romanian context cannot exclude everyday understandings of socialism as an economic and political system, which influenced individual lives for almost 50 years. Political, social and economic aspects were intertwined in such a way that the whole socialist system involved centralised decisions, control and surveillance, as well as individual innovation, creativity and resistance. Central decisions were taken by the Romanian Communist Party, which mainly enforced two large programs: the dissolution and collectivisation of private property, and the industrialisation and centralisation of institutions and services. For the socialist planners, industrialisation was the main instrument of economic development and collective farms provided the agricultural platform for industrial production (Cole 1985). Since the early 1960s, farmers were forced to work the land in cooperative farms (CAPs), conceived as associations based on collective property and the equal participation of members in decision-making processes. In rural areas, these limiting relationships established by the socialist state entrenched an agricultural subsistence economy (Voiculescu 2008) mixed with industrial work. Besides the proletarianisation of a large percentage of the population involved in agriculture, industrialisation involved many other complex transformations: the movement of people from rural to urban areas, the development of public services and infrastructure and the emergence of new social lifestyles. Additionally, through the centralisation and planification of the economy and of industrial production, the socialist state attempted to eliminate individual initiative and minimise involvement in private arrangements for the supply of goods. Nevertheless, the lack of economic rationality and the autarchic model of the socialist economy entailed serious weaknesses: "chronic shortages of goods, labour and investment funds, rather than markets as in capitalism" (Cole 1985: 248). The redistribution of resources and rewards, created to legitimise the communist ideology, was a powerful state apparatus of control over individuals and families (Verdery 1996). Shortages of goods seriously affected the population, especially in the 1980s, when Ceausescu dramatically increased exports (e.g. agricultural products, technical and electric equipment, clothes, etc.) to pay back international debts (Verdery 1993). As a reaction to the regime, people started to get more involved in the 'second'/informal economy by manipulating state resources, such as appropriating products from the workplace and collective farms in order to use them in their households or sell them on the informal markets. This second economy was the tolerated offspring of the state economy's inability to deal with individuals' consumption needs and, as many scholars argued, the two economies cannot be dissociated in the understanding of socialism (Burawoy & Verdery 1999; Hann 2002). The interdependence between the second economy and state production becomes extremely important when we look at individual practices and relations during socialism. An illustration of this comes from my previous research (Voiculescu 2002, 2004), which showed that Roma, like any other Romanian citizens, were often involved in activities outside the socialist state's sphere of control. The Kalderash, who were ambulant smiths and cauldron-makers, used to supply their private activities with copper from large plants. The success of their business was dependent most of the time on the good connections they regularly made with the workers or factory administrators, able to appropriate materials and sell them to the Roma. Generally, the shortages of goods produced by an inefficient centralised economic system generated this kind of informal reciprocal support practices. Thereafter, socialism was not only a planned and highly regulated state and economy, but also a diversity of everyday practices and relations, which transformed people's lives, work and contexts of living. Yet, the capacities to respond by innovation and alternative social practices were different among different social groups. An argument made throughout the book's historical ethnography is that the two Roma groups I refer to had different ways of handling the challenges posed by both socialist and post-socialist economies and state apparatuses of repression. With reference to my field site – Alexandri – the state's paternalism had a significant impact on the Romanianised Roma, who were deeply involved in the socialist state economy, but had less impact on the nomadic Kalderash who showed resistance to and also adaptation to forced settlement programs, formal employment and state policies in general.

Besides care and support programs, the paternalist model of governing the population entailed strategies of control and surveillance, based on both coercive practical methods and ideological strategies. These proved to be critically important in the perpetuation of both the communist ideology and the socialist economy. In Romania, as in other East European socialist countries, the main state control apparatus was embodied in the secret police service – the *Securitate* – which aimed at sourcing information about people, who were suspected of betrayal or of undermining the Communist Party and its ideology (Verdery 1996). Networks of informers, which provided information about dissidents and the internal organisation of various ethnic groups (e.g. Hungarians and the Roma), supported the state mechanisms of surveillance. Hence, local leaders of these groups were not only working in the service of their communities, but they were also collaborators of the *Securitate* providing the constant and updated data needed for their control. These people used to receive various rewards of better jobs, party positions, better supplies of consumer goods and hardly available household equipment and sometimes personal and family protection in exchange. This was the case of many

Roma leaders who became collaborators of the *Securitate* and disclosed information about the Kalderash's gold possessions and their informal activities.

This spying infrastructure led to a decline in social relations and trust among people belonging to the same group or locality. While enhancing the power of the few over the many, the *Securitate*'s use of networks of collaborators disempowered large communities, who became more and more under control of their leaders, party activists and the police state. Most of the people were aware that in this game they lost control over their lives and possessions. For instance, the Kalderash Roma were frequently harassed by the police and forced to divulge information about their own or their relatives' savings and belongings. Although they knew that the main provider of information was their customary leader – *bulibasa* – they were never sure who his collaborators were, people who were often members of their own community.

As Verdery (1991, 1993) documented, the Communist Party used an additional control strategy grounded in a nationalist ideology, aimed at homogenising the society by forcing adherence to the same socialist values. Aiming at erasing differences between ethnic groups and social classes, the state promoted a homogenous proletarian model and morality underpinned by nationalist ideological discursive practices and socio-economic policy. Yet, these goals were never achieved as far as differences have always existed between groups. Different economic practices and modes of existence performed by different Roma groups and distinct conceptions of self-identification (e.g. Romanianised Roma, Kalderash) are a good illustration of the failure of the socialist state's ideological program of homogenisation of cultural differences. Although they were subject to forced settlements, the nomad Roma – Kalderash – continued, after their forced sedentarisation, to travel seasonally, pursue informal activities and resist assimilation. On the other hand, the Romanianised Roma, with no land or commercial abilities, but with a 'sedentary' lifestyle, accessed both seasonal labour opportunities and socialist state's provision of work and social benefits.

In general terms, the socialist state apparatuses developed different forms of repression and control. Yet, the centre was always dependent on the peripheral units in terms of enforcement, ideology diffusion and redistribution of production (Gross 1989, cited in Verdery 1991). As other authors argued (Kideckel 1982; Sampson 1984), state centralisation, which aimed to gain more control over the local administrative units, produced the opposite result. Local populations and authorities domesticated and altered the central state rules. The delegation of responsibilities from the centre to periphery generated tensions between various political and administrative levels of organisation (Campeanu 1986) and, in turn, often resulted in collective resistance to the socialist ideological programs of the state.

To get easier access to resources, many developed informal social connections to local party activists, leaders and nomenclatura (e.g. technical-industrial/agricultural personnel, teachers, physicians), who held privileged positions granted by the Communist Party (Campeanu 1986; Cole 1985). For instance, some Roma customary leaders were concerned to expand and extend their connections to mayors and regional party representatives, who were able to provide them with the necessary goods and services, including protection. These individual accommodations can be considered forms of social innovation, domestication and transformation of the planned rigidities of the socialist regime. Furthermore, the entanglement between socialist forms of organisation and local accommodations to central policies were a source of dynamic power relations between Roma groups and local state representatives and nomenclatura.

After the fall of the Iron Curtain, many Eastern European states experienced not only political changes, but also complex socio-economic transformations, which affected citizens' lives, their practices and projects. Numerous ethnographic studies which investigated everyday practices showed continuity between socialism and post-socialism in its "'regressive' and 'progressive' dynamics simultaneously" (Burawoy & Verdery 1999: 15). The economic reconfiguration of the social led to a complex mixture of 'backward' informal markets based on barter and illegal trade and formal institutions developed to support the markets and private property (Burawoy & Verdery 1999; Verdery 1996). These transformations were expressions of an endless transition in which the large processes of economic liberalisation were interacting with social and economic practices of local institutions and populations from small villages as well as from big cities (Berdahl et al 2000). The very term 'post-socialism' designates a complex process and continuity between two apparently opposed political and economic orders.

Romania, like other Eastern European countries, experienced complex processes of deindustrialisation and de-collectivisation of property. Decentralisation of economic production left a space for massive innovation and engagement with the informal economy that re-linked spheres of production, distribution and consumption in new ways (Burawoy & Verdery 1999). Large unproductive factories were dismantled and sold by the state to international investors, often for small financial gains and with little protection for the workers (Verdery 1996). At the same time, the privatisation of industry often involved corruption and clientelist relations between the government, plant directors and investors. State representatives and plant directors were interested in gaining personal financial benefits by selling the former socialist industrial companies, their machinery and assets. For example, in 2001, DerexGranit[25], the largest South-East European steel plant underwent a privatisation in which the government and the then prime minister, Adrian Nastase, were suspected of corruption[26]. Before privatisation, large parts of DerexGranit were dismantled and its technology was sold to private traders. As both Kalderash and other locals in Alexandri have told me, directors of DerexGranit used to sell materials to dealers and traders. For each transaction, the director would receive an amount of money from traders who were happy to buy cheap and resell dear. During the 1990s, some Kalderash Roma who were used to engaging in trade and who had had sufficient financial resources under socialism bought old pipes from DerexGranit to resell to small firms. This proved to be an important source of enrichment for some of the Kalderash, who filled the gap between old forms of industrial production and the new channels of consumption. The privatisation of industry that created opportunities for the Kalderash to exploit abilities and knowledge they had used under socialism illustrates the continuity between the socialist mode of organisation and new forms of capitalism, which, as many authors stated, are strongly connected and interdependent[27]. On the other hand, as Verdery (1996) documents for Romania, households and individuals coped with the changes and shortages of money by engaging in more than one occupation and by availing themselves of state transfers and interventions. These observations reveal similarities between socialist and post-socialist economies and continuities between the two. In socialism, the state, which held an excessive control over the economy produced shortages of goods and consequently pushed people into the second economy (e.g. exchange of goods, petty trade). In post-socialism, the state, using the rhetoric of liberalisation, withdrew from its own creation and left individuals and groups to deal with a new sector of informal economy generated through deindustrialisation and de-collectivisation (e.g. restitution of property). Without state reforms, deindustrialisation produced high levels of unemployment among the former proletarians, and the restitution of land to farmers resulted in land fragmentation and rural impoverishment[28]. Additionally, it has been argued that the post-socialist state itself was reconstituted using "informal structures and practices utilised by political elites, factory managers, and ordinary citizens alike, which have survived the collapse of communism" (Grzymala-Busse & Loung 2002: 535).

These continuities between socialism and post-socialism, also revealed that different reactions by Roma groups to post-socialist transformations are produced by a complex dynamic of power relations and discursive practices. The rapid post-socialist transformations, connected to socialist legacies, took the form of power struggles and are called throughout the historical political ethnography of this book spaces of power struggle (e.g. the state, politics, the informal economy and religion) within which individuals participate through their relations and practices in the transformation of their own lives. Individuals and groups were driven to experience post-socialist transition as a struggle for connections, resources, adaptation and innovation. All these gave rise to a local dynamics of power struggles. On the other hand, the local level power relations and discursive practices participated actively in the transformation of the groups' and individuals' conditions of existence. They produced constraints or opportunities in the economic conditions of existence for local populations including the two Roma groups I discuss. After 1989, most of the Roma who worked in state farms and factories under socialism were laid off (Stewart 2002) and engaged in informal economic activities such as day labour in agriculture and construction for local farmers or Kalderash neighbours. These practices and relations, which reveal interactions between larger transformations and individuals' practices, generated limited possibilities for adaptation for Romanianised Roma at the local level, which are discussed in the next chapter. They are capillaries of power of a whole dynamic portrayed above. Yet, power relations are not confined to one space of power or another, but influence one another and interact with different discursive practices, which are discussed throughout the book's ethnography. The main form of intersectionality between spaces of power, which emerged under post-socialism is that between the informal economy, the state and politics, expressed locally in the form of patronage politics and individual clientelistic relations. This post-socialist emergence was mainly triggered by large-scale processes such as deindustrialisation, state withdrawal and privatisation of the economy. As shown, Romanian deindustrialisation set in motion a whole world of connections, small businesses and intermediaries. Intermediaries were connected to the state plants' directors interested in selling assets to private companies interested in buying cheap products for their economic activity. Yet, these transactions were publicly translated into a discourse about the Mafia, which emerged in the 1990s in reference to the rampant corruption and informality (Verdery 1996). The 'Mafia' as a discourse was not only an expression of the declining trust that the population had in the chaotic privatisation of the economy, but also an indication of their anxiety about not getting fair access to the market's opportunities and resources. It was a reaction to 'clientelistic relations', 'local bosses'[29] (Humphrey 2002) and what Verdery (1996) called a state of 'statelessness', "in which it is completely unclear who owns what, who is exploiting whom" (p. 218).

In Romania, local patrons have long been called 'local barons'. The ascription is given to people with strong political connections and significant obligations, often representing parliamentary political parties, while at the same time holding local or regional administrative positions (e.g. mayor, prefect, local or county councillor, etc.). Those who are already established as patrons are portrayed by media and popular discourses as people who deal in the 'traffic of influence', who have access to public funds and who abuse their administrative positions to gain large amounts of money, business contracts, protection or to fund electoral campaigns. In 2011, Romanian journalists identified 65 'local barons' corresponding to five political parties, all members of the present parliament: the Social Democrat Party (37), the Liberal Democrat Party (17), the Liberal National Party (8), the Conservative Party (2) and the Romanian Hungarian Democratic Union (1)[30]. The 'local barons' are very well connected to businessmen across the country. The latter can ask for administrative favours and offer their generous financial and political support.

Patronage makes a good case for demonstrating that politics, state and the informal economy act together in the development of post-socialist economic informal networks. In this case, the ruling political party or coalition sets the agenda of interests and power relations and facilitates their enactment by establishing strong connections between the low and high levels of politics. The channelling of resources from the centre to regional and local administrative structures of power is done through the local patrons. As Gadowska (2006) argues for the case of Poland, the redistribution of positions at the local level is conducted on political principles – main political party's directions – and that is the main expression of the way patronage politics works. Similarly, in Romania, a change in the government entails a change in the managerial structure of local institutions (e.g. schools, tax offices, healthcare institutions, etc.). Political favouritism ensures that leading positions are occupied by people who do not necessarily have the skills to run institutions, but who are able to return the gifts by supporting the ruling party and local patrons' interests "even if it would be contradictory to the interest of the office" (Gadowska 2006: 11).

Nevertheless, as long as the 'local barons' or patrons keep their relations and subordinate their actions to the central state representatives, their actions cannot be considered to be, in Verdery's (1996) terms, part of a process of privatisation of power. Verdery's (1996) explanation suggests that these transformations entail a switch in control from the central state structures to local bosses, a 'parcelisation of sovereignty', as Humphrey (2002) argues for the case of post-Soviet Russia. Conversely, as shown in the chapter on political fields, patronage is an expression of a dynamic of power relations between local clients, patrons, followers and central state actors. Moreover, power manifestations are locutions of a temporal dynamic of both horizontal and hierarchical (e.g. clientelist) relations, which produce continuous transformations in the lives of the Roma. Precisely, the analysis reveals power as a set of processes, struggles for authority or control, which can involve both empowerment and subjection to power of the involved actors. This dynamic of power struggles is an egress to changes in the material and socio-economic conditions of the studied Roma groups.

Hence, without confining power to clientelism and patronage, the book's historical political ethnography reveals that power relations encompass clientelist relations. The latter are understood as the expression of the intersectionalities between state, politics and the informal economy. Yet, in all spaces of power struggle, other different relations relevant to the transformation of the historical trajectories of the two Roma groups can be observed. For example, in the sphere of the informal economy discussed in the first chapter, relations between the different groups (e.g. Kalderash, Romanianised Roma and farmers) and the relation with the state in its shift from socialism to post-socialism contain both elements of empowerment and subjection to power. Power and empowerment are entangled in individual and group practices and produce either constraints or opportunities for action and economic improvement for the two Roma groups. In addition, clientelism and other relations between Roma and actors, such as patrons and brokers, are challenged by discursive practices in the sphere of religion, discussed in the last chapter. Pentecostal discursive practices are able to change the Kalderash's locus of authority, their relations with the state and their leaders. All these relations and discursive practices involve simultaneously subjection, contestations of different forms of power (e.g. state, leaders, local patron) and empowerment. Thereafter, social power can be seen as the manifestation of both inter-individual and group relations, and discursive practices. Both categories are entangled in different spaces of power struggle (e.g. the economy, the state, politics, religion), which influence each other and act together in the transformation of Roma populations.

Book Outline

To sum up, in the following, a further specific summary of the book is offered. The main discussions and themes are organised in three parts: 'Book discussion and introduction', 'A historical political ethnography of social power among the

Roma', 'The return to the political: epistemological decolonisation of the subject and historical geographies of power'. In addition to the introduction, the second part of the book comprises five chapters, which are briefly summarised in the following. The first chapter, using Deleuze and Guattari's concepts of smooth and striated space, enquires into different modes of interactions Roma had with transformations of economy as a space of power struggles, from socialism to post-socialism, from within or outside the state institutionalised, regulated space of power. The second chapter reveals similarities between colonial rule and socialist repressive apparatus. It unfolds the transformations of Roma leadership from socialism to post-socialism triggered by transformations of the state and shows how Roma leadership has been progressively incorporated into the state structures. Yet, Kalderash's mobile economy as a source of political subjectivity has been perpetuated as a mode of self-governance alternatively construed to the state's modes of subjection. The third chapter enquires into the historical development of post-1989 Roma politics as a political field, in interaction with other emergent overlapping political fields (e.g. restitution politics, patronage politics and political patronage), which progressively captured its advancement. The fourth chapter, using a Goffmanian dramaturgical perspective, explores Roma's modes of preservation or submission of their political subjectivities to the main state mechanism of subjection: documenting identity. The fifth chapter delves into an alternative mode of subjectification sourced by Roma Pentecostalism, which constructs itself in a dialectical opposition to state's semiology of social integration formulated by expert social sciences. It shows how religious ethics undo the state subject and develop as a form of self-governance, which can engender a political resubjectification of the 'governed'. The third part of the book comprises two theoretical discussions. The first discussion, inspired by Pierre Bourdieu's analysis of fields and power struggles and Deleuze and Guattari's philosophical approach to movement and space, indicates a new way of conceptualising and studying social power as historical geographies of power, a grounded theoretical project, which can contribute to the epistemological decolonisation of the neoliberal subject. Finally, the last discussion, inspired by Jacques Ranciere's political philosophy, advances a new thesis – The return to the political – which advocates for a constitution of a political subject in a dialectical opposition to the 'logic of police' or epistemological apparatus of capital's commandment, which constructs 'the governed' as the neoliberal subject.

Notes

1 Throughout the book I use an Althusserian formula to refer to 'subject' as a concept: "1) a free subjectivity, a centre of initiatives, author of and responsible for its centre of initiatives, author of and responsible for its actions.; (2) a subjected being, who submits to a higher authority, and is therefore stripped of all freedom except that of freely accepting his submission" (Althusser 2008: 56).
2 FRA, UNDP, EC (2012), UNDP (2002, 2006), WB (2000, 2002, 2005).
3 *Subjectification* refers here to a process of constituting a subject, a category to be projected onto a population aimed to be governed or govern itself.

4 I generally refer to the term *semiological apparatus* as a collection of technical language, categories and expert knowledge used by states, transnational organisations and polities to identify, profile populations and exercise governance.
5 I refer here to Jacques Ranciere's (2010) discussion on democracy as anarchic principle. Empirically, it is also a reference to 89' Revolutions as events, which themselves brought a discursive disruption and a search for new modes of political subjectification, not yet institutionalised by the state
6 Ranciere (2010) opposes politics to *the logic of police*. The latter "is characterised by the absence of void and of supplement" (p. 36) or public space, not yet classified and governed by the state and the market, able to reveal individuals' and groups' struggles for political affirmation.
7 *Territorialisation* refers to a process of inhabiting, regulating, classifying a space (e.g. society as social space) or imprinting its manifestations into a conceptual frame by a dominant political force (e.g. sovereign modern State or Reason), which assumes power over space utterances and power to build its institutional pillars of belonging (e.g. nation State building). *De-territorialisation* suggests a de-construction or extraction of a space from its conceptual belongings, metric assumptions and boundaries (e.g. nation State rationality vs. global cosmopolitanism).
8 I refer to *subjectification of labour power by the Capital* as a process through which the waged labour and entrepreneurship devised by neoliberal government are projected as models of self-conduct onto individuals as part of programs of governance grounded in market rationalities. In addition, Karl Marx (1902) makes the difference between labour power and labour. While the first refers to the existing capacity to work, the latter is part of the capitalist production. "The labourer receives means of subsistence in exchange for his labour-power; the capitalist receives, in exchange for his means of subsistence, labour, the productive activity of the labourer, the creative force by which the worker not only replaces what he consumes, but also gives to the accumulated labour a greater value than it previously possessed. The labourer gets from the capitalist a portion of the existing means of subsistence" (p. 39).
9 *Political subjectification* refers to the constitution of a subject empowered to act politically in a dialectical communication with a dominant framework of governing the social and epistemological management of the Other.
10 I refer here to continuous knowledge production for governance, about a population subjected to programs of social and economic intervention.
11 A good example comes from WB (2005) which states the following: "The socially heterogeneous nature of Roma society also influences the integration level of various Roma communities, their political participation, and relations among different Roma groups (p. 12)".
12 In a different understanding, many of the Roma NGOs collaborate and are funded by big transnational actors of development (e.g. WB, UNDP, EU), in this way losing their ideological independence/commitment, submitting to a global neoliberal agenda.
13 The Roma Decade is an EU framework, which monitors states' implementation of policies aimed at reducing the socio-economic gaps between the Roma and the majority populations. It involves a number of European governments: Albania, Bosnia and Herzegovina, Bulgaria, Croatia, the Czech Republic, Romania, Macedonia, Montenegro, Serbia, Slovakia, Hungary, and Spain. It started in 2005 and was planned to run until 2015.
14 Kalderash is a Romani ethnonym. The term can be literally translated: 'Cauldron makers'.
15 Romanianised Roma is the translation of 'Tigani Romanizati', the name Roma, former seasonal labourers and workers in cooperative farms and state factories, use to characterise themselves.
16 I have previously done research with different Roma communities in various localities and regions in Romania. Field research with Roma in Sangeorgiu de Mures – Transylvania has been the basis for an article about identity construction among Roma

communities. Fieldwork with Roma in Atid, Harghita, Transylvania has been the basis for a book chapter on the temporary migration of the Transylvanian Roma to Hungary. Other field researches with Roma have been carried out in Moldavia, as part of an integrated community development project funded by the Open Society Foundation, Romania. The report has been published in the Soros Foundation's publications series.

17 It is worth mentioning that my research on and with the Roma was commissioned by the Romanian government, Soros Foundation, the Research Institute for the Quality of Life, and various NGOs including the West of Scotland Regional Equality Council, Glasgow, UK.

18 Gabors and HaziCigany are Roma who live in Transylvania. Gabors (a Hungarian name), previously nomad Roma, are currently mobile affluent traders, who speak three languages: Romani, Hungarian and Romanian. HaziCigany or House Gypsies, who only speak Hungarian, experiencing poor conditions of living, have always been settled, subjected to consecutive programs of assimilation by the Hapsburg Empire and socialist state.

19 Most of the time identificatory categories are established in opposition to the majority and are mainly based on statistics: "Half of all Roma surveyed are found to live in poverty, and more than one in five live in extreme poverty" (UNDP 2006: 17).

20 The phrase 'local level power relations' is used in correspondence with 'local level politics' conceptualised by Swartz, to argue that local politics is not local per se, but connected through webs of power to central politics.

21 By making references to uncertainties, Burawoy and Verdery (1999) mainly refer to high levels of inflation, difficulties in the restitution of private property, deindustrialisation and high levels of unemployment, difficult access to labour markets, clientelistic relations, etc.

22 For ethical and confidential reasons the name of the locality was changed.

23 In the mid-1990s, in full process of deindustrialisation, the Kalderash started to buy and refurbish old technology and materials, still owned by state plants and resell everything to small private firms all over the country.

24 Historically, Roma have never possessed land and until the mid-nineteenth century they were slaves in Wallachia and Moldavia and serfs in Transylvania (Achim 2004). According to Kogalniceanu (cited in Marushiakova & Popov 2009), a well-known Romanian intellectual active in the 1848 Revolution, in Wallachia and Moldavia "there were three distinct categories of slaves according to whom they belonged to – slaves of the Prince, of the monasteries, and of the boyars" (Marushiakova & Popov 2009: 5). Some of the Roma belonging to first category worked on the rulers' estates, whereas the others were nomad Roma allowed to roam and practice different professions on the condition that they paid annual taxes to the crown. In Transylvania, the situation of the Roma showed some differences. Whereas some Roma living close to regions bordering Moldavia or Wallachia were slaves, other Roma had the status of 'royal serfs' (Achim 2004). The latter were free to roam, with the obligation to pay annual taxes to the crown, "but they were never citizens with full rights" (Voicu & Tufis 2008: 12), neither in the Hungarian Kingdom, nor in the Hapsburg Empire, which included Transylvania at that time. Before the abolition of slavery in all three principalities – mid19th century, according to Alexandri's monograph, whereas Romanianised Roma were domestic slaves working for local boyars, Kalderash were nomadic slaves travelling throughout Romanian principalities practising their traditional occupations.

25 Derex Granit used to be one of the largest steel plants in Eastern Europe. It is an important reference in the book's ethnography. Since socialist times, both Romanians and Romanianised Roma used to be employees of the steel plant.

26 'Plangere penala impotriva Cabinetului Nastase privind privatizarea Sidex' [Penal complaint against Nastase's cabinet regarding the privatization of Derex Granit], Wednesday, 18th August 2009, Available at: www.ziare.com; 'Parlamentarii cer desecretizarea dosarului Sidex' [Members of Parliament request access to Derex Granit dossier], Thursday, 18th June 2009, Available at: www.ziare.com.

58 *Book discussion and introduction*

27 Many authors explored this interdependency. Among those, one can see Berdahl et al (2000), Burawoy and Verdery (1999), Hann (2002), Sick (1994), Stark (1990), Szelenyi et al (1995), Verdery (1996); West and Raman (2009).
28 Farmers, lacking advanced technology, were no longer able to cultivate their land. They were compelled to hire technology or rent out parts of their plots to large farms for relative small amounts of money and were able to exercise only indirect control over the exploitation of their land (Voiculescu 2008).
29 Scholars of Eastern European studies (Hann 2002; Humphrey 2002; Verdery 1996) use different terms to designate the concept of 'local patron': 'local boss' or 'local baron'. Throughout the book, I use the term: 'local patron'.
30 "Cine conduceRomania! Harta baronilor local din Romania. Baronii vechi si noi" [Who is ruling Romania. The map of local barons in Romania. Old and new barons], 11th April 2011, Available at: www.econtext.ro.

Bibliography

Achim, V. (2004) *The Roma in Romanian History*. Budapest: Central European University Press.
Allen, J. (2004) 'The Whereabouts of Power: Politics, Government and Space. Geografiska Annaler'. *Series B, Human Geography, Special Issue: The Political Challenge of Relational Space*, 86(1): 19–32.
Althusser, L. (2008) *On Ideology*. London, New York: Verso.
Badescu, G., Grigoras, V., Rughinis, C., Voicu, M. & Voicu, O. (2007) *Barometrul Incluziunii Romilor [Barometer for Roma inclusion]*. Bucharest: Open Society Foundation.
Balibar, E. (2009) 'Forward'. In Nidhi Trehan and Nando Sigona (Eds.) *Romani Politics in Contemporary Europe: Poverty, Ethnic Mobilization, and the Neo-liberal Order*. London and New York: Palgrave Macmillan.
Barany, Z. D. (1995) 'The Roma in Macedonia: Ethnic Politics and the Marginal Condition in a Balkan State'. *Ethnic and Racial Studies*, 18(3): 515–531.
Barany, Z. D. (2002) *The East European Gypsies: Regime Change, Marginality, and Ethnopolitics*. Cambridge: Cambridge University Press.
Barany, Z. D. (2004) 'Roma Marginality and Politics'. In H. F. Carey and N. Manea (Eds.) *Romania Since 1989: Politics, Economics, and Society*. Lanham, MD: Lexington Books, pp. 255–275.
Berdahl, D., Bunzl, M. & Lampland, M. (Eds.) (2000) *Altering States: Ethnographies of Transition in Eastern Europe and in the Former Soviet Union*. Ann Arbor: University of Michigan Press.
Bigo, D. (2008) 'Security: A Field Left Fallow'. In M. Dillon and A. W. Neal (Eds.) *Foucault on Politics, Security, and War*. London and New York: Palgrave Macmillan, pp. 93–114.
Bourdieu, P. (1977) *Outline of a Theory of Practice*. Cambridge: Cambridge University Press.
Bourdieu, P. (1984) *Distinction: A Social Critique of the Judgement of Taste*. Cambridge, MA: Harvard University Press.
Bourdieu, P. (1985) 'The Social Space and the Genesis of Groups'. *Theory and Society*, 14(6): 723–744.
Bourdieu, P. (1989) 'Social Space and Symbolic Power'. *Sociological Theory*, 7(1): 14–25.
Bourdieu, P. (1991) *Language and Symbolic Power*. Cambridge, UK; Malden, US: Polity Press.
Brubaker, R. & Cooper, F. (2000) 'Beyond Identity'. *Theory and Society*, 29(1): 1–47.

Burawoy, M. & Verdery, K. (Eds.) (1999) *Uncertain Transition: Ethnographies of Change in the Postsocialist World*. Lanham, MD: Rowman and Littlefield.
Burchell, G. (1996) 'Liberal Government and Techniques of the Self'. In A. Barry, T. Osbourne, and N. Rose (Eds.) *Foucault and the Political Reason: Liberalism, Neo-Liberalism and Rationalities of Government.* Chicago: The University of Chicago Press, pp.19–37.
Campeanu, P. (1986) *The Origins of Stalinism: From Leninist Revolution to Stalinist Society.* Armonk, NY: M. E. Sharpe.
Clark, C. (2004) 'Severity Has Often Enraged But Never Subdued a Gypsy': The History and Making of European Romani Stereotypes'. In N. Saul and S. Tebutt. (Eds.) *The Role of the Romanies: Images and Counter-Images of 'Gyspsies'/Romanies in European Cultures.* Liverpool: Liverpool University, pp. 226–247.
Cole, J. W. (1985) 'Problems of Socialism in Eastern Europe'. *Dialectical Anthropology*, 9(1/4): 233–256.
Dean, M. (1992) *The Constitution of Poverty: Toward a Genealogy of Liberal Governance*. London, New York: Routledge.
Dean, M. (2007) *Governing Societies: Political Perspective on Domestic and International Law*. Berkshire, UK: Open University Press/McGraw Hill.
Deleuze, G. & Guattari, F. (2005)[1987] *A Thousand Plateaus: Capitalism and Schizophrenia*. Minneapolis: University of Minnesota Press.
Drakakis-Smith, A. (2007) 'Nomadism a Moving Myth? Policies of Exclusion and the Gyspys/Traveller Response'. *Mobilities*, 2(3): 463–487.
Duffield, M. (2002) 'Social Reconstruction and the Radicalisation of Development: Aid as a Relation of Global Liberal Governance'. *Development and Change*, 33(5): 1049–1071.
EC (2003) Communication from the Commission to the Council, COM. The European Parliament and the European Economic and Social Committee Governance and Development. Brussels, 20.10.2003.
EC (2006) Communication from the Commission to the Council, COM. The European Parliament. The European Economic and Social Committee and the Committee or the Regions. Governance in the European Consensus on Development. Towards a Harmonised Approach Within the European Union. Brussels, 30.8.2006.
EC (2010) Commission Staff Working Document. Roma in Europe: The Implementation of European Union Instruments and Policies for Roma Inclusion – Progress Report 2008–2010, Brussels, 7.4.2010.
EC (2011) Communication from the Commission to the European Parliament, the Council, the European Economic and Social Committee and the Committee of the Regions. An EU Framework for National Roma Integration Strategies up to 2020.
EC (2012) National Roma Integration Strategies, a first step in the implementation of the EU Framework. Communication from the Commission to the European Parliament, the Council, the European Economic and Social Committee and the Committee of the Regions. European Commission Directorate-General Justice: Belgium.
Escobar, A. (2012) *Encountering Development: The Making and Unmaking of the Third World*. Princeton, NJ: Princeton University Press.
Eyal, G., Szelenyi, I. & Townsley, E. (1998) *Making Capitalists Without Capitalists: The New Ruling Elites in Eastern Europe*. Verso: New Left Books.
Ferguson, J. (1994)[1990] *The Anti- Politics Machine*. Minneapolis: University of Minnesota Press.
Fletcher, R. (2001) 'What Are We Fighting for? Rethinking Resistance in a Pewenche Community in Chile'. *Journal of Peasant Studies*, 28(3): 37–66.

Foucault, M. (1980) *Power/Knowledge: Selected Interviews and Other Writings, 1972–1977*. (Ed.) C. Gordon. New York: Pantheon Books.

Foucault, M. (1983) 'The Subject and Power'. In H. Dreyfus and P. Rabinow (Eds.) *Michel Foucault: Beyond Structuralism and Hermeneutics*. Chicago: The University of Chicago Press, pp. 208–229.

Foucault, M. (1984) *The Foucault Reader*. (Ed.) Paul Rabinow. New York: Pantheon Books.

Foucault, M. (1991a) 'Governmentality'. In G. Burchell, C. Gordon and P. Miller (Eds.) *The Foucault Effect: Studies in Governmentality, With Two Lectures by and an Interview with Michel Foucault*. Chicago: University of Chicago Press, pp. 87–104.

Foucault, M. 1991b[1975] *Discipline and Punish: The Birth of the Prison*. London: Penguin Books.

Foucault, M. (2002a) 'Truth and Juridical Forms'. In J. Faubion (Ed.) *Power Essential Works of Foucault 1954–1984*. New York: The New Press, pp. 1–89.

Foucault, M. (2002b) 'Governmentality'. In J. Faubion (Ed.) *Power Essential Works of Foucault 1954–1984*. New York: The New Press, pp. 201–222.

Foucault, M. (2002c) 'The Subject and Power'. In J. Faubion (Ed.) *Power Essential Works of Foucault 1954–1984*. New York: The New Press, pp. 326–348.

Foucault, M. (2003) *Society Must Be Defended: Lectures at the College de France 1975–76*. (Eds.) M. Bertani and A. Fontano, General (Eds.) F. Ewald and A. Fontana. New York: Picador.

Foucault, M. (2005) *The Hermeneutics of the Subject: Lectures at the College de France/1981–1982*. (Eds.) Frederic Gross, Francois Ewald and Alessandro Fontana. New York: Palgrave Macmillan.

Foucault, M. (2008) *The Birth of Biopolitics: Lectures at the College de France, 1978–79. Michel Foucault*. (Ed.) Michel Senellart. London and New York: Palgrave Macmillan.

Foucault, M. (2009) *Michel Foucault. Security, Territory, Population: Lectures at the College de France, 1977–78*. (Eds.) M. Senellart, F. Ewald and A. Fontana. London and New York: Palgrave Macmillan.

FRA (European Union Agency for Fundamental Rights), UNDP and European Commission (2012) *The Situation of Roma in 11 EU Member States: Survey Results at a Glance*. Report prepared for European Commission. Luxembourg: Publications Office of the European Union.

Gabel, G. (2009) 'The Growing Divide: The Marginalization of Young Roma Children in Bulgaria'. *International Journal of Social Welfare*, 18(1): 65–75.

Gadowska, K. (2006) 'Violence in the Area of Clientelistic and Cronyistic'. In Julia Kusznir (Ed.) *KICES Working Papers No. 6. Informal Networks and Corruption in Post-Socialist Societies*. Koszalin Institute of Comparative European Studies (KICES). Koszalin.

Ghani, A. (1995) 'Writing a History of Power: An Examination of Eric R. Wolf's Anthropological Quest'. In J. Schneider and R. Rapp (Eds.) *Articulating Hidden Histories: Exploring the Influence of Eric R. Wolf*. Berkeley, Los Angeles, London: University of California Press, pp. 31–48.

Gill, S. (1995) 'Globalisation, Market Civilisation, and Disciplinary Neoliberalism'. *Millennium Journal of International Studies*, 23(3): 399–423.

Gledhill, J. (2000) *Power and its Disguises: Anthropological Perspectives on Politics*. London: Pluto Press.

Gordon, C. (1991) 'Governmental Rationality: An Introduction'. In G. Burchell, C. Gordon and P. Miller (Eds.) *The Foucault Effect: Studies in Governmentality. With Two Lectures by and an Interview with Michel Foucault*. Chicago: University of Chicago Press, pp. 1–51.

Grzymala-Busse, A. & Loung, P. J. (2002) 'Reconceptualizing the State: Lessons from Post-Communism'. *Politics and Society*, 30(4): 529–554.

Gugliemo, R. & Waters, T. W. (2005, I.) 'Migrating Towards Minority Status. Shifting European Policy Towards Roma'. *Journal of Common Market Studies*, 43(4): 763–786.

Guttman, M. C. (1993) 'Rituals of Resistance: A Critique of the Theory of Everyday Forms of Resistance'. *Latin American Perspectives*, 20(2): 74–92.

Guy, W. (Ed.) (2001) *Between Past and Future: The Roma of Central and Eastern Europe*. Hatfield: University of Hertfordshire Press.

Hancock, I. (2004) 'The Concoctors: Creating Fake Romani Culture'. In N. Saul and S. Tebutt (Eds.) *The Role of the Romanies: Images and Counter-Images of 'Gypsies'/Romanies in European Cultures*. Liverpool: Liverpool University, pp. 85–98.

Hann, C. M. (2002) *Postsocialism, Ideals, Ideologies and Practices in Eurasia*. London: Routledge.

Harris, J. (2001) *Depoliticising Development: The World Bank and Social Capital*. New Delhi, India: Left Word Books.

HCNM (1993) 'Roma (Gypsies) in the CSCE Region'. Report of the High Commissioner on National Minorities Meeting of the Committee of Senior Officials, 21–23 September.

Hindess, B. (2001) 'The Liberal Government of Unfreedom'. *Alternatives: Global, Local, Political*, 26(2): 93–111.

Humphrey, C. (2002) *The Unmaking of Soviet Life: Everyday Economies in Russia and Mongolia*. Ithaca: Cornell University Press.

Ilcan, S. & Lacey, A. (2011) *Governing the Poor: Exercises of Poverty Reduction, Practices of Global Aid*. Montreal & Kingston, London, Ithaca: McGill- Queen's University Press.

Inglis, T. (1997) 'Empowerment and Emancipation'. *Adult Education Quarterly*, 48(1): 3–17.

Iordache, R. (2011) 'Governmental Strategy for the Inclusion of Romanian Citizen Belonging to the Roma Minority for 2012–2020'. Source: European Commission. ww.ec.europa.eu/justice/discrimination/roma/national strategies/index_en.htm

Kalmar, I. D. & Penslar, D. J. (Eds.) (2005) *Orientalism and the Jews*. Hanover, NH: University Press of New England.

Kideckel, D. (1982) 'The Socialist Transformation of Agriculture in a Romanian Commune 1945–1962'. *American Ethnologist*, 9(3): 320–340.

Kothari, U. (2005) 'Authority and Expertise: The Professionalisation of International Development and the Ordering of Dissent'. *Antipode*, 37(3): 425–446.

Kovats, M. (2001) 'The Emergence of European Roma Policy'. In W. Guy (Ed.) *Between Past and Future: The Roma of Central and Eastern Europe*. Hatfield: University of Hertfordshire Press, pp. 93–117.

Ladanyi, J. & Szelenyi, I. (2003) 'Historical Variations in Inter-Ethnic Relations: Toward a Social History of Roma in Csenyete, 1857–2000'. *Romani Studies*, 5–13(1): 1–51.

Ladanyi, J. & Szelenyi, I. (2006) *Patterns of Exclusion: Constructing Gypsy Ethnicity and the Making of an Underclass in Transitional Societies of Europe*. New York: Columbia University Press.

Lee, R. (2005) *Learn Romani: Das-duma Romanes*. Hertfordshire: University of Hertfordshire Press.

Marushiakova, E. & Popov, V. (2009) 'Gypsy Slavery in Wallachia and Moldavia'. In T. Kamusella and K. Jaskulowski (Eds.) *Nationalism Today*. Oxford: Peter Lang, pp. 89–124.

Marx, K. (1902) *Wage-Labor and Capital*. New York: New York Labor News Company.

Massey, D. (1999) 'Entanglements of Power: Reflections'. In J. P. Sharp, P. Routledge, C. Philo and R. Paddison (Eds.) *Entanglements of Power: Geographies of Domination/Resistance*. London, New York: Routledge, pp. 279–285.

Matras, Y. (2004) 'Introduction: The Role of Language in Mystifying and Demystifying Gypsy Identity'. In N. Saul and S. Tebutt (Eds.) *The Role of the Romanies: Images and Counter-Images of 'Gypsies'/Romanies in European Cultures*. Liverpool: Liverpool University, pp. 53–79.

Merlingen, M. & Ostrauskaite, R. (2005) 'A Dense Policy Space: The Police Aid of the OSCE and the EU'. *OSCE Yearbook*, 10: 341–357.

Miraftab, F. (2004) 'Making Neo-Liberal Governance: The Disempowering Work of Empowerment'. *International Planning Studies*, 9(4): 239–259.

Ortner, S. B. (1995) 'Resistance and the Problem of Ethnographic Refusal'. *Comparative Studies in Society and History*, 37(1): 173–193.

Pile, S. & Keith, M. (Eds.) (1997) *Geographies of Resistance*. London: Routledge.

Procacci, G. (1991) 'Social Economy and the Government of Poverty'. In G. Burchell, C. Gordon and P. Miller (Eds.) *The Foucault Effect: Studies in Governmentality, with Two Lectures by and an Interview with Michel Foucault*. Chicago: University of Chicago Press, pp. 151–169.

Ranciere, J. (2010) *Dissensus: On Politics and Aesthetics*. London and New York: Continuum.

Rapley, J. (2004) 'Development Studies and the Post-Development Critique'. *Progress in Development Studies*, 4(4): 350–354.

Rose, N. (1996) Governing "advanced" Liberal Democracies. In A. Barry, T. Osbourne and N. Rose (Eds.) *Foucault and the Political Reason: Liberalism, Neo-Liberalism and Rationalities of Government*. Chicago: The University of Chicago Press, pp. 37–65.

Rose, N. (1999) *The Power of Freedoms: Reframing Political Thought*. Cambridge: Cambridge University Press.

Said, E. (2003) *Orientalism*. London: Penguin Books.

Sampson, S. L. (1984) *National Integration Through Socialist Planning: An Anthropological Study of a Romanian New Town*. Boulder, CO: East European Monographs.

Saul, N. & Tebbutt, S. (2004) *The Role of the Romaninies: Images and Counter-Images of 'Gyspies'/Romanies in European Cultures*. Liverpool University: Liverpool.

Sharp, J. P., Routledge, P., Philo, C. & Paddison, R. (1999) 'Entanglements of Power: Geographies of Domination/Resistance'. In Joanne P. Sharp, Paul Routledge, Chris Philo and Ronan Paddison (Eds.) *Entanglements of Power: Geographies of Domination/Resistance*. London, New York: Routledge, pp. 1–41.

Sibley, D. (1981) *Outsiders in Urban Societies*. Cambridge: Cambridge University Press.

Sibley, D. (1995) *Geographies of Exclusion: Society and Difference in the West*. London: Routledge.

Sick, E. (1994) 'From the Multicoloured to the Black and White Economy: The Hungarian Second Economy and Transformation'. *International Journal of Urban and Regional Research*, 18(1): 46–70.

Stark, D. (1990) 'Privatization in Hungary: From Plan to Market or from Plan to Clan?' *East European Politics and Societies*, 4(3): 351–392.

Stewart, M. (2002) 'Deprivation, the Roma and "the underclass"'. In C. M. Hann (Ed.) *Postsocialism, Ideals, Ideologies and Practices in Eurasia*. New York: Routledge, pp. 133–157.

Stoica, C. A. (2004) 'From Good Communists to Even Better Capitalists? Entrepreneurial Pathways in Post-Socialist Romania'. *East European Politics and Societies*, 18(2): 236–277.

Surdu, M. & Kovats, M. (2015) 'Roma Identity as an Expert-Political Construction'. *Social Inclusion*, 3(5): 5–18.

Swartz, M. J. (1968) 'Introduction'. In M., J. Swartz (Ed.) *Local-level politics: social and cultural perspective*. London: University of London Press LTD, pp. 1-51.

Szelenyi, S., Szelenyi, I. & Kovach, I. (1995) 'The Making of the Hungarian Post-Communist Elite: Circulation in Politics, Reproduction in Economy'. *Theory and Society*, 24(5): 697–722.

Trehan, N. & Sigona, N. (Eds.) (2009) *Romani Politics in Contemporary Europe: Poverty, Ethnic Mobilization, and the Neo-Liberal Order.* Palgrave Macmillan.

UNDP (2000) *Human Development Report 2000.* New York, Oxford: Oxford University Press.

UNDP (2002) *The Roma in Central and Eastern Europe. Avoiding Dependency Trap: A Regional Human Development Report.* UNDP Regional Bureau for Europe and the Commonwealth, Bratislava.

UNDP (2005) *Employing the Roma: Insights from Business.* UNDP Regional Bureau for Europe and the CIS, Bratislava.

UNDP (2006) *At Risk: Roma and the Displaced in Southeast Europe.* (Eds.) M. Collin, C. Grosu, J. Kling, S. Milcher, B. O'Higgnins, B. Slay, A. Zhelyazkova. Bratislava: Regional Bureau for Europe and the Commonwealth of Independent States.

Valverde, M. (1996) '"Despotism" and Ethical Liberal Governance'. *Economy and Society*, 25(3): 357–372.

Van Baar, H. (2011) *The European Roma: Minority Representation, Memory and the Limits of Transnational Governmentality.* Amsterdam: Geborente's Gravenhage.

Van De PORT, M. (1998) *Gypsies, Wars and Other Instances of the Wild: Civilisation and Its Discontents in a Serbian Town.* Amsterdam: Amsterdam University Press.

Verdery, K. (1991) *National Ideologies Under Socialism Identity and Cultural Politics in Ceausescu's Romania.* Berkley, Los Angeles, Oxford: University of California Press.

Verdery, K. (1993) 'Ethnic Relations, Economies of Shortage, and the Transition in Eastern Europe'. In C. M. Hann (Ed.) *Socialism Ideals Ideologies, and Local Practices.* London, New York: Routledge, pp. 169–186.

Verdery, K. (1996) *What Was Socialism and What Comes Next.* Princeton, NJ: Princeton University Press.

Verdery, K. (2002) 'Whither Postsocialism?' In C. M. Hann (Ed.) *Postsocialism, Ideals, Ideologies and Practices in Eurasia.* New York: Routledge, pp. 15–29.

Vigh, H. (2009) 'Motion Squared: A Second Look at the Concept of Social Navigation'. *Anthropological Theory*, 9(4): 419–438.

Voicu, M. & Tufis, C. (Eds.) (2008) *Roma: Life Stories.* Bucharest, Romania: Soros Foundation.

Voiculescu, C. (2002) 'Identity Constructions amongst the Roma in Sângeorgiu de Mureş'. *Romanian Sociology*, 2(1–2): 100–125.

Voiculescu, C. (2004) 'Temporary Migration of Transylvanian Roma to Hungary'. In D. Pop (Ed.) *New Patterns of Labour Migration in Central and Eastern Europe.* Cluj-Napoca, Romania: AMM Design, pp. 145–164.

Voiculescu, C. (2005) *Fighting against Tuberculosis in Roma Communities in Romania* (co-author), unpublished report commissioned to Romani CRISS, Bucharest.

Voiculescu, C. (2008) 'Are Peasants Disappearing in Postsocialist Romania? Rent Regimes and Control Over Land'. *Focaal: Journal of Global and Historical Anthropology*, 52: 77–91.

West, H. W. & Raman, P. (Eds.) (2009) *Enduring Socialism: Explorations of Revolution and Transformation, Restoration and Continuation.* New York, Oxford: Berghahn Books.

Wilson III, E. J. (1981) Orientalism: A Black Perspective. *Journal of Palestine Studies*, 10(2): 59–69.

Wolf, E. R. (1990) 'Distinguished Lecture: Facing Power: Old Insights, New Questions'. *American Anthropologist*, 92(3): 586–596.

Wolf, E. R. (1999) *Envisioning Power: Ideologies of Dominance and Crisis*. Berkeley, Los Angeles: University of California Press.

Wolf, E. R. (2001) *Pathways of Power: Building an Anthropology of the Modern World*. Berkeley, Los Angeles, London: University of California Press.

Woodcock, S. (2007) 'Romania in Europe: Roma, Rroma and Tigani as Sites for the Contestation of Ethno-National Identities'. *Patterns of Prejudice*, 41(5): 493–515.

World Bank. (1992) *Governance and Development*. Washington, DC: The World Bank.

World Bank. (1998) 'World Development Report 1997: The State in a Changing World'. *Overview: IDS Bulleting*, 29(2). Washington, DC: The World Bank, pp. 14–31.

World Bank. (2000) *Roma and the Transition in Central and Eastern Europe: Trends and Challenges*. (Ed.) D. Ringold. Washington, DC: World Bank.

World Bank. (2002) *Poverty and Ethnicity: A Cross-Country Study of Roma Poverty in Central Europe*. (Eds.) Ana Revenga, Dena Ringold and William Martin Tracey. Washington, DC: World Bank.

World Bank. (2005) *Roma in an Expanding Europe: Breaking the Poverty Cycle*. (Eds.) D. Ringold, M. A. Orenstein and E. Wilkens. Washington, DC: World Bank.

World Bank. (2010) *Europe and Central Asia: Economic Costs of Roma Exclusion*. Washington, DC: World Bank.

Zamfir, C. & Preda, M. (2002) *Romii in Romania [Roma in Romania]*. Bucharest: Expert Press.

Zizek, S. (1993) *Tarrying with the Negative*. Durham, NC: Duke University Press.

Part II
A historical political ethnography of social power among the Roma

6 On the move within movement from socialism to post-socialism

Roma interactions with smooth vs. striated spaces of economy

The post-1989 Roma economic practices are specific to the transformations, which occurred in post-socialist Romania and Eastern Europe. The state's withdrawal from the economy (Wallace & Latcheva 2006) left a large proportion of the population unemployed, looking for survival in the informal economic sector (e.g. petty trade, exchange of goods, domestic work, etc.). These changes intensified informal patterns of relations, interactions and reciprocity. As most scholars of Eastern Europe[1] argued, these relations emerged in socialism in the sphere of the second economy[2] and continued to develop further in post-socialism as economies of informal exchange, reciprocal support and coping strategies (Dunn 2004; Stenning et al 2010). Various terms were used to indicate the use of informal economy: 'cash in-hand', 'undeclared', 'shadow', 'informal', 'black' and 'underground' economy (Williams 2009). Some authors (Grabiner 2000; Thomas 1992; Williams & Windebank 1998) identified informal work as the production and commerce of licit goods[3], which are not declared to the state and therefore not taxed, a definition which accurately fits Romanianised Roma's informal work and the Kalderash's informal businesses.

Previous research has shown that informal economy in Central and Eastern European (CEE) countries was practised not only for survival, but also for enrichment (Wallace & Latcheva 2006). In the early 1990s, the lack of clear laws and regulations fostered opportunities for informal commercial activities[4], which were partly developed and formalised later (Okolski 2001; Piirainen 1997). As many authors argued, in post-socialist countries a clear-cut boundary between formal and informal economic practice could not always be established (Williams 2009). Employers used a mixture of formal and informal work practices – informal salary arrangements – in official employment[5], whereas employees were often involved in both formal and informal activities[6]. However, in Romania, the state actors did not consider these qualitative observations and, as Chelcea and Mateescu (2005) argued, the informal economy was heavily criminalised in the 1990s, and 'the informal' was seen as 'illegal'. As they suggested, the ethnography became the most appropriate methodological approach to deconstruct the criminalised image of the informal economy and offer a representation of the subjectivities of those involved in activities considered 'illegal' by the state.

Additionally, drawing further on Granovetter's (1985) argument that economic practices are socially embedded (Swedberg 1991, 2008), authors of post-socialist studies noticed that these informal economic activities have been embedded in webs of social relations, which implicitly configured participants' worlds of meaning, many times alternatively construed to the state or legal ones. In line with this, a comprehensive understanding of social and economic differences among the Roma, but also of their particular subjectivities shaped by adaptations to economic transformations, authorises a careful exploration of the dynamics of their social and economic relations occurring at individual and group level from socialism to post-socialism. In the following, I offer a snapshot of the local economic dynamics in Alexandri, throughout socialism and post-socialism, as an inquiry into the micro-social and economic relations involved.

Alexandri's local economy from socialism to post-socialism

The socialist local economy in Alexandri followed the model of the lowland villages, which underwent the collectivisation of land imposed in the 1950s and 1960s. Alexandri had one cooperative farm where subsistence farmers worked collectively and shared the produce, two state farms and a so-called handicraft cooperative, which used to be the main employer for the locals. In order to obtain both cash and agricultural produce, many Romanianised Roma worked for both collective and state farms. The cooperative farmers and seasonal workers were entitled to a plot of land for family use. Some Romanianised Roma who worked on the collective farm benefited from this entitlement.

From the conversations I had with many Roma, including Ioader, a former state farm team leader and currently an informal Romanianised Roma leader, most of the Romanianised Roma worked in the neighbouring state farms during the warm seasons. They used to receive good payment compared to the cooperative work and large amounts of goods at the end of the season. The disadvantages were mainly related to family life, which was not easy to manage during seasonal work. Many Romanianised Roma were, as they said, 'brought up in farms'. Children were either left in the care of grandparents or joined their parents at the farms, missing several months from school. Yet, seasonal work was not sufficient to provide resources for the whole year, allowing for only daily expenses and food consumption over the cold season when the Roma were largely unemployed.

During the winter, Romanianised Roma used to help local farmers with household work. In exchange for labour, they received either money or goods, and sometimes informal loans with flexible terms of repayment. However, during socialism, unemployment was prohibited and the employment status of the Romanianised Roma during the winter was ambiguous, often subject to negotiation with the local police and the state farms' engineers, who would send evidence of their work on the state farm to Alexandri's local council. These days, Romanianised Roma still provide services for the whole village (e.g. delivering firewood from the forest to the locals) which ensure their survival, rather than bringing about an improvement in their socio-economic condition. Most of them told me that the money gained from the farms was sufficient for food and clothes, but insufficient to invest in their houses, which generally are in bad shape, made of wattle and daub.

During the 1960s, people from Alexandri sought employment in the cities, in the new state enterprises such as the steel plant Derex in Granit. Many small farmers and several Romanianised Roma in Alexandri were permanent employees at DerexGranit. Situated close to the big city, the locals would commute daily for industrial work and work their small plots of land during the weekends. Nevertheless, whereas farmers obtained employment in qualified positions, the Romanianised Roma were the lower grade or unskilled personnel of the factory. On the other hand, Kalderash used to be former nomads, traders and smiths (e.g. cauldron makers) organised in small mobile groups, with one *bulibasa/big boss* representing the group in interactions with local authorities, in negotiations over camping. During the 1960s, they were settled at the outskirts of the village by the socialist state. Since then, their social life has split into two socio-economic forms: a mobile and a settled condition. In other words, the Kalderash were never quite settled. During the warm season, they travelled in small groups based on close kinship relations, trading their copper made products (e.g. cauldrons) over the country. From 1960s onwards, staying in Alexandri or camping in one place over the winter brought them under the direct control of main Roma leaders (Iancu in Alexandri and Traian in Liveni), who would collaborate with state security services.

To sum up, during socialism, the Romanianised Roma and local farmers confined their activities to the state economy and the Kalderash continued to base their existence on mobile customary practices, defined by the socialist state as part of the second economy. The economic landscape altered considerably after 1989 when collective farms and cooperatives were dissolved and large state enterprises in nearby towns and cities were partly dismantled and privatised. The local population faced high unemployment and a retreat to the household economy and agriculture. The dismantling of the socialist state farms and plants left most of the Romanianised Roma unemployed, with no regular source of income, who started to look for day and seasonal labour in Alexandri and nearby localities. Additionally, in the early 1990s, famers received their land back from the state. With inadequate technology, resources and labour they either rented out the land or cultivated it with the help of locals including the Romanianised Roma. On the other hand, many Kalderash families became involved in trading outdated technology and materials, purchased cheaply from Derex Granit and sold to small firms all over the country. Using labour force offered by the Romanianised Roma and farmers, they succeeded to move from their old district and started building their large houses. However, the rest of the Kalderash continued their mobile economic practices as ambulant smiths (e.g. cauldron makers and roof painters).

The reconfiguration and perceptions of local stratification changed, too. The Kalderash started to be considered the wealthiest by the Romanianised Roma and the farmers. On the other hand, the Romanianised Roma were considered to be the poorest by the Kalderash and the farmers. The farmers are considered by the locals to occupy the middle position in this local hierarchy. Generally, these socio-economic differences between the two Roma groups rest upon changes in local perception and changes in the material conditions. Relations and practices they developed during the socialist economy underlie their interactions with the post-socialist transformation and suggest that the two Roma's economic conditions changed in different ways. Starting from these observations, this chapter aims to describe and explain the *socio-economic transformations of the two Roma groups by looking at their interaction with the economic changes from socialism to post-socialism, which released different opportunities and constraints.* This glimpse into their movement, during socialist and post-socialist economy is able to reveal paradigmatic instantiations of their active engagement with the production of their subjectivities and lifestyles, without curtailing the effects induced by the historical movement of economy as a space of power. In order to come to an understanding of the differences between the present socio-economic organisation of the two Roma groups, I look ethnographically at the history of their economic practices starting with the socialist sedentarisation of the 1960s, when the Kalderash settled in Alexandri.

In the following section, I examine the socialist period where the two Roma groups stood in different relations to the state and were involved in different forms of economic activity. The accounts I use in the next sections come from Roma themselves, but also from people who held key positions in Alexandri's socialist socio-economic life: Anton, former director of the local collective farm and handicrafts cooperative, and Pompiliu, a history teacher and former manager of the cultural centre during socialism. Some of the Kalderash were Anton's employees and friends. His narrative focused on the interactions between Kalderash and state institutions. On the other hand, Pompiliu used to teach Romanianised Roma children in school and supervise their parents as performers (e.g. fiddlers) at educational and cultural events organised according to directives received from the centre. He was the mayor of Alexandri in 1991, currently a Liberal Democrat Party member and also the author of an unpublished monograph, which includes references to the history of Roma settlements.

The Kalderash's nomadic subjectivities, the socialist second economy and state repression

According to Pompiliu and other locals, in the 1960s, different mobile groups of Kalderash started to settle in Alexandri. Many Kalderash emphasised, on one hand, the benefits brought by sedentarisation and, on the other, the oppression practised by the socialist state. Xandru and his son, George, who come from a relatively rich family of Kalderash, offered me further accounts about the way their community had to adapt to state repression and to local authorities' management. Xandru's father was a customary Roma leader – big boss/*bulibasa* – for one of the nomadic groups which later settled in Alexandri.

We have been here since the 1960s. My father went to the local council with evidence from Bucharest that we were allowed to get land to build houses. After collectivisation, we received land to build our houses and we did not live in our tents any more. We still travelled a lot, but we were happy to get houses and land.

(Xandru, son of a former *bulibasa*)

C: Why did you decide to settle?
G: They did not let us wander any more. 'Militia' [the former police, under socialism] used to come and check our IDs, check our residence and work permits. If we had none we needed to leave the village [where they settled temporarily] in 24 hours. Then the *bulibasa* decided to give gold for us to receive land for construction. My grandfather went to Bucharest and gave gold and they all received the 'governmental' decision to settle in Alexandri. When the local council saw the document, they distributed land to Gypsies. The whole land was in a single family name. My grandfather, the *bulibasa*, had a house there, but no papers for that, neither did I. No one had.

(George, Kalderash man)

Xandru and George's statements complement each other. Suggesting an improvement in their family's housing conditions, Xandru, the son of a former customary leader emphasises the advantages of sedentarisation. On the other hand, George's narrative reveals that the Kalderash's desire to settle evolved from the constraints imposed by the socialist state on their travelling. Yet, Kalderash became interested in settling as their travel was limited by the evidence of a permanent residence status. However, these arrangements imposed from the political centre created space for debates and quarrels between the local population, Kalderash and the local administration. The Kalderash's decisions to either settle or travel were caught in between the central state decisions of sedentarisation, enforced by regional police, and the local authorities and populations, which often refused them permission to settle[7]. As stated by George and other interviewees, the Kalderash had to negotiate and bribe their settlement in the village. Pompiliu, the school teacher, and other locals claimed that during the 1960s and 1970s, the mayors of Alexandri received gold from the Kalderash groups who were interested in settling in the village:

Mayors at that time, were paid by the Gypsies, but these were unofficial decisions (. . .) The Gypsies gave 24 K gold and 20,000 LEI [by comparison, the value of a car was 70,000 back then] to be allowed to settle here in the village.

(Pompiliu, history teacher)

However, as George stated, after the refusal by the local authorities of permission for his group to settle, his grandfather, a customary leader, suggested that he adopted a different strategy. His grandfather went directly to the central government and bought their right to settle in the village with gold. Other decisions created further discontent among the locals, as the land received by Kalderash was part of the collective farm. Anton remembers his dissatisfaction with the local administration's decision to settle them on the farm's land:

> I was the CAP's [collective farm] director. After 1963, the Kalderash wanted to erect buildings on our vineyards. I brought the issue to the county level where I said: These people are settling on our territory. [County level official]: Comrade Anton, they are citizens of the Socialist Republic of Romania, they have all the rights of a citizen, I was told.
> (Anton, former cooperative farm director)

Anton's conversation with the regional party activist reveals once more the disconnection between central and regional directives and attitudes by local authorities, who were not interested in enforcing the directives. Whereas the locals stigmatised their lifestyle and opposed their settlement, the local administration found governing the Kalderash, a group with a mobile lifestyle and social-political organisation, a difficult and demanding task. The recently settled nomads were almost unidentifiable[8], people with no IDs or birth certificates. The local priests and teachers were supposed to implement the state programs of integration and convince them to get identification papers and go to school. Those involved in these state programs suggested that the requirements involved in ensuring the Kalderash's integration were difficult and time-consuming tasks. It was also very difficult for the local council and state companies to collect taxes and bill payments from them. The Kalderash themselves had to accept sedentarisation and all the consequences to get permission to continue to travel seasonally.

They continued to travel all over the country during the warm season. The railway station facilitated travelling and transport of their tools and materials. Another advantage was the proximity of the steel plant from which, through informal arrangements, they used to purchase working material. Minu and Mirea are two Kalderash in their forties who come from moderately affluent families and still practice their old occupations. They have both experienced the restrictions imposed by the socialist state on their travelling practices and possession of gold. Under socialism, they travelled to Transylvania to make cauldrons for farmers producing alcohol[9]. As ambulant smiths were organised in small groups under the leadership of a customary leader/*bulibasa*, who was authorised to mediate between local authorities (e.g. police and local councils) and the Kalderash who were looking for permission to camp and local authorisation for their economic activities. Cauldron-making for alcohol was forbidden and so was access to the material needed for its manufacture, which was usually not available on the open market. The group's customary leader had to negotiate informally with local police and councils. The arrangements with the local authorities were usually agreed, but the regional police would make periodic controls to seize copper, cauldrons and gold from Kalderash.

M: They confiscated our copper and we ran in the forest. We got beaten.
C: Was it regional or local police?
M: It was the regional police.
C: Did the mayor know that you were making cauldrons?
M: He knew and supported us and after we finished he had an enquiry into who had done what. We used to hide the cauldrons on the river banks and in bushes. We got copper from the state plants.
C: Who were the providers?
M: Romanians – [steel plant] workers, managers, but if we were caught that would have meant arrest. Copper was like gold – valuable and not much available. Regional police once caught us with cauldrons in Bradut [a Transylvanian town] and my family (father, mother, and child) were beaten. They asked me for the copper receipts and I didn't have any. They seized 350 kilos of my copper. In Tormeni [Transylvanian town] they seized my truck, full of cauldrons. What was it like during Ceausescu's time? So much poverty but we were all hard working (. . .).

(Minu, Kalderash man)

Minu's last statement is relevant as it shows that both local authorities and Kalderash supported each other in the socialist second economy. As already mentioned, the Kalderash cultivated good relations with farmers from Transylvania[10] who needed their manufactured products. To secure a living in the restrictive socialist economy, the Kalderash and Transylvanian farmers depended on each other. As many Kalderash explained, exchanges were based on trust and reciprocity. The Kalderash received not only money, but also goods and gifts from farmers, who sometimes became godfathers to their children. These relations between mobile Kalderash groups and local populations were part of the second economy and generated both 'systems of survival' (Voiculescu 2004) and welfare accumulation. Yet, local authorities were not always able to defend them against the socialist state. Regional police and *Securitate* monitored the Kalderash's activities and collaborated with Iancu, a Kalderash customary leader who did not travel too much, but was authorised by the regional police to exercise control over the Kalderash mobile groups resident in Alexandri.

C: Was bulibasa Iancu from Alexandri helpful in negotiating with the authorities?
M: Bulibasa Iancu was a 'communist'.
C: Then, was the other, travelling *bulibasa* helpful?
M: Yes, he helped us to make cauldrons and he worked only with the local police. When they came from Julni, they seized a truck full of boilers. But here, in Alexandri, Iancu didn't always tell us when the police were coming and, in the middle of the night, we would have to run to the forest [to seek refuge]. However, when there were problems at county level the big *bulibasa* Iancu would try to deal with it and he would go with us to the regional police and sort things out.
C: What did you have to do to be supported by Iancu?

74 *A historical political ethnography*

M: I had to give gold, at least 3 gold coins every time. If I had said no, I would have gone to jail. *Bulibasa* Iancu used to tell us how much gold we need to give and the police were there to beat us to make us hand over the gold.
C: Did Iancu have to give any gold?
M: He did not have to. He was our boss. It was so hard during Ceausescu's time. Some say it was better.

(Minu, Kalderash man)

The informal arrangements with the central state representatives were performed by customary leader Iancu, who was supposed to deal with the everyday problems of the settled community and urgent issues raised by the travelling groups. He was also the principal collaborator and source of information for Militia and the *Securitate*, and also a gold collector. He offered information on the Roma's gold possessions and participated, in this way, in the institutionalised gold seizure practices of the socialist state. Minu's narrative and many other accounts coming from Kalderash show also a paradox in the state's activities, which involved restricting their trade in copper and steel products, but also seizing their gold, which was ultimately the product of these trading activities. In addition, Iancu was a *Securitate* collaborator maintaining the state's interests and dealing with its paradoxes. On the other hand, he supported the Kalderash against violent actions by the state.

In his narrative, Minu, like many other Kalderash, showed his dissatisfaction with Iancu's forms of control, which were not used by customary leaders of mobile groups. As many Kalderash characterised him, Iancu was no longer a genuine community representative, but a communist 'boss' to whom they had to listen and subordinate their economic activities. The mobile groups' customary leaders, the *bulibasi*[11], who were subordinated to Iancu, were the real supporters of the Kalderash. As many Kalderash told me, these leaders never acted with duplicity[12], but mediated relations with the local state in the interest of their community. They were the only ones who dealt with the papers required for the activities of the entire teams. As Minu suggested, many Kalderash were poor and unable to pay individually for the work permits. In addition, many had no property papers for the land received from the local councils to build houses. Those proofs of residence were necessary in order to claim individual work permits. Without properties and papers, the Kalderash fell outside the official fabric, while at the same time they were vulnerable in their relations with trans-local authorities who used to raid their settlements and camp sites. In general, they resisted identification, while the local authorities at their residence in Alexandri were either unwilling or unable to bring them into the official structure. Pompiliu's and Anton's accounts reveal the Kalderash's forms of resistance to identification and their independent approach to economic activities.

B: The mayor wanted to open a small bucket shop for them, but they did not want to. The Kalderash said 'we want to practice our profession independently'. The county-level police frequently raided in order to seize their gold and collect taxes. Many used to run to the forest and hide their gold in their carts.

(Pompiliu, school teacher, Alexandri's mayor in 1991)

C: Were they registered?
S: I do not think so, as they have never been army conscripts. The army was a danger for them (. . .) they used police intervention to make them pay taxes, bills (. . .) With these people you cannot impose your will: you must understand that. You won't get anywhere. No one was able to discuss with them in a peaceful way.

(Anton, former cooperative farm director)

Pompiliu's and Anton's statements show that the Kalderash were hardly approachable and identifiable. They also suggest that the Kalderash's expected accommodations with the local authorities were overridden by the regional state administration and police with the collaboration of their main leader, *bulibasa* Iancu. Nevertheless, in Alexandri, as everywhere else, relations between local actors, institutional representatives and Kalderash were based on reciprocal exchanges aimed at meeting the economic demands of the autarchic socialist economic system. *Bulibasa* Iancu and his family used to work and sell their products to the cooperative farms in the Alexandri area. Similarly, in the nearby villages, the Kalderash leaders of settled communities signed contracts with state farms which needed their products for alcohol production. The relations which evolved as a reaction to a restrictive and autarchic socialist economy brought opportunities either for economic survival or wealth accumulation for the groups involved. The Kalderash were able to continue their profession for reasonable returns. The Transylvanian farmers conducted their small alcohol businesses and the Alexandri and neighbouring cooperatives were able to meet the production directives. All these emergent relations play out within two entangled spaces of interaction: nomad and sedentary [space] corresponding to two similar types of subjectivity: "nomadic assemblages and war machine" vs. "sedentary assemblages and state apparatuses" (Deleuze & Guattari 2005: 415). In Deleuze and Guattari's (2005) understanding, the first are construed in opposition to the state, acting creatively against arborescent models of power. As they argue, traditional metallurgy is entangled with nomadism, which not only polarise spaces of social exchange, but configures their overlapping(s). Ambulant smiths' political subjectivities are configured in opposition to the state as a centralised and stable apparatus of power and their lives are configured at the borderline of these two spaces, in relation with the sedentary Other. They are itinerant artisans, organised in small "groups of the rhizome type, as opposed to the arborescent type which centers around organs of power" (Deleuze & Guattari 2005: 358), such as state. Yet, Kalderash's mobile economic practices were highly repressed and leadership confined to its surveillance and repressive apparatuses, which nonetheless did not bring about the subordination of their ways of life and economic organisation to a sedentary state ideology. Most continued to travel seasonally in small groups across the country and maintain a relative independence in relation to state institutions and structures. To sum up, whereas the 1960s settlement restricted Kalderash's territorial movement, leadership was centralised by the state, which nonetheless did not bring a dissolution of their nomadic[13] subjectivities and lifestyle. A series of relations, which continued to develop with small farmers in Transylvania and local authorities in Alexandri,

Romanianised Roma at the margins of the socialist state economy

As compared to the Kalderash, the Romanianised Roma have been for centuries constituted as sedentary subjects[14] who, during socialism, fell within the ambit of the state. In the 1960s, none of them owned land as they started to work for the Alexandri and neighbouring state farms. Whereas some were employed as low-skilled workers with Derex Granit and other state factories, others were unskilled labourers in state and collective farms. As unemployment was criminalised by the state, the local police used to inform the regional authorities about the unemployed and asked them to keep them under surveillance. Romanianised Roma, temporarily employed as seasonal labourers or freelancers (e.g. fiddlers), had to show periodically proof of their work. Nevertheless, their employment status was not always confirmed by the state farms and the Romanianised Roma were sometimes fined or asked to do community work.

For the Roma fiddlers and the Kalderash, as for all the other people with liberal professions, the situation was different. They were required to hold work permits provided by the local councils of their place of residence, to whom they paid annual taxes. However, all fiddlers I talked to and held permits, under-reported their incomes in order to pay lower taxes. These days, they are the richest among the Romanianised Roma and are involved in local and regional politics and leadership. Adrian comes from a fiddler family and his condition is more modest than his siblings. His father was a fiddler, and his mother an informal trader. He is an informal labourer for local farmers' and Kalderash's households. He is not satisfied with the temporary work and low payment he gets in Alexandri.

A: At Tiones [pub] we made a lot of money as fiddlers. During Ceausescu's regime my mother traded cigarettes, chocolate – she was a trader. I was 9 years old and my father played music with other people from our family. Later, when I was 12 I got a contract of my own and played myself. We had permits for our profession.
C: Were there many fiddlers at that time?
A: No! My father and [his] family. My father played for a lot of cash. Although we were not allowed to bribe the police, my father gave gifts to policemen (. . .). With the money, he bought two houses on a large area of land.
C: Have you ever worked for the state farms?
A: Yes, since I was 14. Many people say life was much better then. At the farm, it was crowded, dirty, but we had work and a salary (. . .).

(Adrian, Romanianised Roma man)

Adrian's story shows how working in the socialist second economy permitted some Romanianised Roma families to negotiate their relationship with state representatives and generally moderated their subjection to state forms of social and economic organisation. These activities were sometimes mixed with agricultural work in state farms. His portrayal of agricultural work in the socialist state farms is constructed in comparison to current informal labour he performs locally for farmers or Kalderash, which is temporary and uncertain. Although demanding and performed in insalubrious conditions, regular work and salary in state farms produced a minimum of stability for the Romanianised Roma. Nevertheless, wealth did not come from seasonal agricultural work, but from an independent activity – fiddling. The latter depended on clientele and the performer's skills, fame and their ability to broaden trans-local connections.

Most Romanianised Roma relied, however, on work offered by the socialist centralised economy. Their socio-economic practices were connected to the fixity of state arrangements and institutions. This created a relative dependency on the state, also reflected in their statements. When asked to compare their socialist and post-socialist experiences, they emphasised the advantages of the socialist economy (e.g. jobs provided and decent salaries), and less its forms of repression, which were more enforced against the nomadic Kalderash.

Notwithstanding, the Roma fiddlers are an example of an independent approach in relation to the socialist state economy, which comes closer to the Kalderash's approach. Except for the Iancu's family, who collaborated closely with *Securitate* as a customary leader, most of the Kalderash struggled to live and act outside state structures, continuing to perform a mobile lifestyle throughout the country. On the other hand, the fiddlers, already identifiable and governable subjects of the state, negotiated the state's rules from within its structures and thus occupied the best socio-economic position among the Romanianised Roma. This domestication of the state's institutional practices took place from within its own structures, and from inside its fragile boundaries of control confined by the second economy.

The Kalderash's social navigation within the post-socialist economic uncertainty

After 1989, the state proceeded to the restitution of private property seized during socialism. Farmers started to reclaim their land and the Kalderash, their gold. Through government-initiated programs in collaboration with the National Bank of Romania, Kalderash were able to claim their gold by using their confiscation certificates, which registered the amounts to be compensated. The gold restitution has been a long process mediated by customary leaders. Not all the Kalderash in Alexandri received the full amount confiscated by the state, and some confessed that they donated a part to *bulibasa* Iancu who helped them make the applications. The restitution started during the Social Democrat governance and was associated by Kalderash with the party leader Ion Iliescu. For these reasons many Kalderash have been long-time supporters of the Social Democrat Party[15]. Along with the restitution, the state started dismantling and privatising large inefficient plants like Derex Granit. These processes created opportunities for various middlemen to facilitate trading between large factories and small firms seeking to utilise the reclaimed technology. Many Kalderash families sold some of their gold and mediated such transactions around the country. Both the local farmers and the Kalderash claimed that these businesses were the main source of the Kalderash's enrichment.

> They [Kalderash] made a fortune from Granit and dealt with former managers and other state officials, including the mayor of Derex. After 1989, they went there with cash, bought materials and sold them somewhere else, until the new owner came. Until then, the Romanian managers made big businesses with the Gypsies from Alexandri, Tieni and Liveni [neighbouring villages]. They asked for huge bank credits and never paid them back. At that time there were roughly 100 unregistered firms. When they came here in 1960s, they [Kalderash] just made cauldrons – it was their job.
> (Pompiliu, school teacher, PDL councillor, village mayor in 1991)

As shown in Pompiliu's statement and confirmed by many other informal conversations with the locals, all seem to emphasise the 'illegal' aspect of the Kalderash's practice, which, from their viewpoint, produced fast and illegitimate enrichment. However, these narratives ignore the Kalderash's trading skills and their mobile commercial approach. The narratives seem to be part of a larger discourse about transitional informal economy in Romania and its post-1989 nouveaux riches[16]. Many Romanians who struggled with poverty in the first years after 1989 considered themselves 'cheated'. Transition was characterised by a regulatory void, marked by state corruption and complicity in shady state factories' privatisation[17]. In this context, state representatives and politicians were "interested in 'grabbing' state resources in their own interest" (Wallace & Latcheva 2006: 83; Sik 1994). Notwithstanding, insofar as no clear laws and taxation systems existed in order to regulate transactions, many informal activities cannot be considered 'illegal', but rather 'a-legal' or unregulated activities (Wallace & Latcheva 2006)[18]. From this viewpoint, the Kalderash's businesses were not necessarily 'illegal', but informal ways of exploiting legal and economic gaps. The 'transition' from cauldron makers to intermediaries between companies is also intriguing. What seemed to be a 'traditional', rudimentary occupation was actually the performance of their trader's abilities and connections to an expanded network of relationships. Travelling around the country during socialism brought them into contact not only with local populations, but also with state company managers from whom they bought copper informally and other materials they needed for their work. In relation to their constant territorial mobility and ambulant economy detached from state assemblages of power, the Kalderash as itinerant artisans continuously moved within the moving/self-transforming space of informal economy.

Gold was an important start-up resource, although not all Kalderash who possessed it were able to invest in this kind of business. As many locals claim, Kalderash families who succeeded in doing big business with Granit were well connected to state factory managers and supported by high officials who were involved in privatisation. The cash involved was not always documented, but negotiated between the parties according to their personal interests. These informal connections between state representatives and Kalderash via various companies in good business relations with the state were made possible by the new clientelistic relations, which emerged in the 1990s and generally dominated politics and economy. Notwithstanding, some Kalderash families never succeeded in getting into this sort of business, while others were not able to keep on with it and faced progressively substantial decline in their cash flows. Mixed occupations – selling pipes and copper metallurgy – started to prevail among Kalderash in the last years. During informal conversations, they showed that they expect this business to end at some point, and that they will need to look for other opportunities. Former state-owned large factories were privatised and the new owners were no longer interested in selling old materials, as the former managers were. In this context, the Kalderash's good economic position had to be maintained through other connections on the market. It is not only financial resources that made them persevere in strengthening their socio-economic and symbolic status, but something else which differentiates them from the Romanianised Roma, who regard the state as a source of both welfare and pauperisation. The explanation emerged in many informal conversations with Kalderash families, who have never been middlemen involved in pipe businesses, and especially from an interview I had with a young man coming from a middle income Kalderash family who travels seasonally and practices 'traditional' occupations (e.g. cauldron-making, roof painting).

N: I bring money from Ardeal [Transylvania]. Here I could starve, I have no job here, but in Ardeal I make cauldrons. This year I left the village for 7 months, May until November (. . .) If you come here in the summer you will not find anyone in our district. We all leave. We [his family] have our rented house there and have been staying there for 6 years now.

C: How long will you keep on doing it for?

N: I also wonder how long it is going to last. But, you know how it is if you see all the Gypsies [the Kalderash] leaving the village (. . .) I would manage here as well, but not as comfortably as I do there.

C: How much money did you make last year?

N: Last year we, as a family, brought home almost 27 000 RON (approximately 6000 Euro).

(Nicu, Kalderash man)

Nicu and his family travel seasonally to make and sell their cauldrons to support the construction of their children's houses. Many families struggle to make sufficient money to build large beautiful houses for their boys married at early ages (e.g. 5, 6 to 12 years old), as they claim that waiting too long would make it harder for parents to find partners for them later. The cash they claim to get in a six-month period is almost two times the minimum annual salary a Romanian citizen can expect to earn[19]. It is not certain whether my respondent judged his earnings correctly, but all the Kalderash who travel to Transylvania to make cauldrons or paint roofs reported high earnings, usually invested in buildings and decoration of new houses.

Although relatively well-off and active, Nicu's family could not involve itself in the pipe business: 'this occupation was invented by someone – we do not know where it came from. My father tried that, but it did not work'. There is also an interesting contradiction between two statements he makes: "Here I could starve, I have no job here" and "I would manage here as well". Whereas the first is a pragmatic vision on local resources and work opportunities, the latter is an optimistic vision on life management. An optimistic outlook is rare among the locals, including the Romanianised Roma, farmers and local bureaucrats, but is often expressed by almost all Kalderash. In Alexandri, as elsewhere in Romania, people show a reserved approach to the 'management' of their lives, most of the time connected to their mistrust of state institutions, quality of institutional services and low-salaried jobs available on the market. On the other hand, the Kalderash, who always cultivated a sort of self-reliance and lived most of the time outside the state structures and formal markets without being direct subjects of their institutional framings, do not experience this disappointment directly. They use their flexible forms of socio-economic practice to produce wealth.

Nicu's narrative, also common among other Kalderash families, explains his optimistic vision on life management. It also suggests how these Kalderash, unable to get involved in the pipe business, still avoided poverty and coped with situations of scarcity and uncertainty. By referring to the role of state education and occupation played in his life, Nicu offered me a key explanation for his family's economic status management:

C: Do you find formal education useful?
N: No. Someone asked why I do not want a degree. Why should I have one? Gypsies [Kalderash] will never have a profession as they say, a qualification in their life.
C: Are you sure?
N: I cannot say for sure because you can't be sure what is going to happen in the next 5–6 years. First, they were with the cauldrons, and then they *started to invent something new* [my emphasis]. Painting roofs was invented. We saw it works and we decided to keep doing it.

(Nicu, Kalderash man)

The statement indicates a demystification of formal education, which is not always capable of offering stable employment and a reliable way of adapting to an uncertain economic environment. Instability is given by corruption, low salaries and unemployment, which offer less than expected. Yet, as already discussed, most of the Kalderash, when asked what they would do if their activities were no longer available or lucrative, invariably answer: "I will always find something else." The statement indicates their trust in relations they already have or which can be developed with economic partners in the sphere of informal economy. In addition, the term 'to invent' he uses comes close to, but differentiates from what usually Romanians call in their everyday life '*a te descurca*', which in English translation is 'to cope'. However, the term '*a te descurca*' goes beyond the English understanding of 'to cope'. It is rather connected to informal ways (e.g. connections, bribes, etc.) of getting access to services and wealth, or overcoming difficulties created by an inefficient bureaucracy and an unstable economic environment. On the other hand, the verb *invent* used by Nicu suggests a different interaction with economic uncertainty. The actor adapts to uncertainty through invention and improvisation, acting in an ad hoc way, rather than searching for clear-cut, permanent solutions. *Invention* captures both the activity of the agent in an uncertain and fast-transforming economic sphere and the imaginary adaptation to opportunities to be exploited. Following Deleuze and Guattari (2005), Kalderash's 'invention' can also be seen as the ambulant's "intuition in action" (Deleuze & Guattari 2005: 409) within a nomad space, outside the state, which shapes their political subjectivities. It is the Kalderash's own fluid approach to labour and economic practice, a mechanism of 'social navigation' through which they devise 'tentative mappings' "entailing that the map is never a static set of coordinates but a dense imaginary, which is constantly in the process of coming into being" (Vigh 2009: 428).

The relation between resources and movement, between gold possession and *invention* is intriguing too. Gold is clearly a valuable resource and the preferred form of accumulation among the Kalderash. Nicu offered a further explanation for that:

C: Why do Gypsies buy gold?
N: It is a long story, since they travelled by carts. When travelling, they could not buy and keep so many things and were obliged to invest everything in gold and carry it on their journeys.
C: But now don't they keep their money in bank accounts?
N: Yes, but the gold was 12 units last year and it is 13 units this year. Gold's price rises each year.

(Nicu, Kalderash man)

As Nicu explained, gold has been a form of accumulation perfectly suited to their mobile lifestyle. This form of accumulation lies outside institutional control (e.g. state, banks) and is an expression of their independent way of life. In this case, the possession of gold is not an indication of a fixed form of resource accumulation, but of a mobile and autonomous form of wealth. In addition, the Kalderash still avoid contact with the state. Their possessions – houses, cars – are often unregistered and in this way almost non-existent from the viewpoint of state institutions. Due to their unofficial character, possessions are compatible with their seasonal mobility and unrecorded possessions are no longer constraints. They are objects which do not necessarily belong either to state authorities or banks as identifiable resources. They lose fixity, escape attachment to sites of power and become part of the flow of possibilities and opportunities, part of the movement beyond the boundaries of institutionalised forms of power. Therefore, invention, the ambulant's "intuition in action" (Deleuze & Guattari 2005: 409), symbolises the way Kalderash interact with the transforming economic sphere and navigate

82 *A historical political ethnography*

across its constraints and opportunities, avoiding the first and exploiting the latter. Distinctly, the next section concentrates on Romanianised Roma interactions with informal economic practices and sedentary space of the state re-emerged under post-socialism.

Figure 6.1 Kalderash man in Alexandri demolishing the farmer's old house in the courtyard of his new property in order to build a house for his son. On the roof the Kalderash owner. Behind him stands a Romanianised Roma man hired as construction worker for the new house to be built. Another Romanianised Roma man stands on the site's ground.

The longing for stability across survival possibilities: the Romanianised Roma interactions with informal economy

After 1989, the Romanianised Roma either lost their temporary jobs or fell into long-term unemployment and became the most pauperised group in Alexandri. Almost all families sold their plots and started surviving on state benefits and local seasonal work in agriculture and construction. Approximately ten families have members who left for Italy and Spain to work seasonally in agriculture. The others rely on the local labour offered by farmers' subsistence agriculture and by Kalderash families who build their large houses or need other casual labour. More accounts about their daily living come from Romanianised Roma themselves. For instance, Adrian is a 33-year old Romanianised Roma who worked as a guard for a company. Now he works locally for Kalderash and farmers and receives social benefits that guarantee free health care to his family.

A: That is the main source of income – the Kalderash. They wait here for them [Romanianised Roma] each morning to be taken to work.
C: How do you make a living?
A: Look at the scrap there, plus the transport I do for local stores! This morning I made three trips to carry concrete by cart, and I made 60 RON (approximately 15 Euros). It is not like that every day, but now I do it every two days. My brothers do that and have their pockets full of money (. . .).
C: Are there more people who were imprisoned here than among the Kalderash?
A: Yes, sure. The Kalderash travelled to other villages and worked, but these ones here started stealing – a horse, a cow – and they went to jail. It is hunger here! If they [the Kalderash] leave and return in the autumn, they make no problems here.

(Adrian, Romanianised Roma man)

Adrian, like many other Romanianised Roma, considers that the main source of living comes from Kalderash, who can offer work more often than the aging farmers who practise subsistence agriculture. However, it frequently happens that Kalderash do not offer them work and the Romanianised Roma often get involved in scrap collection throughout neighbouring villages. However, these small informal activities bring low returns compared with the amount of cash the Kalderash make from copper metallurgy sold all over the country. In addition, Adrian's statements suggest that the Romanianised Roma's petty 'criminality' is the product of a local approach to limited economic possibilities, in contrast with the Kalderash's mobility, which brings opportunities on the move. It is a way of survival the Romanianised Roma employ as a reaction to severe unemployment they experienced after the 1990s. Formerly employed as low-skilled workers, many of them emphasised the insecurity and uncertainty that characterise their lives. Nicu is a Romanianised Roma who worked in a mining town for 16 years and experienced good salaried work. After the mines were closed, Nicu returned to Alexandri as an unemployed man with serious worries about his future.

C: How did you earn your bread when you got back from Moldova Noua?
N: I came back in 2004, and I worked as a day-labourer in agriculture and pipe-cleaner for Kalderash.
C: What were the relations with the Kalderash, before 1989?
N: *At that time, there were no relations. There were no businesses* [my emphasis]. They travelled with their tents, had no cars, but only their traditional occupations. Since I got back I have mostly been working with them, I had no other jobs. They [the Kalderash] are different. They travel and have gold. As for me – I am just like you. I have education, I learned a profession in school, I obtained a qualification as a mechanic, and since 1986 I worked as a mineworker. I was an army conscript, like everyone else. I have done everything.
C: Were you happy as a mineworker?
N: Sure – I had a job, good money, and my wife was employed too. I was a stable man. I was on a par with the others. I had holidays, a flat in town and many benefits. There were people who did not know what a permanent job was as they just worked as day-labourers for state farms.

(Nicu, Romanianised Roma man)

Like other Romanianised Roma employed in socialist state factories, Nicu expresses here his longing for the stability offered by the socialist state from which he got education, a profession and a permanent job. Interestingly, he emphasises that he followed the state's prescriptions. He did what the state expected and got access to resources and stability. However, the benefits of his attachment to the state's structure and economic organisation were severely challenged in the 1990s. His statement – "at that time there were no relations; there were no businesses" – is crucially important for the Romanianised Roma experience of post-socialist transformations and their understanding of the new socio-economic reconfigurations.

During socialism, the Romanianised Roma were mostly inactive within the second economy, and relations with the farmers and Kalderash were not locally developed. After 1990s, alienated from the state's organised field of opportunities, Romanianised Roma were forced to seek survival in local relations with other locals, which rather acted as constraints, limiting their likelihood of improving their socio-economic conditions. On the other hand, these local relations facilitated the Kalderash's exploitation of opportunities offered by the new informal markets. Many Kalderash travelling for business around the country made use of the Romanianised Roma's cheap labour force in their pipe businesses and construction of their houses. These connections produced either constraints or opportunities for the two Roma groups and built a power relation within which the Romanianised Roma were not yet totally subjected to its forces. On the other hand, these informal economic possibilities held a serious risk of non-payment for the Romanianised Roma and consequent legal sanctions. Ian, a Romanianised Roma, one of my fieldwork friends, was for a short time a permanent employee and, after 1996, he worked for the Kalderash's pipe business. Similar to Nicu, he cleaned and painted pipes, and also dismantled metal structures from former state companies. In the summer of 2010 he was worried about his last collaboration with the Kalderash and he wanted to share his experience with me. He did tell me a week in advance that he was about to leave with a Kalderash man to work near Bucharest. In two days he got back, disappointed.

I: They did not pay us. They had a different business there which we didn't know about. We did not like that and left for home. I do not want to go to jail. I prefer not to eat, but to be able to sleep on my pillow. I was convicted in the past so I did not want new trouble.
C: What happened after you left?
I: They took other boys from here. It was their [Romanianised Roma] chance to make money and be imprisoned.
C: Were they not afraid that you could report them to the police?
I: No, because we were there too and now we are in the same boat.

(Ian, Romanianised Roma man)

Ian did not receive any money for his work and left for home after he realised the informal aspect of the Kalderash's work. Generally, the Kalderash know that the Romanianised Roma are a cheap labour force and amongst the few willing to get involved in risky deals. On the other hand, due to the bad treatment and shady businesses which could trigger imprisonment, some Romanianised Roma gave up working with the wealthy Kalderash and relied instead on casual agricultural work, scrap collection, begging and state benefits. However, this renunciation contributed to a local discourse about them as uneducated, lazy, offenders and inefficient. Yet, as often portrayed by the Romanianised Roma themselves, this renunciation can be seen as a contestation of informality and risk and the constraining power of the socio-economic relation with the Kalderash. The power of relation is produced by the reciprocity of exchange between parts, which creates constraints, but also survival possibilities for the Romanianised Roma and opportunities for economic improvement and wealth for the Kalderash. Therefore, Romanianised Roma are still able to *socially navigate* locally and access survival possibilities[20] through Kalderash's informal opportunities as far as informal economic activities are used as a form of security by all those left at the margins of the formal labour market, as Chelcea and Mateescu (2005) argued. Yet, these actions involve high insecurity, risk of conviction and even imprisonment. They are not work relations, but arrangements, which involve forms of indirect economic exchange. In this sense, both Kalderash and Romanianised Roma unequally exchange favours in the dynamics of the informal economic sphere produced by deindustrialisation, experiencing the lack of state involvement in minimising the market effects.

These contradictory approaches in relation to Kalderash that Romanianised Roma have shown both subjection to the power of an interdependent relation and its implicit contestations. Yet, the constraining and sometimes exploitative relations the Romanianised Roma have with the Kalderash are counterbalanced by the reciprocal ties they developed with the local farmers over time. Many Romanianised Roma buy on credit from local shops and borrow money for undetermined periods from farmers, who sometimes pay their labour in kind. In this way, farmers with low cash resources ensure cheap labour for their subsistence agriculture, whereas the shopkeepers can keep their survival entrepreneurial source of income going with the help of the Romanianised Roma clientele. As shown in an article on socio-economic relations between Roma and Hungarian peasants in Transylvania (Voiculescu 2004), these relations between unemployed Romanianised Roma and farmers form local systems for survival, which come close to what Sahlins (1999) called 'generalised reciprocity'. Compared to the socio-economic relations they have with the Kalderash, their relations with the local farmers and shopkeepers maintain social characteristics that prevail and are often strengthened by the kinship ties they establish (e.g. farmers act as godparents for Roma children). These economic interactions foster relationships and intensify communions between locals, which can surpass the uncertainty and instability of a neoliberalised economy, which fails to deliver its promises.

Notwithstanding, these relations and interactions between Romanianised Roma, Kalderash and farmers seem contradictory and constantly changing. These contradictory aspects can be explained by the content of these relations, which involve, as any power relation, both 1) confinement to a restrictive form of exchange, and 2) multiple forms of contestation. The Romanianised Roma sometimes work with Kalderash and farmers, whereas at other times they refuse them and go for scrap collection or begging in neighbouring towns. They often mix all these activities in their everyday life. Notwithstanding, most of them consider that all local relations have more disadvantages than advantages and sometimes look confused about their day by day prospects, as they are never sure what work they will get the next day. The contradictory and restrictive content of these relations push the Romanianised Roma into a sort of irregular movement. It is the *navigation of a local social labyrinth* with limited and restrictive possibilities for economic practice.

The Romanianised Roma themselves confirmed that these types of exchange and relationships confined to the local do not offer them economic opportunities: "What can we do here? There is nothing to do". In Szelenyi and Ladanyi's (2003) terms, the Romanianised Roma's movement within the relational sphere of informal economy can be seen as 'navigation within poverty', which generally indicates a passive approach. However, in my view, this movement across socio-economic relations constitutes a form of *social navigation within a locally restrictive labyrinth of the informal economy*, a dynamics of power struggles in which the Romanianised Roma are actively involved. The emphasis is on the local character of these struggles, which are limited to local resources and possibilities of survival, within a sedentary space as Deleuze and Guattari (2005) would call it. Hence, the Romanianised Roma's material conditions of existence are not only the product of structural transformations reproducing their marginal economic position, but also the outcome of their interaction with post-socialist informal economy, generally subjected to a sedentary ideology enforced by the state over time. As already mentioned, this mode of interaction varied, however, among the Romanianised Roma, who, since socialism, had an approach to the economic sphere of varying degrees of independence. The fiddlers involved in socialist second economy are a case in point. In post-socialism the fiddlers integrated well with state and political structures and became Romani political representatives (e.g. Corina, Roma expert at the Derex prefecture) or even local employers of the poorest Romanianised Roma (e.g. Cristian, local entrepreneur in construction). These influential Roma were connected to patronage politics as a field of opportunity in which members of the local patronage (e.g. mayor, vice mayor, local administrator/patron) supported and promoted their positions in the local economy and politics. A detailed analysis of the field of patronage politics is developed separately in the chapter on political fields.

Conclusions: interactions with nomad-smooth vs. sedentary-striated spaces of economy

This chapter presented a historical comparative analysis of the two Roma groups' informal economic practices and relations and developed a dynamic understanding of individuals' and groups' historical trajectories, which are not solely the result of state policies, but arise out of interactions with an economic space in continuous transformation. As the data shows, the sharply different socio-economic conditions of the two groups can be explained by two relational patterns within the power space of economy which is crosscut by two other spaces: sedentary vs. nomad space as suggested by Deleuze and Guattari (2005).

1 *Interactions with the sedentary/striated space of state economy and its model of economic practice* is aligned with the state policies of integration and assimilation, a centuries-old model, with its roots in Roma slavery, which was massively reinforced under socialism. As Deleuze and Guattari (2005) argue, the sedentary space is the striated space, a product of state regulations, which does not necessarily stop movement, but establish conduits, routes of action and thought subordinated to its arborescent powers over and constitutive to its subjects. It is a space of surveillance and subjection especially established through formal employment, which is framed by state institutional architecture. The Romanianised Roma gravitated around this model. They were identifiable subjects of the state, workers in state and cooperative farms and welfare recipients. Most of them were seasonal or unskilled workers and, therefore, were able to act on the margins of the socialist economy. Yet, the fiddlers acted within the second economy or 'nomadic space', which emerged as a reaction to excessive regulation/striation by the socialist state, a metamorphosis and reversed movement emphasised by Deleuze and Guattari (2005) themselves. Fiddlers approached state more independently, which prepared them better for an active interaction with the uncertainty of the rapid post-1989 transformations. Yet, the Romanianised Roma, moving within the striated space of state and economy, had limited mobility across relations confined to a local *field of possibilities*[21] *within the local labyrinth*, preserving their ideological subjection to the sedentary space of the state.

2. *Navigation within the nomad/smooth space of the informal economy.* As compared to the state sedentarist model, Kalderash continued as ambulant smiths within the space of informal economy, a nomad/smooth space, "nonmetric, acentered, rhizomatic" (Deleuze & Guattari 2005: 371), performative in its transformations which can "be explored only by legwork" (p. 371), through continuous creativity or "intuition in action" (p. 409). Notwithstanding, the state sedentarisation of the 1960s striated Kalderash's smooth space, imposing a metric aspect to their mobility which remained a characteristic "of a 'moved body' going from one point to another" (Deleuze & Guattari 2005: 386), from new settled places (e.g. Alexandri) to temporary ones in Transylvania. Most of them continued and extended their connections and relations, developed in the informal economic space, from socialism to post-socialism and *navigated fields of opportunities* by the use of *social invention*, preserving their *nomadic subjectivities*.

In this case, invention is related to the concept of *social navigation* coined by Vigh (2009), which brings back the dynamic perspective on the socio-economic environment. Social navigation refers to the individuals' movement within a socio-political-economic sphere in a state of change, "an environment that is wavering and unsettled" (p. 420), and reflects the interaction individuals have with the self-transforming contexts, or what I call spaces of power struggle (e.g. economy, politics, state, etc.). Vigh (2009) mainly refers to African countries where socio-economic contexts underwent dramatic transformations, while populations had to face everyday uncertainties, adopt short-term strategies and imagine what he calls 'tentative mappings'. Similarly, as Burawoy and Verdery (1999) documented for Eastern Europe, post-socialist transformations[22] generated high uncertainties and an irregular movement of the economy in which groups of people became unemployed and, released from the state control mechanisms, needed to adapt to fast transformations. Furthermore, post-socialist transformations unleashed informal economy from the anxious and repressed socialist second economy and raised its velocity through deindustrialisation, which generated irregularities able to be exploited as opportunities and possibilities. This movement of the economic space stimulated movement of individuals and groups – *movement within movement* – and relationality became an interaction with uncertainty, experienced as a field of possibilities by Romanianised Roma, ideological subjects of the state, and as fields of opportunity by Kalderash, ambulant artisans opposing state assemblages of power.

To conclude, the chapter's analysis contributes to a decolonised understanding of Roma as active subjectivities, suggesting that a historical analysis focusing on both individuals and groups should not concentrate solely on state policies or the accumulation of resources, but also on two forms of movement: the movement/transformation of spaces of power (e.g. state, politics, economy) and the movement of actors within these spaces. The following chapters focus on the social dynamics of Roma power relations in connection with these two forms of movement involved in each space of power struggles – state, politics and religion.

Notes

1 See Stark (1986,1990), Szelenyi (1988), Williams (2009).
2 See the section 'Historical entanglements of power: from socialism to post-socialism in Romania'.
3 'Licit goods' is a reference to all goods which are allowed to be sold on the free markets. Example of illicit goods would be drugs, guns, etc.
4 From my experience of living in Romania, in the early 1990s, when the state had no clear taxation system, people used to sell everywhere in the streets and opened shops, paying no taxes.
5 See Samers (2005), Williams (2009).
6 Lee (2006), Neef (2002), Round et al (2008), Sedlenieks (2003).
7 Local people including the Romanianised Roma were against the Kalderash's settlement in Alexandri. The Kalderash, called 'nomads', were considered by the locals 'dirty' and 'uncivilized'.
8 All Kalderash are called Mateiescu, by family name, and that constituted the most problematic issue in their identification.
9 In Transylvanian villages, in the hilly areas where the collectivisation of land was not possible, famers used to produce plums and apples in large quantities, usually used in small private alcohol production.
10 Due to its hills and mountains, Transylvania is not suitable for agriculture. In many areas farmers involved in fruit production (e.g. plums and apples) used to make alcohol for informal markets.
11 Before the 1960s there was not a clear hierarchy among big bosses/*bulibasi*. They were leaders of the small mobile groups. After sedentarisation, *bulibasa* Iancu stopped traveling himself and, with support from outside, took the leadership of all Kalderash mobile and settled groups resident in Alexandri.
12 Duplicity refers here to the customary leaders of the settled groups who, during socialism, gave their support to both *Securitate* and other state authorities, and Roma communities.
13 *Nomadic* refers here to Deleuze and Guattari's (2005) discussion on nomadology as a war machine, which emphasises an independent, decentralised, rhyzomatic form of political subjectivity construed in opposition to arborescent models of power such as state.
14 For more details, see section 'The field site', part of the Book discussion and introduction.
15 The details on politicisation of restitution of gold are offered in the chapter on political fields.
16 Details about 'nouveaux riches' phenomenon in Romania is discussed in the introduction, section – 'Historical entanglements of power: from socialism to post-socialism in Romania.'
17 See Eyal et al (1998), Szelenyi et al (1995).
18 In the early 1990s in Romania, there was no clear taxation system and laws to organise commercial activities. Therefore, Kalderash were not obliged to pay taxes for their economic transactions and establish firms for money transfers. In the mid and late 1990s this double taxation was enforced by the state (e.g. tax for commercial company, money transfer-VAT) and Kalderash's businesses were categorised by the state as 'illegal' or part of the 'black economy'.
19 In January 2015 the minimum monthly salary in Romania was 218 Euro/month. Source: Eurostat News release-National minimum wages in the EU, 33/2015–26 February 2015.
20 Compared to 'opportunity', which refers to a mix of high risks and high financial returns, 'possibility' implies low economic returns and high levels of social insecurity. Whereas the first category is associated with informal commercial activities, the latter is mainly an expression of the post-socialist economic survival.

21 I refer to 'field of possibility', and later to 'field of opportunity' as expanded spatial expressions of possibilities and opportunities, not necessarily factual, but created, increased or reduced through individual interactions with the post-socialist informal economy.
22 Post-socialist uncertain transformations refer to state withdrawal from economy, privatisation of property, deindustrialisation, inflation, which subsequently involved uncertainties on the labour markets and high levels of unemployment.

Bibliography

Burawoy, M. & Verdery, K. (Eds.) (1999) *Uncertain Transition: Ethnographies of Change in the Postsocialist World.* Lanham, MD: Rowman and Littlefield.

Chelcea, L. & Mateescu, O. (2005) 'Introducere'. In L. Chelcea and O. Mateescu (Eds.) *Economia informala in Romania: Piete, practici sociale si transformari ale statului dupa 1989.* Bucharest: Paideia, pp. 5–33.

Deleuze, G. & Guattari, F. (2005)[1987] *A Thousand Plateaus: Capitalism and Schizophrenia.* Minneapolis: University of Minnesota Press.

Dunn, E. C. (2004) *Privatising Poland: Baby Food, Big Business, and the Remaking of Labor.* New York: Cornell University Press.

Eyal, G., Szelenyi, I. & Townsley. E. (1998) *Making Capitalists Without Capitalists: The New Ruling Elites in Eastern Europe.* Verso: New Left Books.

Gibson-Graham, J. K. (2006) *Post-Capitalist Politics.* Minneapolis, MN: Minnesota Press.

Grabiner, L. (2000) *The Informal Economy.* London: HM Treasury.

Granovetter, M. (1985) 'Economic Action and Social Structure: The Problem of Embeddedness'. *American Journal of Sociology*, 91(3): 481–510.

Ladanyi, J. & Szelenyi, I. (2003) 'Historical Variations in Inter-Ethnic Relations: Toward a Social History of Roma in Csenyéte, 1857–2000'. *Romani Studies*, 13(1): 1–51.

Lee, R. (2006) 'The Ordinary Economy: Tangled Up in Values and Geography'. *Transactions of the Institute of British Geographers*, 31(4): 413–432.

Neef, R. (2002) 'Aspects of the Informal Economy in a Transforming Country: The Case of Romania'. *International Journal of Urban and Regional Research*, 26(2): 299–322.

Okolski, M. (2001) 'Incomplete Migration: A New Form of Mobility in Central and Eastern Europe. The Case of Polish and Ukrainian Migrants'. In C. Wallace and M. Stola (Eds.) *Patterns of Migration in Central Europe.* Basingstoke: Palgrave, pp. 105–129.

Piirainen, T. (1997) *Towards a New Social Order in Russia: Transforming Structures and Everyday Life.* Aldershot: Dartmouth.

Round, J., Williams, C. C. & Rodgers, P. (2008) 'Everyday Tactics and Spaces of Power: The Role of Informal Economies in Post-Soviet Ukraine'. *Social and Cultural Geography*, 9(2): 171–185.

Sahlins, M. B. (1999) 'On Sociology of Primitive Exchange'. In M. Banton (Ed.) *The Relevance of Models for Social Anthropology.* London: Tavistock, pp. 139–186.

Samers, M. (2005) 'The Myopia of "Diverse Economies", or a Critique of the "Informal Economy"'. *Antipode*, 37(5): 875–886.

Sedlenieks, K. (2003) 'Cash in an Envelope: Corruption and Tax Avoidance as an Economic Strategy in Contemporary Riga'. In K.-O. Arnstberg and T. Boren (Eds.) *Everyday Economy in Russia, Poland and Latvia.* Stockholm: Almqvist & Wiksell, pp. 37–52.

Sik, E. (1994) 'From the Multicoloured to the Black and White Economy: The Hungarian Second Economy and Transformation'. *International Journal of Urban and Regional Research*, 18(1): 46–70.

Stark, D. (1986) 'Rethinking Internal Labour Markets: New Insights from a Comparative Perspective'. *American Sociological Review*, 51(4): 492–504.

Stark, D. (1990) 'Privatization in Hungary: From Plan to Market or from Plan to Clan?' *East European Politics and Societies*, 4(3): 351–392.

Stenning, A., Smith, A., Rochovska, A. And Swiatek, D. (2010) *Domesticating Neo-Liberalism: Spaces of Economic Practice and Social Reproduction in Post-Socialist Cities*. Malden: Blackwell.

Swedberg, R. (1991) 'Major Traditions of Economic Sociology'. *Annual Review of Sociology*, 17(1): 251–276.

Swedberg, R. (2008) 'Economic Sociology'. In B. Turner (Ed.) *The New Blackwell Companion to Social Theory*. Malden: Blackwell, pp. 360–378.

Szelenyi, I. (1988) *Socialist Entrepreneurs: Embourgeoisement in Rural Hungary*. Madison: University of Wisconsin Press.

Szelenyi, S., Szelenyi, I. & Kovach, I. (1995) 'The Making of the Hungarian Post-Communist Elite: Circulation in Politics, Reproduction in Economy'. *Theory and Society*, 24(5): 697–722.

Thomas, J. J. (1992) *Informal Economic Activity*. Hemel Hempstead: Harvester Wheatsheaf.

Vigh, H. (2009) 'Motion Squared: A Second Look at the Concept of Social Navigation'. *Anthropological Theory*, 9(4): 419–438.

Voiculescu, C. (2004) 'Temporary Migration of Transylvanian Roma to Hungary'. In D. Pop (Ed.) *New Patterns of Labour Migration in Central and Eastern Europe*. Cluj-Napoca, Romania: AMM Design, pp. 145–164.

Wallace, C. & Latcheva, R. (2006) 'Economic Transformation Outside the Law: Corruption, Trust in Public Institutions and the Informal Economy in Transition Countries of Central and Eastern Europe'. *Europe-Asia Studies*, 58(1): 81–102.

Williams, C. C. (2009) 'The Hidden Economy in East-Central Europe'. *Problems of Post-Communism*, 56(4): 15–28.

Williams, C. C. & Windebank, J. (1998) *Informal Employment in the Advanced Economies: Implications for Work and Welfare*. London, New York: Routledge.

7 Transformations of the state and Roma leadership

Self-governance, state capture and Roma brokers

The previous chapter discussed the different historical trajectories of the Roma groups, their relations with the state and interactions with the transformations in the space of economy. This chapter focuses on an important theoretical and methodological aspect of the analysis of social power, brokerage, the expression of the interaction Roma leaders have with the state power space: Roma brokers' relations and practices, which connect different power levels and reveal either alternative modes of political subjectification or subjection to state power.

Roma leaders often acted as brokers, connecting or mediating between the Roma communities and two different sources of state power: socialist apparatuses of control and surveillance, and post-socialist governance and state social integration apparatuses. Distinct forms of mediation performed by Kalderash and Romanianised Roma leaders created various forms of Roma subjection to a changing state power structure that generated further socio-economic and political constraints and opportunities for the two Roma groups discussed.

The Roma leadership in Alexandri does not reveal a stable, homogeneous category. As this chapter shows, it comprises a diverse, unstable, fluid relation between Roma leaders, state, politics and patronage actors. Under socialism, both Romanianised Roma and Kalderash leaders were informal, with roles adapted to the social organisation of their Roma group. During the state enforced sedentarisation of the 1960s, a part of the Kalderash leadership was co-opted as *Securitate* collaborators – the socialist state's main apparatus of repression and control. The *Securitate* aimed at protecting the Communist Party's achievements and continually sought to extend its network of informers and collaborators into every domain of activity (e.g. education, commerce, industry, culture, politics, etc.). Collaborators were appointed to collect information about all those acting against the ruling party, to work with local police and persecute so-called 'conspirators'. In relation to the Kalderash, the socialist state wanted to seize their gold, as the private accumulation of gold was illegal. On the other hand, the customary leaders who signed up with the *Securitate* were expected to provide information about Kalderash possessing large amounts of gold. This chapter argues, among other things, that their activity and collaboration with the state apparatus of control produced critical transformations in the institution of the Kalderash's customary leadership (*bulibasa*) and in its meanings. These transformations in the institution of leadership resemble to some extent the changes in traditional chiefdoms which occurred in former African colonial states, when colonial governments co-opted 'traditional' leaders from rural areas into their administration (Bennett 2004; Keulder 2010; Murray 2004). A number of the local African chiefs agreed to support the administration and received "local administrative and court responsibilities" (Miller 1968: 189). This was a colonial administrative mechanism used to build colonial states (Ray 2003) and govern extended rural areas. In the Romanian case, the socialist state was interested in expanding its sovereign and administrative power, but less preoccupied with the social governance of Kalderash. As mentioned in the previous chapter, state institutions were more interested in seizing their private possessions, restricting their mobility and associated economic activities which constituted them as nomadic subjectivities.

In colonial Africa, the reconfiguration and absorption of indigenous forms of polity into colonial rule was made using customary law enforced by the local chiefs, who had extensive coercive powers over local populations (Keulder 2010). Similarly, in Romania, during socialism, Roma customary leaders (*bulibasi*) were given coercive powers over the Kalderash groups and were empowered by the state as the main leaders of settled communities[1]. Nevertheless, unlike the *colonial chiefs*, Kalderash customary leaders formed no part of the socialist state's administration and were not officially paid for their informal positions.

In post-socialism, following EU directives, the Romanian government initiated social inclusion projects as part of the larger 'Roma decade 2005–2015' program[2]. As part of the social inclusion strategy for the Roma, in 2007 the government formalised and developed a parallel form of governance and a network of Roma experts and mediators for public institutions in all localities with large Roma populations[3]. The project aimed at improving relations between Roma communities and public institutions and implementing the program of social integration of Roma communities, concomitantly extending the state infrastructure into its peripheries or less governed communities. The Roma mediators have specific roles related to education, public order and health, and they connect institutions to communities. The second category of leaders formed by the Roma Decade is the Roma expert and comes closer to the understanding of brokerage and representation of state inside the Roma communities. Roma experts engage in mediation with local public institutions and are expected to implement the government's social inclusion strategy at the local and regional level. These days, both Romanianised Roma and Kalderash's forms of leadership are split between leaders who perform their roles of mediation and representation in an informal way, and Roma experts who work for the local council and are part of the state programs of social integration. This relative formalisation of the Roma leadership was accepted by some informal leaders, but rejected by others.

Furthermore, as part of the same strategy, the government has built a multilevel infrastructure of governance and communication involving both informal leaders and Roma experts, who are part of regional level joint working groups (JWGs), local initiative groups (LIGs), and local working groups (LWGs) (NAR 2014). Generally, the groups include representatives of local public institutions (e.g. mayors, deputy-mayors, teachers, doctors, lawyers and police officers), local council members and representatives from NGOs. Regular meetings are organised and all leaders are invited to participate. All the local Romanianised Roma and Kalderash leaders in the county are supervised by a regional Roma expert, Corina, a Romanianised Roma woman from a main family of fiddlers – Sotu. Thus, new forms of Romani leadership became an expression of Roma interactions with transformations of the state, and variation in the relations that Roma leaders progressively established with a multitude of actors from different spaces of power struggle, especially with state and political actors. In this chapter, these interactions and multiple, sometimes contradictory relations are explored. The next section provides a brief examination of the Kalderash and Romanianised Roma leaders in Alexandri and neighbouring localities Liveni and Medeleni under socialism and post-socialism.

Leaders and forms of leadership in Alexandri

In the first years of socialism, from late 1940s to 1960s, when the state had no clear policy of assimilating the Roma, the Kalderash leaders were the product of idiosyncratic social and political community organisation. They were customary leaders travelling with small groups and had the role of settling everyday disputes and negotiating interactions with local authorities in the places where they used to camp. These mobile groups did not have a lot of contact with each other and were autonomous in their forms of socio-political organisation. However, links between groups were created through marriage[4]. The customary leaders of different Kalderash groups knew each other and cooperated, but without this having any effect on the groups' hierarchies and leadership. From the 1960 onwards, the socialist state initiated a coercive program of sedentarisation for nomadic Roma, including the Kalderash. Many groups and leaders settled in Alexandri and neighbouring villages (e.g. Liveni and Medeleni). In Alexandri, Iancu, one of the Kalderash leaders, was co-opted and agreed to collaborate with the *Securitate*. His aim was to get the necessary support for a position of authority over all the groups settled in Alexandri, which, at that time, had different customary leaders. On the other hand, the *Securitate* was interested in getting information about the possession of gold by the Kalderash and in seizing it. *Bulibasa* Iancu often provided information and assisted the police in raids against Kalderash families. He was able to impose himself as the main leader for the settled community in Alexandri, part of which continued to travel in small groups organised by other *bulibasi*. However, the customary leaders of small groups became subordinated to *bulibasa* Iancu who was recognised as the main 'boss'.

In Liveni, a neighbouring village, Traian was the settled *bulibasa*, whereas in Medeleni the most powerful position went to Casian's father. Both were collaborators with *Securitate*. While supporting some Kalderash families, they assisted in the persecution and harassment of others they considered to be acting against their own interests. The *bulibasi* from neighbouring localities considered that Iancu from Alexandri had the most power and their decisions were often subject to his influence. In interviews and informal conversations I had with Kalderash and former socialist authorities, Iancu was portrayed as a man who was prepared to use his influence against even those prosecutors who opposed his actions.

> 'Bulibasul' had unlimited powers, I can't say powers on life and death over his community members, but anyway (. . .). He had the power to say: 'Hey you! The police want to see you. Follow me to the post'. He was called in whenever there was any litigation. When two families had a quarrel they would ask bulibasa to help them.
>
> (Racov, former head of police in Alexandri)

C: Was Iancu working for the police?
I: My understanding is that he defended his Gypsies who had problems during their travels. On the one hand, he helped them. On the other, he disclosed information about them and asked them for bribes, to keep Gypsies out of the hands of the police. One day he beat up a prosecutor. His nephew killed a man in a car crash. Iancu went to the hospital and he beat up the prosecutor who was there (interrogating Iancu's sibling).
C: Why did he beat him up?
I: He just had power to do that then.

(Ioader, Romanianised Roma informal leader)

Racov, former police officer in chief in Alexandri, suggests that *bulibasa* Iancu was able to act with all the authority and impunity of the police, to interpellate[5] Kalderash and force them to comply with Securitate's orders, which were often illegitimate. When Racov says '*bulibasa* had unlimited powers', he is referring to Iancu's ability to threaten Kalderash families with action by the police as he pleased. Ioader also suggests that Iancu acted within dual frameworks of power. On one hand, he was empowered to lead the Kalderash community and help them in their dealings with the regional police when needed. On the other hand, he was subject to the security services' power and was therefore expected to provide information about the Kalderash who possessed gold. However, as Ioader suggests, *bulibasa* Iancu could challenge and overrule local and regional police officers' decisions to imprison Roma prosecuted for informal trade. He could also use violence, not only against his community, but also against people from the institutions of the socialist state (e.g. prosecutors).

These observations identify further similarities between the Kalderash *bulibasi* under socialism and customary political leadership in colonial Africa. Colonial leaders were given "extensive powers, especially power of coercion" (Keulder 2010: 150) over populations. Adopting administrative colonial positions, "many traditional leaders transformed themselves from custodians of their people into custodians of the colonial order" (Keulder 2010: 151) and became 'local despots' (Mamdani 1996). Similarly, under socialism, the main settled Kalderash *bulibasi* performed the role of local despots as informal Security officers, ruling over

96 *A historical political ethnography*

Kalderash communities. On the other hand, empowered by *Securitate*, they were able to bypass the local authorities' violent impositions over mobile Kalderash, all over the country. Bridging these two role performances strengthened their relation with two sources of power: socialist *Securitate* and Kalderash groups forming communities while settled. In other words, this dialectical relation, which involved both subjection to socialist state surveillance authority and empowerment to rule over community was a form of brokerage, which maintained them as the main leaders till the early 1990s.

Under post-socialism, the leadership changed dramatically. In Alexandri, the aging *bulibasa* Iancu lost his support from the state institutions and, consequently, his authority over the Kalderash. In the 1990s, the Kalderash started businesses and some of them got rich. The new affluent, including Iancu's son, Lucretiu, started claiming the role of customary leader. However, these days Lucretiu fulfils only a limited version of his father's role. He mediates between community and local police in matters of local fighting or disputes, but he is not always recognised as a legitimate mediator by some Kalderash families, nor does he occupy the same kind of privileged position with the authorities that his father had. The other two competitors – Victor and Silviu – come from wealthy rival families connected to Iancu through kinship ties. Victor is the son of a former Kalderash *bulibasa* of a small mobile group who accepted Iancu's collaboration with the *Securitate* under socialism. Silviu is considered by many Kalderash in Alexandri to be the wealthiest Roma and the most successful businessman. As the other Kalderash *bulibasi*, Silviu acts as a broker for political parties and persuades the Kalderash to vote for one party or another during elections. In Liveni, Traian, former collaborator of Security services, is still a *bulibasa*, but with dramatically diminished authority over Kalderash. He is in competition with another Kalderash family which claims the leading position. Traian is also a Pentecostal convert enjoying very good relations with the Kalderash believers in Alexandri. Yet, the regional Roma expert that oversees the other leaders' activities in the region is a Romanianised Roma woman, Corina Sotu, originally from Alexandri. However, while talking with Romanianised Roma about leadership in their community, almost all of them told me that they never had leaders. The members of the Sotu family, who acted for a considerable period as mediators with the local council, are not generally considered as legitimate leaders. However, their conception of leadership is different from that of Kalderash: 'We do not have leaders, we do not have *bulibasi* like the Kalderash do'. Rather they suggest they just have mediators. Today there are two Romanianised Roma from the Sotu family who claim to be local leaders in Alexandri: Ioader and Doru. Doru is Corina's brother and Ioader is her cousin. During socialism, Ioader used to organise seasonal work at state farms in the neighbouring villages and was a regionally well-known fiddler. Both were informal mediators between local council and the Romanianised Roma community.

Yet, the development of the Romanianised Roma leadership took shape after 1989, when the Roma were recognised by the state as a minority and allowed to set up NGOs, which could also function as political parties[6] and participate in elections. In the early 1990s, the Roma Party developed a nationwide network of activists. The Roma Party representatives were more or less informally appointed at each administrative level[7]. Upon Corina's recommendations, the Sotu family became the informal representatives of the Roma Party in Alexandri. At some point, both Doru and Ioader ran for a position of local councillor for the Roma Party. However, only Doru, supported by his sister Corina, was elected councillor for 4 years. Notwithstanding, when the government started the Roma expert program in 2005, he undertook a period of training and, in 2007, he became a local Roma expert in Alexandri. The position was funded by the central government between 2007 and 2013, with the intention to be transferred to the local council. Doru, as a local Roma expert, is expected to represent and mediate on behalf of all Roma in Alexandri. However, he rarely visits the Kalderash's district, which is mainly under the customary leaders' control. However, he is known by both Roma groups as the 'local council man'. On the other hand, Ioader undertook a police mediators' training course and he considers himself to be a Roma mediator with the local police. He principally acts as an informal leader. The Romanianised Roma recognise both Doru and Ioader as mediators, but not necessarily as legitimate Romani representatives or their leaders.

Brief questions and theoretical references

The roles of Roma leaders within socialism and post-socialism show no clear-cut distribution and classification of leadership forms among the two Roma groups. These forms of leadership are produced in interaction with transformations in state control and governance (e.g. *Securitate* under socialism, the state's Roma expert and mediator networks under post-socialism), politics (e.g. the Roma Party's need for local representativeness), informal economy (e.g. the Kalderash's businesses) and religious discursive practices (e.g. authority transfers from customary leaders to God[8]). Arising from the observations made in the previous section, the questions this chapter seeks to answer are the following:

How did these interactions, between Roma leaders and the transformations within the state power space, constitute or alter Roma leadership? Did these transformations in Roma leadership from socialism to post-socialism constitute Roma as subjects of state power?

Leadership has been conceived either as an individual entity or as a social-relational construction (Uhl-Bien 2006). The entity perspective individualises action and conceives of individuals as entities somewhat separated from their environments. They also emphasise 'positions' and 'resources' 'owned' by two categories of actors related to each other through exchange: leaders and followers (Brower et al 2000; Graen & Uhl-Bien 1991, 1995). From the same perspective, hierarchical and relational 'realities' are already organised 'out there', and are easy to represent (Dachler 1992). Social network theory can be considered an example of an entity-approach as it looks at individuals and their interactions as instruments for network enactment (Uhl-Bien 2006). It is a way of mapping social relationships "concerned with description (e.g. who talks to whom, who is friends with whom) and taxonomy (e.g. friendship network, advice network, ego network) of relational links (. . .) rather than [with] how relational processes emerge and evolve" (Uhl-Bien 2006: 660).

On the other hand, the relational approach sees the production of transformative power in relations and emphasises the capacity of relatedness (Uhl-Bien 2006; Pearce et al 2007). From this perspective, leadership is always shared, collaborative "with others for the construction of a particular understanding of relationships" (Dachler & Hosking 1995: 15). It is not a pre-established organisational reality, "but an emergent reflection of socially constructed realities in constant change" (Dachler 1992: 171). The relational constructionist approach (Meindl 1995) looks at leadership as a process in which both individuals and relationships undergo transformations in a historically and socially self-transforming environment (Uhl-Bien 2006). Therefore, an analysis of leadership as a process is less about "traits, behavioural styles, or identifying particular types of leaders or people management techniques" (Uhl-Bien 2006: 662), and more about interactions between state, political and economic transformations and the leaders' actions. It is a relation established between Roma leaders, state apparatuses of control and communities through which "both collaborators and leaders are all doing leadership" (Rost 1995: 133). The remaining parts of the chapter explore different forms of Roma leadership by looking at individual interactions with historical transformations in the state and its programs of assimilation and social integration. The next section concentrates on the history of relations between Kalderash and the socialist state and the ways customary leadership transformed.

The Kalderash in socialism: nomad governance, state capture and brokers

Until the 1960s, the Kalderash were nomads, barely subjected to the control and identification mechanisms of the state. They were organised in small mobile groups under the guidance of an experienced Kalderash man or customary leader able to deal with identification, documentation and authorisation issues as they arose in various places of work and settlement. These customary leaders called *bulibasi* were part of the Kalderash's form of self-governance aimed at representing community needs in dealings with local authorities. Yet, the 1960s' sedentarisation brought about a period of stability for governance and state control over the Kalderash. It was also the period during which all travelling Kalderash groups from Alexandri came under *bulibasa* Iancu's control. Iancu was also the regional coordinator of all the other main settled customary leaders (e.g. Traian from Liveni, Torea's father from Medeleni) from neighbouring villages, who were, at their turn, collaborators with *Securitate*. The main leaders served as the channel by which oppression by the socialist state of Kalderash communities operated. Notwithstanding this, the Kalderash continued to travel during the warm seasons, led by other *bulibasi* who had travelling responsibilities[9], but less influence. George is one of the Kalderash from Alexandri who, after the 1960s, continued travelling around the country. He frequently experienced state abuse and *bulibasa* Iancu's control over his trade.

C: Who helped you when the police came?
G: He [the *bulibasa* for the mobile group] had been taking care of our tents as he was a *bulibasa* for our group. For instance, when I was caught by the regional police, they beat me and asked me where I was living, and with whom. Then, they went to the local police station to ask how many people were camping there and how much equipment they had with them. Our *bulibasa* [for the mobile group] begged the local police to intervene [and mediate] and asked them to understand that our people could not give any information about that.
C: What was then the difference between the leaders organizing the camping groups and those organizing the settled one?
G: The one organizing the camping supported us while the other one [*bulibasa* Iancu] supported the police.

(George, Kalderash man)

From George's statement it is clear that the *bulibasi* for mobile groups were those who acted on behalf of the Kalderash and supported their interests. Yet, *bulibasa* Iancu, empowered by the *Securitate* had better connections with the regional police, which was subordinated, as a Ministry of Interior's institution, to the *Securitate*. The Kalderash's statements show that Iancu enforced the often violent rules of the state in his community, and that he provided information to the authorities about the Kalderash's identities. Documenting identity was not an easy job for the police. The Kalderash had the same surname: Mateiescu. To seize their gold, the police needed to collaborate with *bulibasa* Iancu, who disclosed the official identities of those possessing gold. Large amounts of gold and work tools and equipment were thereby seized by the state.

The weakness of the links between the Kalderash *bulibasi* for mobile groups and the regional authorities often proved to be a disadvantage in the Kalderash's encounters with the police and administration. These leaders had good links with local institutions, but had no connections in the central and regional authorities. They were less able to protect the Roma mobile groups. George and Alexandra, two other Kalderash from Alexandri, told me about their vulnerability in relation to regional authorities who used to team up with *bulibasa* Iancu.

G: Even if a [local] mayor knew us, when we were caught by the regional police, the local police would refuse to honour the arrangement that they made with us, pretending that they didn't know anything about our presence: "We don't know when they arrived here". They used to seize our buckets, our tools; we were pushed into wagons and sent home. Our children were beaten, and then our wives, they came with dogs to search for us. We were sad, we lived in hard times.

(George, Kalderash man)

C: Was it possible to escape the police control by showing your trading license?

A: If you gave something to the mayor, you could get a paper, but it was only valid for that village. During Ceausescu's regime, we were severely punished. They confiscated our papers, everything they found on us.

(Alexandra, Kalderash woman)

As George and Alexandra suggest, the Kalderash always negotiated their activities with the local authorities (e.g. police officers and mayors). Yet, the man who could negotiate the issues was the *bulibasa* of the travelling group. The other people, lacking ID cards and birth certificates, were almost non-identifiable. The *bulibasa* for mobile groups was the legible and 'legal' actor for the local state authorities. He always had an ID and was supposed to have a trading license too. Getting work permission for an area was, however, not sufficient for full protection in their relations with the regional authorities, who had the right to engage in unannounced controls and seize their gold and copper. In this case, the main *bulibasa* Iancu was the only one who could resolve disputes and legal actions initiated by the regional police against the travelling Kalderash.

Although sharing some of the Kalderash's interests and sometimes rendering useful service, this new form of leadership tended towards a distant and non-democratic form of governance of the Kalderash. Nonetheless, the main *bulibasi* received significant support from their own communities who were many times protected from the state violent actions. As Bennett (2004) argued in the case of colonial Africa, the customary leaders who acted against the community's interests were repudiated. Hence, in order to maintain their positions, *main bulibasi* had to address their community's problems. Traian, sedentary customary leader, confirms his dual position and shared form of leadership with the socialist state.

C: What was the advantage from your relation with *Securitate*?
T: It was good because they used to help you. If you wanted to help someone who was arrested they were ready to free him. If it was about someone in jail, they lightened his sentence. If it wasn't a serious accusation, a theft or fight, we used to go to the prosecutor and the head of police would intervene and say: 'We'll let him off'.
C: Which policeman? At the county-level?
T: Yes, someone from the regional level. They were lieutenants, assistant-lieutenants. They arranged everything and told me: 'Traian, you bring us 3 golden coins if you don't want your Gypsy to spend 2 years in jail'. He would give the gold to the police officer and then go to the prosecutor to declare that the Gypsy had donated some gold. And immediately they would release him.
C: Where did the gold go?
T: It was sent to the state bank and the police officer to a higher position.

(Traian, *bulibasa* Liveni)

The interview with Traian reveals exchanges of favours between the socialist state and the main customary leader. Police officers and prosecutors represent here the state's pragmatic interest in the Kalderash's gold, but also its ideological commitment to capturing and transforming individual property into collective property. The gold was not appropriated by police officers, prosecutors or governmental representatives, but taken to the state bank as the collective property of the socialist state. However, in order to seize their gold, the police had to exercise violence against the Kalderash and raid their settlements regularly. Generally, the socialist state manipulated a double form of violence: (a) visible coercion and physical abuse and (b) symbolic power (Bourdieu 1989), the state's ability to manufacture 'services', empowerment for *bulibasi* and 'support' for common Kalderash.

Furthermore, its aim to patronise and capture individual properties and assets introduced the Kalderash main *bulibasi* to the higher power structures where the secret police, central state representatives and local authorities were formally and informally connected. At the same time, s*edentary institutional space of the state*, productive of authority and centralised commandment, captured customary leaders willing to rule over the Kalderash mobile groups*, as nodes of its arborescent power (state brokers). This constituted a mechanism of state manoeuvre and capture of Roma leadership and indirectly of their form of self-governance into the repressive state apparatus.* Yet, the socialist 'destructive empowerment', made as in the African context by the administrative state, disturbed and transformed sedentary leaders' selfhood, belonging and legitimacy as leaders and damaged Kalderash's customary forms of self-government based on mobility and representativeness. The main *bulibasi* performed leadership in a dynamic relation with opposing actors, and oscillated between support for their community and the enforcement of state rule. On the other hand, the less influential travelling *bulibasi navigated a smooth space* of flexible relations with local authorities, their extended families, and generally maintained an idiosyncratic *form of self-government* based on *reticulated movements* and small family group administration of resources and distribution of economic activities. The small group customary leadership and its forms of administration were based on continuous negotiation of prestige and collective avowal, involving "no instituted weapon other than prestige" (Deleuze & Guattari 2010: 12). It embodied an almost non-hierarchical "complex mechanism that does not act to promote the strongest, but rather inhibits the installation of stable powers, in favour of web of immanent relations" (p. 13). I call this form of social and political organisation, built up in dialectical opposition to the state centralised power apparatus and grounded in agnatic solidarity, *nomad self-governance.* The new term does not necessarily emphasise dichotomies between state and external forms of governance, but dialectics of forms of governmental power, as self/group vs. state governance, which seamlessly configure the architecture of political subjects and subjectivities. To sum up, Kalderash leadership was constituted by contradictory relations between leaders, communities and state, which took the character of a power struggle. *Power struggles defined the Kalderash's customary forms of leadership as a power relation continuously transformed through its main actors' performances that changed and redefined the Roma leadership under socialism.* Notwithstanding, the *bulibasi* for travelling groups became less and less important and visible for their communities and state authorities, and in time lost their leadership roles. The socialist state centralised the Kalderash's leadership and the institution itself became a site of contestation by Kalderash themselves.

Post-socialist Kalderash forms of leadership: from state capture to multiplicity and loss of authority

The centralised production of repression dissolved after 1989. The state's withdrawal from the economy and politics brought rapid transformations and unpredictable socio-economic changes (e.g. deindustrialisation, informal economy, corruption and patronage politics) which transformed the Kalderash's forms of leadership, their claims and their meanings. Kalderash no longer forced "to donate" gold to the state, did not need the *bulibasa*'s "support" services. On the other hand, many Kalderash got wealthy and had no interest in following a leader who might serve to limit their authority. No longer supported by the repressive state apparatus, the main *bulibasi* have largely lost their authority and legitimacy in relation to all members of their community. Power, no longer centralised by the state, was shared with other Roma leaders and mediated through local patronage politics (e.g. the mayor and deputy-mayor's political interests). The 'despotic' rule of the Kalderash *bulibasi* ended. The *bulibasa* slowly became a peaceful mediator of community problems, positioned in a loose relationship to local and regional public institutions.

Many members of the Kalderash community made the comparison between aggressive socialist leaders and new ones who seem no longer as important and influential as they had been. Without representing one or the other, the Kalderash *bulibasi* reached a balance between the support offered to their community, on one hand, and to state authorities on the other. Traian from Liveni told me about his experience of losing his authority.

C: How was *bulibasa* after 1990?
T: It wasn't the same as during Ceausescu. He [*bulibasa*] was much stronger then. He had good relations with the state and police and everyone was afraid of him. Now Gypsies expect you not to disclose any information about them. When there was such a thing as *bulibasa*, there was more authority [for the leader]. Gypsies and even the police officers were afraid. *If you want to be bulibasa for your people you need to be useful. But how can you work in this way without denouncing your Gypsies* [my emphasis]? I am *bulibasa*, but I no longer have the authority to send a Gypsy to jail.
C: Is it important to have a lot of money and houses to become a *bulibasa*?
T: To become a *bulibasa* you need to support both the police and the Gypsies. Since I became a Pentecostal I stopped harming people. My *bulibasa* position is now lost.

(Traian, *bulibasa* Liveni)

Traian's statement shows the contradictory workings of the 'destructive empowerment' produced by the socialist state: being able to do harm in order to 'help', restore what was damaged and then to be able to harm again. As many Kalderash suggested, the *bulibasi* had the power to do good and bad things altogether. Without support from the authorities, the main *bulibasi* would have not been able to pass on information about Kalderash, or to send them to prison. They would have neither been able to offer support for the evil done nor to restore their legitimacy undermined by acting as agents of state violence. This shows that in socialism, the power of the Kalderash's main *bulibasi* was produced by the way they enforced state violence, which created a space for them to perform the manufactured "help". In his last sentences, Traian suggests that in so far as he is not able to support the police and produce harm in order to "help", he is no longer able to be a *bulibasa*. Also, his 'lost' much-criticised position, has been replaced by a religious discourse of reconciliation inspired by the practice of Pentecostalism.

Immediately after 1989, the state weakened its control apparatuses over Roma. The Kalderash *bulibasi* had to find new ways of preserving or reinventing their authority and legitimacy. Traian and Iancu started to get involved in the state's reparation and restitution of seized gold. They continued their collaboration with high-level state representatives and this time both the Kalderash and their leaders had some benefits. *Bulibasa* Traian narrated the story of the restitution of gold to the Kalderash.

C: After 1989 you continued your links with the police?
T: Yes, as we gave the gold back to the Gypsies. After the Revolution me, Iancu, King Adrian [the self entitled king of the Gypsies] went to Bucharest for a week. We knew the people whose gold had been confiscated. I would be lying if I didn't say that the Gypsies always gave us something in exchange. When I was a *bulibasa* and a Gypsy asked me to get him out of jail, I demanded 500 RON in exchange. From that I gave 300 to the policemen, and the rest of 200 was mine. It was a bonus and he was happy that I had helped him.

(*bulibasa* Traian, Liveni)

Traian suggests that Kalderash offered money to *bulibasi* when they needed their support in matters of mediation with the police. However, after 1989, many Kalderash chose to deal directly with the state institutions and rely less on the *bulibasa's* ability to mediate with the local and regional authorities. Through informal economic practices and through new religious practices they strived to become independent from any external form of power (e.g. leaders, state). In Alexandri, Lucretiu took over the main responsibilities from Iancu, his father, and continued to mediate at a lower level between the local council and police. However, the institution of *bulibasa* is now much more locally based and is being challenged by other wealthy Kalderash. There are three people who all claim the same leadership position: Lucretiu (Iancu's son), Victor, and Silviu. They all collaborate with the local authorities, but lack the necessary legitimacy from the Kalderash who think that 'they claim to be *bulibasi*, but no one appointed them so' and that 'they are *bulibasi* for themselves'. In addition, *bulibasi* themselves consider that the *bulibasa's* institution is dying, being challenged by the new relation towards the transformed state institutions. For example, Lucretiu considers it no longer appropriate to support the police and provide information about Kalderash engaged in informal economic practices.

C: What's changed for the *bulibasa* now?
L: Now they all have money and do whatever they want. It is very different now.
C: Were they afraid before?
L: Yes, they were because the police forced them to hand over gold and every week someone would ask my father for help. Now it is different – they only come to me when there is a scandal or something. I only get involved in minor issues – I can't help with serious problems. If some of them fight and injury others, I can't secure their release from jail.
C: How many claim they are *bulibasi* in the Kalderash's district ?
L: My father was a *bulibasa*, but now others claim that they are *bulibasi* too. Whenever I go anywhere I don't tell anyone that I am a *bulibasa*, I just introduce myself as Lucretiu. If I go to the police, they know me, but if I go to somebody else who does not know me I would not tell them: 'You know who I am? I am *bulibasa*.' I don't have to praise myself. Nobody pays me for that.
(*bulibasa* Lucretiu, Alexandri)

Similar to Traian, Lucretiu suggests that he cannot offer the manufactured "help" any longer. Neither can he overrule local authorities' decisions and secure the release of someone from jail. For these reasons, he even avoids using the term – *bulibasa* - which is associated by Kalderash with socialist state violence. Most of the current customary leaders are trying to distance themselves from the former meanings through different kinds of interactions with the restructured state and its newly devised forms of governance aimed at Roma inclusion (e.g. meetings for Roma leaders and Roma experts organised by the government). Both the Kalderash and Romanianised Roma leaders, interested in developing and strengthening their leadership positions, have been involved formally and informally in the government's strategy of Roma integration (2005–15). The lack of financial resources meant that some local informal Roma leaders began to occupy positions of Roma experts and become paid state employees working for local councils or regional administrations. Roma expertise is held by those with modest resources obliged to work for and from within the state structures. The next section details Roma leaders' occupational histories and largely concentrates on Roma experts and their relations with Roma communities and local authorities.

The post-socialist state and Roma experts as state brokers

As already mentioned in the first section of this chapter, Doru, a local Roma expert, expected to work with both Romanianised Roma and Kalderash, and link them in with local institutions. As a state employee, he gets paid by the central government and is expected to implement locally the governmental strategy for Roma social inclusion, which targets four aims: 1) "to increase the level of Roma representation in the structures of public administration for all 8 regions of Romania (...)"; 2) "the sustainable development of a national Roma expert network, which can support the implementation of measures for social inclusion (...)"; 3) "the development of the institutional capacity of the local public administration (...)"; and 4) "facilitating the constitution of local working groups for the identification, organization, and implementation of actions that can lead to the socio-economic inclusion of Roma" (NAR 2011). Generally, the Roma expert network program aims to transfer community knowledge to central institutions through Roma experts, who are expected to follow the state's governance by being subordinated to local state authorities. It is also implied that the Roma experts are expected to mediate access and penetration of the state structures into the lives of the Roma. Hence, the Roma experts can be considered to be state brokers within Roma communities, rather than Roma representatives within state structures. Their official roles and implications trigger multiple difficulties for the Roma experts, who struggle to get recognition from their communities and be accepted as leaders. In Alexandri, Doru supports the Romanianised Roma by solving their difficulties related to identification papers, health and education services. In the early 1990s he has been an informal leader and a Roma Party representative teaming up with the present informal leader Ioader. As Doru stated in an interview, his early leadership positions and actions were part of the Roma Party's national program for forming local action groups on Roma issues, a project initiated in the early 1990s by Nicolae Paun, president of the Roma Party.

C: When did you start to deal with Roma issues? Was it a question of being a Roma representative?
D: Since 1991. Yes, Mr. Nicolae Paun organized us in teams and since then I have worked voluntarily for the local council. We were all members of the Alexandri-Derex team.
C: Were you a Roma Party member?
D: I was a member of the Alliance for Roma Unity and after a while I changed my membership to Roma Party. These are not proper political parties, but NGOs, and at some point, they amalgamated. They didn't collect sufficient numbers of signatures and that is why they are still NGOs. You know how Gypsies are. They do not want to see me as their boss, everyone would like to be in charge, and everyone would like to be a boss. So we get King Adrian with his supporters, Emperor Octavian with his, Nicolae Paun with his followers.
(Doru, Romanianised Roma man, Roma expert, Alexandri)

Doru's statements show the weak representation and support for the Roma parties and the limited political power of the Roma as an ethnic group. In the early 1990s, Roma political options were unevenly distributed amongst stronger parties (e.g. SDP, NLP, LDP[10]) and small Roma political organisations. The Romanianised

Roma, who started to receive state benefits, and the Kalderash, who received their gold back, both supported SDP, the governing party at that time. On the other hand, the Roma political parties, with minimal support from the Roma, remained in inchoate forms and never succeeded in getting into parliament. In the context of weak or almost non-existent Roma politics, the local Roma Party representatives Doru (local level) and Corina (regional level), with less financial resources, chose to work as Roma experts for the government, in the local and county councils, respectively.

In Alexandri, the Sotus are known as a respectable, well-off family. During socialism, they used to be renowned fiddlers. In this way, they differentiated themselves from other Romanianised Roma. After 1989, using their influence, they succeeded in securing key positions as Roma Party representatives. Corina is now the president of the Roma Party for the entire South-Eastern region, the president of Romani women at the county level, and the prefect's councillor on Romani issues. Her cousin, Ioader, remained an informal Roma leader and a Roma Party representative. He ran for an official Roma Party councillor position at the local council, although with no success. Yet, to strengthen his informal leadership in the Romanianised Roma community he trained to be a police mediator. On the other hand, Doru, Corina's brother, between 2000 and 2003 worked as a school mediator as part of the government project for Roma inclusion. New regulations were imposed and those with no high-school education were no longer eligible for the program. However, he decided to pass his position on to his daughter and run instead for the position of a Roma Party local councillor. In 2004, supported by his sister Corina, who convinced the Roma to vote for her brother, he was elected as a Roma Party councillor. He held this position until 2007, when the Roma expert network program was launched and gave him the opportunity for formal employment. Doru explained the disadvantages that the Roma expert's position poses in terms of representing the Roma communities. After the 2009 presidential elections, significant cuts in social welfare benefits were made by the local council. All councillors, including the SDP representatives and a SDP Romanianised Roma local councillor were no longer interested in the Roma's votes and decided to re-evaluate social benefit applications and raise the threshold for informal day labour and household expenditure included in the calculations of the minimum guaranteed income. The Romanianised Roma, local state welfare recipients, were much affected. Doru described his position in this situation.

D: I asked the mayor, 'Why did you reduce the number of social benefits?' and he replied: 'Doru, it was not mine, but the councillors' decision'.
C: What would have happened if you had been a local councillor?
D: I would have shown them my fist.
C: But you resigned from your councillor's position.
D: Yes, I did, because I'm an old man and I have to get my pension, how am I supposed to live, otherwise? When I was councillor, Mr. Septimiu [Alexandri's administrator] knows, I showed my fist and I did what I wanted. Cristian Sotu [another Romanianised Roma] who represents the Social Democrat Party in

the local council should have refused to vote for lower social benefits for the Roma. I reproached him: 'Why didn't you raise your hand?' [against the local council decision]. Gypsies have nothing to reproach me with. I helped them get water and electricity in their district. I sent their children to school. This is my role.

(Doru, Roma expert)

Doru was not able to get involved in local decision-making, in so far as the Roma experts are state representatives and their roles are confined to mediation between local authorities and the Roma community. On the other hand, Cristian, a SDP councillor, a Romanianised Roma himself, had no objections to local council decision and he supported his political party. Doru suggested that whereas a Roma Party councillor has some control over decisions, a Roma expert has none. His change in position from being a Roma Party councillor to a Roma expert entailed a loss in his capacity to represent the interests of the Roma and participate in local council decision-making. The Romanianised Roma themselves confirmed that Doru is no longer a Roma representative, but a local council employee who cannot afford to do more than what his superiors (e.g. the administrator, mayor) say. As Doru stated, becoming an expert was an opportunity for some Roma to get a monthly salary with the promise of a pension and secure life. In a similar, but also contrasting way, another example comes from a Kalderash leader Casian, a Roma expert in a neighbouring village, Medeleni. His father was a *bulibasa* for 50 years, but Casian decided to formalise his leadership position and became an employee of the local council.

C: Why did not you run for a councillor's position at the local council instead?
I: The problem was money. It was a problem for me then. It is still a problem for me now. You cannot do too much for 4 children with 480 RON, which is my salary. As a local councillor you receive 120 RON – can you believe that? And you have responsibilities for 1,730 souls [the Kalderash in Medeleni]. When it is about elections – yes, we vote for the candidate who supports us.
C: You said that that the presence of 1–2 Roma councillors at the local council would [positively] influence local decisions.
I: Yes, it would be different as I can't make decisions alone, from my position at the moment. But I am respected as a colleague (. . .) there are 22 of us employees [at the local hall].

(Casian, Kalderash man, Roma expert, Medeleni)

Keeping the customary leadership power seems difficult when individual access to economic resources is low. Due to the lack of a stable income, Casian, like Doru, chose becoming Roma experts, state employees with a regular salary. As Roma experts, both have experience of the impossibility of making political representation on behalf of the Roma concerning their queries and social problems. The alternative of being a local Roma councillor offers more possibilities for representing the Roma in local decision-making, but with lower and symbolic remuneration. In both cases, the low-income Roma leaders were drawn into the state's organised forms of leadership and brokerage. Nonetheless, Casian suggests that by working for the state, he gets training, state knowledge and access to formal governmental networks, which are helpful for the poorer Kalderash, who need access to state services. In addition, he thinks he still has an influence over community opinions, which can be used during local or national elections to get control over the local distribution of votes and strengthen his connection with the local patronage.

C: Who do you help more: the Roma or the institutions?
I: I think I help the institutions: the local council and even institutions from Bucharest were happy with the votes I secured from Gypsies.
C: Are Roma supported in any way?
I: They get support from the 416 Law [the social benefits law]. They also get 'support' from lies and unfulfilled promises politicians make to them, but the story is going to be different from now on. In the next elections I will provide the voters' names list, but no one will go to vote!

(Casian, Kalderash man, Roma expert Medeleni)

Casian's statements express a discontent and reveal the Roma experts' practices. They are expected to help institutions to deal with Roma issues, but not directly help their communities. Interestingly, when he says he helps institutions he makes reference to patronage politics and vote-buying practices, which in Romania cannot be disconnected from state institutions and are an established feature of the post-socialist politics. As Casian suggests, these clientelistic exchanges – votes for social benefits – upheld by Roma experts, seem to bring little benefit to the Roma communities. With no access to the local decision-making, Casian considers that he can use voting behaviour as the only instrument of control over a local governance and patronage that pays minimum attention to the community's needs. Similarly, both Corina and Doru need to follow both the state's interests and the interests which arise from the local and regional patronage politics. From this viewpoint, community representativeness and active political participation by Roma experts in local governance are limited by the state's definition of Roma experts as institutional representatives, and also by the dynamic of local patronage politics. To sum up, post-socialist state structures of governance aiming at social inclusion of Roma captured informal structures of leadership, mainly the leaders with poor financial resources. Romanianised Roma leaders were mostly affected, on one hand, by these parallel forms of state governance and on the other, by the weakness of Romani politics' early development stifled by development of two political fields, patronage politics and political patronage of Romani politics, discussed in the next chapter.

Discussion

The Roma leadership underwent substantial changes in parallel with the state transformation from socialism to post-socialism. Going back to the parallel between colonialism/post-colonialism and socialism/post-socialism, the customary leadership was always in communication with the state apparatuses and institutions. In colonial states, customary leadership was almost wholly absorbed by the British administration and untrained leaders became in effect state functionaries. This form of state governance, 'decentralised despotism' (Mamdani 1996), gave extensive coercive powers to local leaders to serve the interests of the colonial states. However, some writers (Keulder 2010) have argued against this interpretation and have suggested that customary leaders often challenged colonial rules. The situation was analogous to Romanian socialism. Although the main *bulibasi* were empowered by the *Securitate* to serve the interests of the state, the customary Roma leaders for small groups were not drawn into its politics of violence. Additionally, in their struggle for legitimacy over their fellows, the main *bulibasi* challenged the state's actions too.

Notwithstanding, it is more than clear that the legitimacy and the democratic workings of these forms of self-governance were seriously affected during both colonialism and socialism. Furthermore, the Kalderash's institution of customary leadership and its associated form of government, *nomad self-governance*, was centralised and captured by the socialist state. The latter, as any state, "defined by the perpetuation or conservation of organs of power" (Deleuze & Guattari 2010: 12) engaged mechanisms of capture of customary leadership as independent form of self-government, transforming its leaders into state brokers or men of the state. In other words, customary leadership, as an expression of a *war machine*[11], built in dialectical opposition to centralised, stable forms of power and ideological domination, became an organic part of the repressive state apparatus.

During both colonialism and socialism, tradition was also "used as a strategic resource" (Keulder 2010: 152) to give "rapid and recognizable symbolic form to developing types of authority and submission" (Hobsbawm & Ranger 1994: 237). However, the 'traditional' leader's authority was not necessarily connected to *tradition*, but to *custom* (Keulder 2010), which "does not preclude innovation and change up to a point" (Hobsbawm 1994: 2). Customs were not 'real' or 'invented' (Keulder 2010), but continuously in a state of change and in communication with social, cultural and political meanings and practices. In this sense, *customary law* was both "the mechanism to enforce the colonial order" and the "site of contestation and struggle" (Keulder 2010: 151) within which 'chiefs' accepted some colonial claims while rejecting others. Similarly, *bulibasa* was the Kalderash's institution of leadership informed by customary forms of organisation, which were captured and used by the socialist state as forms of control and oppression against their communities. Nevertheless, as it is shown in the chapter on religion as a form of self-government, *nomadic subjectivities* of Kalderash were not destroyed, but preserved through seasonal mobility and mainly reconstituted through religious practice and reflexivity centred on a dialogical religious self.

In post-socialism, restoration of customary leadership was not an aim for the Romanian post-socialist state, as it was for the post-colonial states (Murray 2004; Ray 2003). There was no special interest in supporting those Roma's customary forms of self-governance and leadership that had existed prior to socialism. On the other hand, the Roma expert network works as a parallel structure of governance, which serves the development and penetration of the administrative apparatus of the state into the lives of Roma communities. Roma experts are mainly state brokers, part of a mechanism of community knowledge transfer to central state institutions, but also state government exercise at the local level, which constitute nodes for its arborescent architecture of power. For the Romanianised Roma, the constitution of leadership through the Roma Party's networks and state structures of governance did not bring them the necessary representation, but a consolidation of their subjection to state governance and patronage politics, as will be discussed later in this book. The negotiations from within patterns of subordination (e.g. patronage politics, state governance) performed by their leaders encouraged Romanianised Roma to become dependent on the state and local patronage politics, which blocked the development of alternative forms of self-government, which could have created opportunities for lucrative socio-economic practice.

To conclude, Roma leadership can be primarily seen as a power relation and, therefore, as a form of government for two reasons: 1) it releases power to transform the leaders' positions and actions through interactions with other leaders and political actors, and 2) it has the capacity either to transform or restore Roma subjection to state power. Moreover, Roma leadership, as a power relation, transformed itself in interaction with post-socialist transformations in the state and politics. The dynamic between local state actors, Roma, central state and political leaders revealed similarities with the customary and colonial leadership in African states. It shed light on Roma leadership as a continuous process of power struggles and contestations, but also as a state mechanism of expert knowledge production and governance, capturing alternative forms of self-government or deterring the emergence of new ones.

Notes

1 When talking about *bulibasa* Iancu in socialism, the Kalderash alternatively used terms like 'security officer' and 'communist boss'.
2 See 'Decade of Roma Inclusion 2005–2015', www.romadecade.org/about-the-decade-decade-in-brief. Last seen 20/10/2015.
3 See Romanian Government, the National Agency for the Roma, www.anr.gov.ro.
4 The Kalderash always looked for marriage partners from other Kalderash groups and that provided an opportunity to meet and establish horizontal kinship relations with other mobile groups.
5 I make here a direct reference to the police mode of interpellation, discussed by Luis Althusser, which constitutes individuals as subjects to state ideological power: "all ideology hails or interpellates concrete individuals as concrete subjects" (Althusser 2008: 47).
6 To be officially registered, political parties need a large number of members. Like other small Roma organisations, the Roma Party did not succeed in collecting the required number of signatures and established itself as an NGO. For this reason, the government allowed the Roma NGOs to act as political parties.
7 Details of the post-socialist transformations in the Roma politics are discussed in the chapter on political fields.
8 Transformations in the Kalderash's political leadership and its meanings are discussed in the last chapter on religion and self-governance.

9 They used to negotiate various issues with the local councils and police at the places where they travelled: temporary settlement, work matters and taxes.
10 SDP – Social Democrat Party; NLP – National Liberal Party, LDP – Liberal Democrat Party.
11 Following Deleuze and Guattari (2010), *war machine* is an affirmative force, elaborating against state apparatus and warding off its constitution, manifested and engaged by non-state populations, but also by philosophers, local knowledge(s) and forms of art and creative mechanisms, which oppose themselves to sovereign reason.

Bibliography

Althusser, L. (2008) *On Ideology*. London, New York: Verso.
Bennett, T. W. (2004) *Customary Law in South Africa*. Lansdowne: Juta and Company Ltd.
Bourdieu, P. (1989) 'Social Space and Symbolic Power'. *Sociological Theory*, 7(1): 14–25.
Brower, H. H., Schoorman, F. D. & Tan, H. H. (2000) 'A Model of Relational Leadership: The Integration of Trust and Leader–Member Exchange'. *The Leadership Quarterly*, 11(2): 227–250.
Dachler, H. P. (1992) 'Management and Leadership as Relational Phenomena'. In M. V. Cranach, W. Doise and G. Mugny (Eds.) *Social Representations and Social Bases of Knowledge*. Lewiston, NY: Hogrefe and Huber, pp. 169–178.
Dachler, H. P. & Hosking, D. M. (1995) 'The Primacy of Relations in Socially Constructing Organizational Realities'. In D. M. Hosking, H. P. Dachler and K. J. Gergen (Eds.) *Management and Organization: Relational Alternatives to Individualism*. Avebury: Aldershot, pp. 1–29.
Deleuze, G. & Guattari, F. (2010) *Nomadology: The War Machine*. Seattle, WA: Wormwood Distribution.
Graen, G. & Uhl-Bien, M. (1991) 'The Transformation of Professionals into Self- Managing and Partially Self-Designing Contributors: Toward a Theory of Leadership-Making." *Journal of Management Systems*, 3(3): 49–54.
Graen, G. & Uhl-Bien, M. (1995) 'Relationship-Based Approach to Leadership: Development of Leader–Member Exchange (LMX) Theory of Leadership Over 25 Years: Applying a Multi-Level Multi-Domain Perspective'. *The Leadership Quarterly*, 6(2): 219–247.
Hobsbawm, E. (1994) 'Introduction: Inventing Traditions'. In E. Hobsbawm and T. Ranger (Eds.) *The Invention of Tradition*. Cambridge: Cambridge University Press, pp. 1–15.
Hobsbawm, E. & Ranger, T. (1994) *The Invention of Tradition*. Cambridge: Cambridge University Press.
Keulder, C. (Ed.) (2010) *State, Society and Democracy: A Reader in Namibian Politics*. Windhoek: Macmillan Education Namibia (Pty) Ltd.
Mamdani, M. (1996) *Citizen and Subject: Contemporary Africa and the Legacy of Late Colonialism*. Princeton, NJ: Princeton University Press.
Meindl, J. (1995) 'The Romance of Leadership as a Follower-Centric Theory: A Social Constructionist Approach'. *The Leadership Quarterly*, 6(3): 329–341.
Miller, N. N. (1968) 'The Political Survival of Traditional Leadership'. *The Journal of Modern African Studies*, 6(2): 181–198.
Murray, C. (2004) *South Africa's Troubled Royalty: Traditional Leaders After Democracy*. The Federation Press in association with the Centre for International and Public Law.: Faculty of Law. Law and Policy Paper 23. Canberra: Australian National University.
National Agency for the Roma (NAR) (2014) Romanian Government's Social Inclusion Strategy for Romanian Citizens Belonging to Roma Minority, for the Period 2014–2020. www.anr.gov.ro/docs/Site2014/Strategie/Strategie_final_18–11–2014.pdf

112 *A historical political ethnography*

National Agency For The Roma (NAR) (2011) National Network of Roma Experts, Support Mechanism for the Implementation of Measures of Social Inclusion of Roma, Vulnerable Group Subjected to Social Exclusion. Romanian Government's Report. www.anr.gov.ro/docs/proiecte_pdf/2275.pdf

Pearce, C. L., Jay, A., Conger, J. A. & Locke, E. A. (2007) 'Shared Leadership Theory'. *The Leadership Quarterly*, 18(3): 281–288.

Ray, D. I. (2003) 'Rural Local Governance and Traditional Leadership in Africa and Afro-Caribbean: Policy and Research Implications from Africa to Americas and Australasia'. In D. I. Ray and P. S. Reddy (Eds.) *Grassroots Chiefs in Africa and the Afro Caribbean Governance*. Calgary: University of Calgary Press, pp. 1–31.

Rost, J. C. (1995) 'Leadership: A Discussion About Ethics'. *Business Ethics Quarterly*, 5(1): 129–142.

Uhl-Bien, M. (2006) 'Relational Leadership Theory: Exploring the Social Processes of Leadership and Organizing'. *The Leadership Quarterly*, 17(6): 654–676.

8 Mapping power relations through political fields

Patronage politics, political patronage and Romani politics

As showed in the previous two chapters, Roma relations under post-socialism occurred at the intersection of spaces of power struggle (e.g. state, politics and informal economy), which emerged in the wider post-socialist society. Hence, politics cannot be treated separately or independently from the transformation of the state and informal economic practices. They come together at the level of local politics and political processes (e.g. patronage politics), without being confined to local or central instantiations. Romani politics has been transformed through these local and trans-local temporal dynamics of power relations, which occurred simultaneously at different administrative levels in interaction with patronage politics, a characteristic of post-socialist political space.

In Romania support for the ruling party became a necessity for access to business, social connections and public positions and goods and, overall, the intersectionalities between party politics, the state and the informal economy favoured the development of patronage politics. As argued in the first chapter, post-socialist transformations did not necessarily bring about a "privatisation of power" in the shape of 'chiefdoms' able to act independently from central government, as Verdery (1996) suggests, but led to a general politics of clientelism, in which local patrons become state representatives, in control of local resources and distribution of welfare, but dependent upon and subordinated to central governmental and political actors.

In general terms, clientelism was a constant both in socialism and post-socialist capitalism. In socialism the Communist Party aimed at restricting and controlling individual initiative and action. Nevertheless, as Burawoy and Verdery (1999) argued, party bureaucrats and locals, through their everyday practices, domesticated the restrictive centralised distribution of resources by the Party. In other words, socialism was a patrimonial system, a paternalistic, authoritarian system dominated by clientelism, not always following the rules of the centre (Eyal et al 1998).

In post-socialism, the withdrawal of the state from the economy, privatisation and the decentralisation of economy and politics generated informal inter-dependencies between the spaces of power struggles (e.g. politics, state, economy), which gave way to the development of new forms of clientelism, patronage and a neopatrimonial system as a whole based on democratic elections.

114 *A historical political ethnography*

Clientelism (e.g. dyadic relations between a person with a higher rank and a client with a lower rank) and patronage politics (e.g. distribution of administrative positions by actors organised around a political party) became a rule for both local and central level politics. As discussed in the introduction, politicians became the main supporters of business actors and were often implicated in cases of corruption. Central and local level politics were of equal importance in the complicated process of post-socialist transformation.

The aim of this chapter is to analyse the transformations of Romani politics in the context of these larger political transformations, which took place in Romania after 1990 and explore their relevance for the Roma's forms of governance and representation.

Local level politics and political fields: local and regional political organisation of Romani leadership

The early 1990s were characterised by the emergence of a political pluralism and democratisation in the space of party politics mainly through the practice of free elections at both national and local level. At present, the Roma Party is the most important Roma NGO and political organisation with its president, Nicolae Paun, occupying a deputy's chair in the parliament. For each region, there are Roma Party representatives who many times work as Roma experts for county councils or prefectures. The distribution of Roma Party representatives runs in parallel to a complex hierarchical bureaucratic apparatus of monitorisation of Roma communities devised by the government as part of the national strategy 2014–20 (NAR 2014) for the inclusion of the Roma, which includes local and regional offices concerned with Roma issues. Regional Offices for the Roma (ROR) "are functional structures organised at county level within the prefecture".

> There are maximum 3 experts/bureaucrats, part of the executive apparatus and one of them obligatorily has to belong to Roma minority (. . .). Members of the JWG [regional Joint Working Group] have planned team activities, organise visits for assessing and monitoring situation of communities of Romanian citizens belonging to Roma minority, collect data and information at the local level which they need to centralise at the county level. JWG is subordinated to the prefecture under technical coordination of National Agency of the Roma.
>
> (NAR 2014: 43)

Together with *local initiative groups* and *local action groups*, *regional offices for the Roma* act as supervisory and epistemological apparatuses of the state, expanding its administrative power throughout its peripheries, and as discussed in the chapter on Roma leadership, incorporating Roma leadership into its arborescent architecture. Corina is the regional Roma Party representative and the Roma expert nominated by the prefect of Derex. The Derex ROR includes both informal and formal Roma leaders from Alexandri: a) Doru, Roma expert and Roma

Party representative; b) Ioader, Roma Party representative, police mediator and Romanianised Roma informal leader; c) Victor, informal Kalderash leader; and d) Lucretiu, informal Kalderash leader, *bulibasa*.

At the local level, the governmental strategy includes local initiative groups (LIGs), organised by the Roma expert with local Roma, and local working groups (LWGs) composed of "the local Roma experts, representatives of the public institutions, members of the local council (including Roma councillors), members of the NGOs and a local Roma community representative, part of the LIG" (NAR 2014: 44). LWGs aim at implementing and incorporating "local plan of social inclusion into the local council strategy of local development" (NAR 2014: 44) and communicating these to the ROR. The LWGs are organised by the local council. Besides the Roma leaders I mentioned above, during my fieldwork in Alexandri, I talked to three local council members, who were frequently active in the LWG: a) Dan, the president of the local Liberal National Party (LNP) organisation; b) Ovidiu, first mayor of Alexandri, a LNP local councillor and sports teacher at the school attended by Kalderash and c) Rodan, a Liberal Democrat Party (LDP) councillor. I intentionally chose to talk with councillors from local political opposition groups (LNP, LDP), who could offer accounts of Roma leadership in relation to public institutions, different from that presented by the main local SDP patronage actors: mayor Tiberiu and the deputy mayor and local administrator Septimiu. Whereas Tiberiu is the main supporter of Romanian inhabitants and known for his anti-Roma views, Septimiu is a Romanian who grew up among Romanianised Roma. He was a teacher and a director of the school attended by Romanianised Roma. He has always been a supporter of the Roma interests and helped their families directly (e.g. social services, employment and cash). Officially, he is the administrator of the village, while informally he serves as the local patron. On the other hand, mayor Tiberiu has ruled the local council since 2000, the year when, in order to get political support from the ruling party, he chose to join the Social Democratic Party just after the local elections and he appointed his SDP running mate Septimiu, as a deputy mayor. In 2008, Septimiu became a councillor of the Minister of the Interior Octavian (SDP), a period during which he channelled governmental money to Alexandri. In 2009 he returned and he was appointed by the same mayor as the local administrator of the commune. These days both SDP leaders are interested in convincing the Roma to vote for their party in exchange for local council services or cash.

However, at the county level, the administration adopts a different approach to the patronage politics. From 2005, a situation which changed only in 2012, representatives of the liberal and conservative parties – NLP and LDP – held the position of prefect[1]. In order to serve as senior state officials, the prefects, as representatives of the government appointed by the Minister of Interior, have to abandon their official political positions[2]. However, despite this official renunciation, they continue to maintain informal links with their political parties. The prefects' political interests often clash with their administrative roles. In this context, Corina, the Roma Party representative and the regional Roma expert, appointed by the prefect, is expected to follow either the prefect's political interests (LNP

116 *A historical political ethnography*

or LDP), which are opposed to the Roma Party's and Alexandri's patronage politics (SDP) described above. This overlap between state administrative roles and patronage politics, which occurs at different administrative levels (e.g. SDP in Alexandri and LNP or LDP in Derex) causes conflicts among Roma experts and state actors dealing directly or indirectly with Roma issues. The present chapter looks at these inconsistencies and collaboration between the Roma leaders and patronage actors at different administrative levels, in order to inquire into the Romani politics from within the local level politics, which presents itself as an *incomplete field of action* in relation to central level politics. As Swartz (1968) suggests, local-level politics is not local per se, but has to be analytically examined and treated as *an incomplete field of action*, involving negotiations with regional and central politics, in which local actors and their practices are engaged with outside actors at different levels in the political structure (e.g. national, regional, cross-regional). Patronage politics is a good example of political incompleteness, a mechanism whereby power is manifested and negotiated through practices and relationships between local, regional and central politicians and state actors. It is a sphere of action and power struggle "defined by 'the interest and involvement of the participants' in the process being studied and its contents include the values, meanings, resources, and relationships employed by these participants in that process" (Swartz 1968: 9). The local and central levels are not fixed points of reference in the individual's relations and practices, but nodes in a complex web of power relations. Moreover, as Swartz (1968) argues, "the spatial and temporal extension of political processes" are incorporated in the term of *political field* that "is composed of the actors directly involved in the processes being studied" and involves "both continuity and change in the relations among participants in politics" (p. 6). In this case, *post-socialist patronage politics* is an illustrative example of a political field in which patrons and their followers, as representatives of parliamentary political parties, operate within different spaces of power struggles (e.g. politics, state, economy) and connect local and central politics. Generally, *patronage politics* is an expression of the transformations occurring in the neopatrimonial space of power, an effect of "the spatial and temporal extension of [delocalised] political processes" (p. 6), which might interact and overlap with other political fields (e.g. political patronage). In practical terms, *patronage politics* refers to the way in which the local patron and his followers make use of their political party membership to stabilise power of a main political formation locally and get control over the local distribution of positions and resources. The patron maintains and develops relations with local clients and political brokers[3], clients and upper-level party members for whom he often becomes a broker himself (Hilgers 2008; Remmer 2007).This chapter delves into the historical emergence and transformation of *Romani local level politics as an incomplete field of action* in interaction with other political fields, within the post-socialist neopatrimonial political space of power. The following questions deserve attention:

> *Does Romani politics constitute an independent political field able to channel power to the Roma communities? If not, what exactly prevented the*

development of Romani politics and diminished the effectiveness of Romani leadership in the local decision-making process and political representation of Roma at the local level?

I answer these questions by exploring connections between local and regional political organisations as they interacted with the larger transformations of the post-1989 Romanian politics as a neopatrimonial space of power.

The local dynamics of patronage politics in the development of the Romanian neopatrimonial political space

After 1989, the entanglement between party politics, social and institutional local life became the norm in the everyday local practices. In Romania it is generally known that political allegiance is the main criterion in the distribution of institutional positions and that a change in the government is usually followed by a change in the managerial structure of public institutions. Managers of public institutions are required to be members of the ruling party and pursue the governing party's interests at the local and institutional level. In my field research, Ovidiu, a sports teacher and the local representative of the National Liberal Party in Alexandri, indicated a strong connection between local institutional practices, the distribution of local positions and the growing interdependence between party politics and local public administration:

C: Do you think that education is much more influenced by party politics now than before 1989?
G: Yes, it is. It has never been worse than now. Once I was at the regional inspectors' office and I heard a discussion in the hallway when the general inspector was telling to his deputy: "We need to change 65 directors in Derex county". The deputy replied: "We need to slow down". However, the general inspector said: "No, we have the necessary leverage, we will change everything and we'll get our people in".
G: There has never been a politicisation like it is right now, not only in education, but in all areas. I used to talk with an engineer who was head of police. He got fired and they installed a man coming from a completely different field. While the first was a member of the NLP, the new man was the member of LDP [the governing party]. The new employee was looking for people to help him do his work. He didn't have a clue what he had to do, but the LDP man had to be there to oversee the institution.
(Ovidiu, first mayor of Alexandri, school director and member of the local NLP organisation)

Politicisation refers here to the direct intervention of the central ruling party in the distribution of managerial positions in local public institutions (e.g. schools, financial offices, hospitals, etc.), which is called here patronage politics. In this context, managers of public institutions can get easier access to central resources

118 *A historical political ethnography*

and connections. However, problems appear when central government is ruled by a party different from the local or regional patronage party. In cases where the local government (Alexandri – SDP patronage) has a different political orientation from the central government – LDP, the distribution of local public resources to public institutions lead by LDP representatives is blocked by the local council administration, which generally follows the direction of local patronage politics (SDP)[4].

Ovidiu makes references to the last decade (2004–08) when central government was run by a LDP majority, and representatives of the local public institutions such as schools were replaced by people who were not necessarily qualified for those positions, but who were members of the LDP. Similarly, in 2008, when the LDP won the parliamentary elections and formed the government, the regional LDP office asked him either to change his political membership from LNP to LDP, or to resign. At that time, Ovidiu considered that it was more important to keep his LNP membership and risk his position as head of the school. Later on, the regional education management replaced him with a LDP teacher who was less well qualified. From the accounts given by public institution managers and local teachers including Ovidiu, all those who were in the LDP kept their managerial positions, whereas others, from other parties, were either fired or demoted. Similarly, Dan, head of the LNP local organisation, currently a local councillor in Alexandri, expressed his discontent with the post-1989 politics and economy.

D: I expected the 1989 Revolution to change the values and bring them back to their right place, but the opposite happened. Values were reversed: if you had money, you had everything. It does not matter if you are smart, educated, or if you work hard. You need to have money. It does not matter how you get it. And now we have the Gypsy-like model: arrogance and disdain are at the governmental level. The Kalderash have become rich, they speculated for 5–6 years and were attached to a party.
C: Which party?
D: First, they were with the SDP [the Social Democrat Party], then with the LDP [the Liberal Democrat Party]. They did the same and they got rich.
C: Do you think they would have been able to succeed without being attached to a political party?
D: No. Without public money you cannot succeed. Don't you see that all businesses are legal.

(Dan, head of the NLP, local organisation Alexandri)

It is interesting to observe that Dan does not make a clear differentiation between local and central politics. On the contrary, he considers that all economic and political practices, local and central, are part of the same socio-political context. The post-1989 reality is not a one-way process from central to local practices, but a complex transformation in which politics and informality come together in the development of patronage politics and extended clientelistic relationships between individuals with unequal positions. In his analysis, Dan transfers the characteristic of the Kalderash's economy – informality – developed during both socialism and post-socialism, to the whole post-1989 neopatrimonial system. Similarly, in the Romanian context, it is a common perception that associates the Roma's informal economic activities with the side effects of an uncertain transition, becoming in the process a symbol of informality and 'illegality'. Dan's non-specific answer to my question 'which party?' also suggests that clientelism was a constant in the Kalderash's informal economic activities irrespective of the political orientation of the central or local government. Kalderash's clientelistic dyadic relations were developed in connection with representatives of both central and local ruling parties, thus alternating between the SDP and the LDP.

The so-called 'reversal of values' is the result of a transition from a centralised authoritarian system to the uncontrolled emergence of overlapping spaces of power (e.g. state, politics and informal economy) in which the political favouritism became the main basis for ensuring personal relations, institutional practices and success in business. This state of affairs was reflected and accommodated within local-level politics where patronage[5] developed through successive forms of political governance and favouritism. Starting with the 2000 local elections as a time reference, the history of patronage politics expanded through the local council actors' connections to central level politics. In 2004, Septimiu (SDP deputy mayor) came in contact with Octavian, a SDP vice-president of the central executive bureau of the SDP regional organisation. In 2009, Octavian, who had been named vice-prime minister in 2008, became the country's Minister of the Interior, and Septimiu, now his councillor, left his deputy mayor position in Alexandri to work for the central government. Septimiu used his position in the government to channel financial resources to Alexandri and develop local infrastructure (e.g. water, gas facilities, sports facilities for a local school, an open-air market, etc.). In this context, he paid special attention to the Romanianised Roma district where he grew up. He supported developmental projects in the area with both information and money (e.g. water facilities and road improvement). He was highly appreciated by the locals, especially by the Roma, who generally considered him the most important political leader involved in the development of locality. The help he was able to extend, owing to his position in the central government, recommended him as a 'local patron'. In exchange, he expected allegiance for his party – SDP – from the locals and especially the Roma. These new bonds between local state representatives (e.g. mayor, vice-mayor and followers) and SDP representatives situated at upper level politics created the local level patronage politics, which, since 2004, has started to act independently from central elections and government. Local patronage politics thus developed can also stand as the main explanation for the political continuity of the Alexandri's dominant party – SDP – since 2000. For Alexandri, Septimiu is the main actor in local patronage politics, connecting higher political levels to the local politics. His legitimate power or *stabilisation of power*, in Graziano's (1976) terms, comes from his relations with higher-up party members, in the field of patronage politics, which enables him to get access to governmental funding and therefore gain support from the locals.

120 *A historical political ethnography*

Notwithstanding, *patronage politics* is more than a simple patron-client exchange relationship, a classical relation of domination, as in Scott's conception, in which the patron exercises control over resources (Scott 1977). It is the binding power between the ruling party and state institutions and the link between central and local politics, developed in parallel with the structural transformations occurring in the post-1989 Romanian society at large. Patronage politics is *a political field* with its own constitutive and interactive history, a manifestation of a web of power struggles between leaders, voters, political parties, state and institutional representatives (e.g. local council and schools), which extend from local to central politics. From within this field, the patronage team controls local resources, voting behaviour and governance. The latter is more than governance. It is patronage politics and affects the way the Roma communities are represented by their leaders in local decision-making.

Roma allegiances: from restitution politics to patronage politics

For the Roma, patronage politics was less important in the 1990s and gradually became more prominent in the 2000s when the mayor and the deputy mayor became part of the same SDP patronage grouping. However, in the early 1990s, Roma, especially the Kalderash were greatly affected by a different form of politics, which I call here *restitution politics*, directly related to the activities of the central state. The Social Democrat Party, at that time (RSDP) aimed at reinforcing its legitimacy and solidifying its political power through the restitution of land to peasants and gold to Roma (Kalderash). In the 1990s and early 2000, *restitution politics* was a source of political power for the SDP. Dan, the president of the local NLP, as well as many other party representatives and Kalderash present a picture of Roma allegiance to SDP politics and its emblematic figure, former president Ion Iliescu.

> In 2000, the Kalderash supported the SDP and voted for the existing mayor. I had been in their houses. Inspectors from the regional financial offices came to look for them, but they were afraid of going alone to the Kalderash's district and for that reason I joined them. I went inside their houses and I saw posters with Iliescu [head of the RSDP, president in 1992–96, and 2000–04] on the walls, just like you sometimes see orthodox icons in Romanian farmer's houses.
>
> (Dan, head of the NLP local organisation Alexandri)

The analogy between religious and political icons made by my respondent is a proof of the symbolic process in which *restitution politics* endowed the head of the SDP with authority and, in Graziano's terms, with 'pure power' (Graziano 1976) produced in a unilateral relation. The latter is an indirect exchange between the president of the country – a symbolic patron – and the Roma as clients, in which the patron expects returns – votes – by creating *obligations* among his clients. Compared to a classic client-patron relationship, which implies a direct exchange of goods or money for votes, the 'pure power' the national SDP leader addresses is sourced by one single form of exchange (e.g. gold restitution-SDP allegiance), established as authority exercised at distance – symbolic patronage – manifested as respect and endorsed by its clients – Kalderash – in a long-lasting relation attached to a symbolic iconography of power. Many Kalderash families were able to become affluent by investing gold in their businesses with state enterprises. In this context, President Iliescu, who opened the door for these opportunities, has for a long time been a symbolic patron and authority figure in their everyday lives, the symbolic iconography of the *restitution politics*, which substantially changed the Kalderash's life trajectories.

Gold has been perceived as a major benefit brought by the act of restitution itself. However, the emergent symbolic entanglement between gold/land restitution and the SDP developed into what I call *restitution politics* as part of a larger discourse on justice and reparation of previous socialist forms of injustice. In a search for legitimacy, this type of discourse was promoted by both RSDP members and its leader Iliescu, who were accused by liberal political formations and parts of population of harbouring former 'communist' convictions. Similarly, the RSDP ideology was considered to be a rehashing of the former Communist Party. *Restitution politics* was integral to the party's electorate strategy for the first democratic elections, which took place in 1992. That explains, how in the 1990s, not only the Kalderash were happy to claim they voted for RSDP and Iliescu, who gave their gold back, but also the farmers, who considered that Iliescu gave them back[6] their land. The restitution was deeply influenced by party politics and created a relative stable SDP electorate among those Roma and farmers who were able to get their gold or land back.

By managing the local restitution of gold, the *bulibasi* were still important as Roma leaders and directly connected to the central politics and people holding important positions in the government. The old *bulibasa* Iancu of the Kalderash community from Alexandri, a *Securitate* broker under socialism, acted as a mediator for the gold restitution process. He was the main link between the Kalderash community, central government and the National Bank, where the gold had been stored. In the late 1990s, other Roma representatives started to exert influence on the Kalderash's voting behaviour. I offer here two examples of the way local Roma leaders, both formal and informal, Kalderash and Romanianised Roma, created power relations through *patronage politics*. Casian is a Roma expert in Medeleni and, as discussed in the chapter on Roma leadership, he became a leading supporter of the local patronage party the mayor's party (NLP).

C: What happened in the 90s when you came into contact with the local council?
I: It was not a connection, but all of the candidates were looking to get more voters. And a part of us, the Roma, voted. Some went with the SDP, others with the NLP, the LDP. In the late 90s we went with the NLP.
C: Why did you choose the NLP?
I: For the first elections in the 1990s we voted for the SDP because of President Iliescu who gave the gold back to us, along with all the rights taken away

122 *A historical political ethnography*

> under socialism. President Iliescu came here in 1992 for the elections: 'vote for me' (. . .).
>
> Before 1992, our mayor was from the SDP. Then we went with the NLP [the new mayor's party]. The mayor is a respectful and polite person. He didn't differentiate between Roma and Romanian children. He was always considerate to everyone and my father [former *bulibasa*] talked to the Roma telling them that it was good to vote for him.
>
> (Casian, Kalderash man, Roma expert,
former *bulibasa*'s son, Medeleni)

This narrative shows a transition from *restitution politics* to *patronage politics* in Roma everyday politics. Casian's answers differ in relation to the time reference. When talking about politics and voting in the early 1990s, Kalderash leaders and other Kalderash tend to make references to the SDP and the emblematic President Iliescu. However, in the late 1990s, local informal Roma leaders in Alexandri and Medeleni became state-patronage politics brokers for their mayors' political parties (e.g. Alexandri – the SDP, Moroieni – the LNP) in both presidential and local elections. In the interview Casian suggests that, together with his father he convinced many Kalderash to follow the mayor's political party and vote for the NLP in the last elections. In 2000, patronage politics became important for Romanianised Roma leaders in Alexandri, too. Ioader, the informal Romanianised Roma leader, offers a detailed account of his progressive allegiance to the SDP.

C: Were you interested in the SDP?
I: Yes, we were interested because we support the SDP. I mean my brother-in-law works for Vega [a regional gas company]. And if he works at Vega we support the SDP.
C: Why? Is Vega a SDP company?
I: Yes. It is Octavian's company and we go with Octavian [former Minister of the Interior]. Since the 1990s I have been friends with Octavian.
C: How did you meet?
I: In official meetings. In the first meeting we had, he asked me who the Roma leader was? Ioader! [the respondent]. He came here telling us to vote for him.
C: When was that?
I: In 2004, when he was campaigning for the SDP, and he invited me to the meeting. Septimiu and Tiberiu were in the same political party and I asked them to be candidates of different parties. One of them could work with the government, directly with Octavian. I took Septimiu to the local school [the district where the Kalderash live]. Octavian came with 12–15 people there, important people, and he asked me: What should we do with Septimiu? And I said, Septimiu should lead the SDP local organization and after that he [Septimiu] became the head of the local SDP.

(Ioader, informal Romanianised Roma leader)

This interview excerpt illustrates how informal leaders circulate and connect central and local levels of power by the negotiation of local political positions, on the basis that Roma have always been a good electorate source for SDP. Assuming that Ioader's story is accurate, it is intriguing to notice that in the distribution of the local SDP positions, Octavian[7], a representative of the central level SDP politics, asked an informal Roma leader for advice. By taking responsibility for Roma voting behaviour, Ioader, an informal Roma leader, operated as a broker not only between the Roma community and local authorities, but also in relation with representatives of central politics. In the interview he also mentions Vega, the regional gas company associated with Octavian's interests, as an important reference for his voting options. He also mentions that he personally knew Octavian from meetings organised by the Roma Party, most probably from 1999 onwards when the Roma Party established a political coalition with the SDP. The statement also shows that his main interest lies in connecting with higher level SDP political representatives and acting as a *power broker*, able *to circulate and link* different levels and spaces of power (e.g. politics, police/state mediation).

Similarly, other informal Romanianised Roma leaders such as Ioader and Kalderash *bulibasi* in Alexandri, who convince the Roma to vote for different political parties, act as *power brokers* across *loose webs of power*. The latter connect different political levels, exploit boundaries between *spaces of power struggle* (e.g. informal businesses, local authorities, politics), and even give advice to central and local political leaders. Roma power brokers' actions show how local and central-level politics are entangled and act together within the *field of patronage politics which progressively replaced from below the field of restitution politics*. On the other hand, Roma experts act from within state bureaucracy's *tight webs of power* and are *state-patronage brokers*.

Romani politics: political patronage and patronage politics

In the early 1990s, the Roma were recognised as a minority and according to governmental Act 8/1990 they were allowed to set up political parties and NGOs. On the other hand, in agreement with governmental Act 21/1994 minorities, have the opportunity to launch candidates in the local and presidential elections[8]. Since 1990, the Roma have had a Roma deputy in parliament, a representative of their main political formation, the Roma Party. In 1994, 23 other Roma organisations joined the Roma Party, which became the main Roma political organisation. Nevertheless, 1999 was the year when the Roma Party agreed to have an official, open-ended political partnership with SDP, for both presidential and parliamentary elections and nationwide local council elections. According to this, Roma Party representatives are required to extend political support to SDP candidates. In exchange, the Roma Party expects to receive support in the promotion and representation of the Roma projects related to education, social welfare and cultural rights. This political partnership engendered *political patronage* at different administrative levels in which both formal and informal leaders who are also Roma Party representatives[9] are expected to convince the Roma to vote for the SDP in local and national elections.

Notwithstanding, the transition from *restitution politics* to *patronage politics* and *political patronage* (SDP-Roma Party coalition) discouraged the emergence and development of ethnic politics among the Roma groups. The *political patronage of Roma politics*, which institutionalised at the central level, strengthened *SDP local patronage* power locally and in Alexandri, too. However, in other locations, like Medeleni, or at the regional level – Derex's prefecture – the *general political patronage* orientation (SDP) did not correspond to the political orientation given by the *local patronage politics*, the mayor's or prefect's political party (e.g. PDL/LNP). These inconsistencies between the mayor's or prefect's political orientation and the SDP-Roma Party coalition generated conflicts between Roma leaders, especially Roma experts, who follow either one political option or the other or alternate between parties.

Most of the Sotu family members are either informal or formal leaders in Alexandri and are Roma Party representatives in the regional area. Corina, as a regional Roma expert and prefecture employee, is expected to be a state representative for the Roma communities, including those from Alexandri, and at the same time a political broker for the NLP regional patronage politics (the prefect's party). In addition, as a Roma Party representative she needs to support both the Roma Party and the national Roma Party-SDP political alliance. From her positions, the NLP *regional patronage politics* offered by the prefect's political orientation and *national SDP political patronage of Roma Party* are contradictory political fields through which Corina needs to negotiate and mediate her position. On the other hand, in Alexandri, all her family members including Doru, local Roma expert, support the local SDP patronage. These divisions between Alexandri and Derex's political orientation often generated conflicts between the two leaders Corina and Doru. Each of them was interested in persuading the Roma to vote for one political party or another. Thus, the interference of *SDP political patronage of Roma party* and the variation in *patronage politics* at different administrative levels alter the role of Roma experts, who are not primarily interested in representing or handling Roma community problems, but rather in representing different political parties' interests.

Nevertheless, the informal Roma leaders, Romanianised Roma and Kalderash, acting as power brokers have more space for negotiation inside the two political fields: political patronage and patronage politics. Ioader, the informal Romanianised Roma leader in Alexandri, narrated a brief history of his political brokerage and the transformations in Roma local voting behaviour.

C: How were the Roma Party representatives established in Alexandri?
I: We announced that one week in advance. Who came then? The state secretary of the Roma, who is also a Roma representative for the Roma Party in Derex. Corina, who works for the prefecture, invited him. Corina told me: 'he is going to nominate you'. Now it is not as it was before: public elections. We had 500–600 people [attending the meeting].
C: Who were the other candidates?
I: Only people from the Sotu family (. . .). Those from Bucharest said [to all Romanianised Roma on the stadium] 'raise your hands' and they all raised the hands for me.

C: And in 1992 you had the first elections for the local council. Whom did you vote for and how did you advise Roma to vote?
I: Votes were distributed randomly. People [candidates] came with packs [of food] and asked the Gypsies to vote for them, and Gypsies divided between different parties.
C: And how did you tell Roma to vote?
I: It was not our elections to tell them not to vote for somebody.
C: Does that mean you had no interest in any candidate?
I: No, none.
C: When did you start to get interested in voting for one candidate or another?
I: Since Tiberiu came, in 2000. I started, because we knew each other from the cooperative state farm.

(Ioader, informal Roma leader Alexandri)

This interview fragment shows how in the early 1990s Romani politics started to take shape locally through community elections under the coordination of the Roma Party, which aimed to build an infrastructure of local political activism in all the regions of Romania. As Ioader claims, these were community elections amongst the Roma, which were later formalised in local or regional elections for the position of Roma Party councillor, a position difficult to obtain in competition with main political parties (SDP, NLP, LDP). In the early 1990s, the first community elections for the positions of Roma Party representatives were organised only among Romanianised Roma. More than that, Roma Party candidates were all from the same family of fiddlers – Sotu, who succeeded, after 1990, in becoming local or regional leaders and later on active political brokers in local and *regional patronage politics*. In this context, Romanianised Roma themselves were susceptible to vote buying and split their votes between different political parties. On the other hand, the Kalderash, who always acted as a separate group, did not participate in these elections and were still organised around the main *bulibasa* Iancu. More than that, in the early 1990s, Kalderash were connected to *restitution politics*, showing allegiance to the SDP and former president Ion Iliescu.

Interestingly, Ioader's statement about 1992 local council elections, "It was not our elections, to tell them not to vote for somebody", suggests that in the early 1990s, Roma leaders were not already represented politically in the local council and local mayoral elections were of little interest to Roma. Ioader became interested in political brokerage in 2000, when the local SDP patronage team (e.g. mayor Tiberiu and deputy mayor Septimiu) was constituted and Roma leaders were asked by the local patronage actors to influence the Roma's voting options in exchange for favours. That can be applied both to Romanianised Roma and Kalderash leaders, formal and informal, who found in the new SDP local patronage a source of power, which enabled them to strengthen their leadership positions. Forms of Roma leadership (e.g. Roma experts, Romanianised Roma informal leaders and *bulibasi*), weak in terms of legitimacy, became valuable in terms of political brokerage for the local SDP patronage battling with the opposition. From 2000 *local patronage politics* became a common political practice organised locally by Septimiu – local patron – and his followers' co-SDP team members such as mayor Tiberiu and Roma expert Doru, but also by Ioader and other local SDP councillors and supporters. Ioader told me more about the complicated voting options informed both by the Roma Party and SDP local patronage.

C: Did Corina Sotu support the SDP or the Roma Party?
I: She was with the SDP then. When we did not have problems with our votes, we were with the SDP, for the parliamentary elections. When we needed votes for the Roma Party, we told them 'brothers, we cannot vote for two people because Gypsies would vote for different people and thus cancel out each other's votes'. Those from the SDP said, 'It's okay, Mr. Ioader'.

(Ioader, informal Roma leader, Alexandri)

Ioader suggests that voting options for the Roma Party needed to be negotiated with the local SDP patronage actors and central Roma Party representatives, who in 1999 entered a political coalition with the SDP, thus allowing Roma leaders to support their Roma Party during different elections. Nonetheless, in other situations, the Roma leaders Corina, Doru and Ioader were expected to support alternatively regional or local patronage politics (e.g. prefecture's LNP/LDP, or Alexandri's SDP), the Roma Party or the coalition SDP-Roma Party. This intricate picture created by overlapping(s) between *patronage politics* (the mayor's or prefect's party) *and political patronage* (SDP-Roma Party alliance) is able to generate conflicts between Roma experts, who act as both *patronage politics and political patronage brokers* at different administrative levels where mayors or prefects may have different political membership and voting options. That provides the main explanation for the different voting patterns proposed by local and regional Roma experts. Doru, Roma expert in Alexandri, explained why he votes for the SDP rather than offering his support to the Roma Party.

C: Who do you actually support?
D: I go with the SDP.
C: Why not the Roma Party?
D: I also go with the Roma Party, but did the Roma Party come here to help me? I'm asking you. Did the Roma Party help me? Or was it the SDP?
C: So why did they [SDP patronage team] help Roma?
D: Because I was here and I told him: 'Mr. Septimiu, they are poor'. Septimiu has known the Gypsies since he was a teacher. They were his pupils at school. Go into Tiganie [the Roma district] and you'll see that no one speaks badly about Septimiu. Only a mad person would say something bad about him. All of them support him. Do they have water, electricity, gas? [a rhetorical question].

(Doru, Roma expert, Alexandri)

As Doru suggests, the Roma Party cannot offer the same benefits and social and economic support that the local SDP patronage offers them. On the other hand, Doru's actions for the Romanianised Roma community are strongly supported by the local patron Septimiu, who generally channels funding into local community development projects. From this perspective, Doru is a *local patronage broker* who needs to convince Roma to vote for the SDP, but less able to support the Roma Party. In the interview, he mentions that Corina, regional Roma expert, is the person who actively supports the Roma Party but, as shown, her actions are caught in the same entanglement of contradictory political fields. These days the only way for Doru to support Romanianised Roma's community interests is to ask local patronage actors for help. In this way his leadership actions are subordinated to SDP local patronage, being less able to express critical views on the local governance for the Roma.

C: How important is politics in the life of the Roma?
D: They [Romanianised Roma] are not interested in politics. They vote because I tell them who to vote for. I go there and tell them: 'Look, Septimiu is running for election in 2012. You know this man and you know what he does for you. If you could not get a paper because you did not pay the council tax, he went and put a word in for you. You didn't have food, one day. You didn't have money. You went and asked for money, and he gave you money and that didn't happen only during elections'. If someone else is elected, it means nothing to me. Nothing can happen to me. I could be fired. So what? If someone else comes into the council I can choose not to cooperate with him as I do with Septimiu and we minorities always have support in the government, as they need the Roma as institutional representatives. They can nominate someone else. If he does not appoint me as a Roma expert, the Roma Party will.

(Doru, Roma expert, Alexandri)

Doru suggests that, in terms of politics, Romanianised Roma do not have ideological options and they mainly follow his advice in terms of voting. Additionally, from the discussions I had with Romanianised Roma, it is clear that the voting goes through the local patronage politics and is not only influenced by Doru, but also by local patron Septimiu who, through a long-term relationship and direct exchanges (e.g. cash, services for votes), convinces the Roma to vote for his party, SDP. In this context, Doru's last statement shows the way he plays the game of independence from within constraining power relations: local SDP patronage, Roma Party and central state. By looking at the contradictions in his multiple subordination relations within and across overlapping spaces of power – patronage politics and state governance – he envisages a possible escape route. Either the Roma Party or central government can nominate him as a Roma expert, but collaboration with local patronage actors is the most important factor for his role and leadership activities. Through this collaboration he is able to support the Romanianised Roma in matters of social benefits, or applications for identity papers. Nevertheless, as one of the Septimiu's followers and supporter of his political options, he cannot afford to be critical of local patronage politics, progressively developed and maintained through local distribution of public resources and welfare.

128 *A historical political ethnography*

In the early 1990s, when the state had very few social welfare programs for those classified as 'disadvantaged groups', including the Roma, local patronage politics and clientelistic relations were nearly non-existent and there were almost no informal exchanges between the mayor/local administrator and the Roma. As there were fewer things to be exchanged (e.g. votes for social benefits/services), the Roma and local governance actors were less interested in each other. Things changed from 1995 onwards when the state initiated the provision of social benefits for families with low incomes (Zamfir 1999). The program was designed to be implemented and organised by the local councils, who were responsible for distributing government funding (Lazar 2000). Since then, relations between the Roma and local council employees intensified, and welfare distribution started to work through clientelistic relations and later through the established local patronage politics. As Lipsky (1984) suggests, the extensions or rather cuts in the welfare provision for minority or poor groups changes their relation with the state, increases or diminishes their political participation as citizens in the local decision-making. In this context, the effect and reaction to the institutionalisation of state welfare provision were different for the two Roma groups. The Kalderash with high levels of autonomy became very eager to claim their citizenship rights, from an external independent position. On the other hand, the Romanianised Roma's previous subjection to state power resumed as an everyday patriarchal relation with the state. Furthermore, from 2000 onwards, the relation of Roma with the state started to be mediated through local SDP patronage politics, and the ways it was managed revealed the Kalderash's high levels of externality in relation to local patronage and the Romanianised Roma's high levels of subjection to patronage politics. In this sense, Rodan, a LDP councillor, explained his discontent with local SDP patronage, which makes use of local welfare distribution to create a monopoly on Roma political voting options.

C: Are the Roma politically important?
R: They are not only important, but extremely important for a certain political group.
C: Why are they not so important for the opposition?
R: Because they are manipulated through the social benefits they receive from the government. Everything is done through the local council where the same team has been in power for 12 years now. There are people who have been working there since 1990 and have control over the Gypsies.
C: Do you have any Roma who support your party?
R: We try, but everything is monopolized. It does not work with those from the valley – [the Romanianised Roma]. I talked to them personally and they promised they would vote for my party; then, on the next day, the whole SDP commando [ironically – representatives and supporters] were there, putting pressure on the Roma. They use pressure and blackmail.

(Rodan, LDP local councillor)

Rodan's statements suggest that the local distribution of state welfare, which is made through the local council, has become a key instrument of political monopoly for those who lead the local governance (e.g. mayor, deputy mayor and administrator) and their followers. The local patron/administrator of the village, Septimiu, is surrounded by council employees, who need to please his *Roma clients* and the *state-patronage politics brokers* (e.g. Roma experts and informal Roma leaders). In some cases, as Rodan suggested and Romanianised Roma confirmed, Roma voters are threatened by the main local patronage actors with losing their local social benefits. Moreover, the Roma state-patronage brokers or Roma experts and their followers, who also engage in political campaigns, maintain the local patronage politics and do not leave space for representatives of other political parties or the Roma Party itself to get support from the Roma electorate.

Conclusions

The main pattern of change that affected the post-1989 Romani politics is the change from *restitution politics to patronage politics and political patronage*. The early 1990s development of *the political field of restitution politics* and later on *the political field of patronage politics*, emerged at the local party politics level, prevented both Kalderash and Romanianised Roma from voting for Roma parties and precluded the local development of Romani politics. Furthermore, from 1999 onwards the political alliance between the SDP and the Roma Party established a central *political patronage within Romani politics*, which extended to local levels and partially captured Roma Party representativeness and leadership. Roma Party representatives who were local Roma leaders were expected to support the SDP in elections and extend their support to the Roma Party only in negotiation with the SDP representatives. *To sum up, whereas in the early 1990s, the field of Romani politics was overshadowed by the political field of restitution politics, in the late 1990s it was almost totally absorbed and captured by two other political fields: patronage politics and political patronage.* At the local level, these two political fields, which overlapped or contradicted each other, complicated the positions and actions of the formal and informal Roma leaders, who needed to accommodate both. It generally obstructed the active participation of Roma experts in the local decision-making process, but also obstructed Roma communities' political support for the Roma Party, the main Romani political formation.

Tracing the practices of mediation between public institutions and the Roma communities, I described the Roma experts as *state-patronage brokers* and the informal Roma leaders as *power brokers*. Being directly connected to central level political actors, informal Roma leaders/power brokers are able to give preferential support to the local patron or political actors from the opposition, but do not necessarily represent Roma communities. Nevertheless, neither the Roma experts/ patronage brokers, nor the informal Roma leaders/power brokers can be characterised as genuine Roma representatives, who focus primarily on Roma's interests and actively participate in their communities' development. Additionally, the transformations occurring in Romani politics through power relations established at the centre – SDP political patronage of the Roma Party – and also locally through patronage politics, hampered the development of idiosyncratic forms of political organisation among Romanianised Roma, which had been encouraged by the Roma Party in the early 1990s. On the other hand, Kalderash were precluded from reformulating their form of customary leadership, which transformed in time into political brokerage. However, the power brokerage performed by *bulibasi*, aimed at convincing Kalderash to vote for different parties, did not repress Kalderash's subjectivities, shaped by a mobile approach, and the emergence of a religious form of self-mastery and political re-subjectification, discussed in the last chapter. To conclude, the transition and overlapping(s) between extraneous political fields – restitution politics, patronage and political patronage – *undermined the development of an independent field of Roma politics*, which could have become a bridge between different Roma groups and a strong source of Roma representation and participation in both central and local decision-making processes. Finally, the chapter contributed to an improved analysis of the political space, which needs to take account not only of the power relations between individuals and groups, but also of the multiple constitutive political fields, which have different moments of emergence and categories of actors, follow different temporalities and spatial/relational extensions, interact, support or overshadow and capture each other in the process of enactment and expansion of the fields themselves.

Notes

1 NLP prefect of Derex county ruled between 2005 and 2008 and LDP prefect ruled between 2009 and 2012.
2 See www.dreptonline.ro/legislatie/lege_institutia_prefectului_340_2004_2008.php. Last seen on 28/10/2015.
3 I refer here to political brokers, especially Roma leaders, who mediate between local communities, local governance and higher upper level politics and convince Roma to vote for one political party or another (Scott 1977).
4 School directors – LDP members – complained that the mayor, the local administrator Septimiu and SDP local councillors refused to provide funding for renovating a workshop classroom and school access to the gas supply. Gas infrastructure was developed through a local council project made with governmental money channelled by the local patron Septimiu – SDP member, at that time councillor of the Minister of Interior.
5 Patronage refers here to a local team supporting one political party with access to local resources and distribution of resources.
6 These interpretations are grounded in my extensive fieldwork experience, based on interviews with Roma, bureaucrats and farmers in Romania, that I have carried out since 2001.
7 Since 1996, Octavian has held important positions in the parliament and the Social Democrat Party: deputy in the Chamber (since 1996), deputy-president of SDP Derex county, member of prime minister's cabinet, 2000–2004 and Minister of the Interior in 2008.
8 More information can be found at: www.partidaromilor.ro/despre-noi/scurt-istoric. html, last seen September 2013.
9 I refer here to Corina (regional Roma expert), Doru (Romanianised Roma expert), Ioader (Romanianised Roma informal leader) and some other Kalderash informal leaders.

Bibliography

Burawoy, M. & Verdery, K. (Eds.) (1999) *Uncertain Transition: Ethnographies of Change in the Postsocialist World*. Lanham, MD: Rowman and Littlefield.
Eyal, G., Szelenyi, I. & Townsley, E. (1998) *Making Capitalists Without Capitalists: The New Ruling Elites in Eastern Europe*. Verso: New Left Books.

Graziano, L. (1976) 'A Conceptual Framework for the Study of the Clientelistic Behaviour'. *European Journal of Political Research*, 4(2): 149–174.

Hilgers, T. (2008) 'Causes and Consequences of Political Clientelism: Mexico's PRD in Comparative Perspective'. *Latin American Politics and Society*, 50(4): 23–153.

Lazar, F. (2000) 'Statul Bunastarii din Romania in cautarea identitatii' [Welfare State in Romania Searching Its Identity]. *Calitatea vietii: Revista de politici sociale* [*Quality of Life: The Journal of Social Policy*], 1–4: 7–38.

Lipsky, M. (1984) 'Bureaucratic Disentitlement in Social Welfare Programs'. *Social Service Review*, 58(1): 3–27.

National Agency For The Roma (NAR) (2014) Romanian Government's Social Inclusion Strategy for Romanian Citizens Belonging to Roma Minority, for the Period 2014–2020. www.anr.gov.ro/docs/Site2014/Strategie/Strategie_final_18–11–2014.pdf

Remmer, K. L. (2007) 'The Political Economy of Patronage: Expenditure Patterns in the Argentine Provinces, 1983–2003'. *The Journal of Politics*, 69(2): 363–377.

Scott, J. C. (1977) 'Patron-Client Politics and Political Change in Southeast Asia'. In S. W. Schmidt, J. C. Scott, C. Landé and L. Guasti (Eds.) *Friends, Followers, and Factions: A Reader in Political Clientelism*. Berkeley: University of California Press, pp. 123–146.

Swartz, M. J. (1968) 'Introduction'. In M. J. Swartz (Ed.) *Local-Level Politics: Social and Cultural Perspective*. London: University of London Press LTD, pp. 1–51.

Verdery, K. (1996) *What Was Socialism and What Comes Next*. Princeton, NJ: Princeton University Press.

Zamfir, C. (1999) *Politici sociale in Romania (1990–1998) [Social Policies in Romania 1990–1998]*. Bucharest: Expert.

9 Street level bureaucracy, documenting identity and subjection of Roma to neopatrimonial state power

The state has always been an important actor for the Roma, defined and approached differently in various periods. Whereas the socialist state was a centralised and repressive structure with harsh mechanisms of control and surveillance, the post-socialist political and economic transformations generated gaps of legal authority. As previously discussed, in the introduction of this book, immediately after 1990, the withdrawal of the state generated a high level of insecurity and inequality due to monopolies of power[1], but also informal opportunities to be exploited further. Additionally, as analysed in the previous chapters on Roma leadership and political fields, representatives of the local patronage have control over the distribution of welfare and documenting identity process, and Roma relations with the local state bureaucracy are often mediated through patronage politics. Hence, state bureaucracy constitutes itself as a space of power struggles for identification, governance and constitution of subjectivity from within which Roma can actively contest or accommodate forms of membership and belonging to state structures. The current chapter explores variations and differences in the relations and interactions Roma groups establish with the local state, which reveal differential access to opportunities/constraint, self-governance and distinct subjectivities. It enquires into the state's main mechanism of subjection – documenting identity – through which the Roma are constituted as subjects and identifies changes brought by post-socialism in the relations Roma have with the street level bureaucracy. In the following, a brief overview of the main respondents is offered.

Main respondents and questions

During my fieldwork, I made regular visits to the local council administrative and social work offices, where I actively observed the interactions between the Roma and state workers. I have many times participated as an active observer in the interactions Roma had with the local council workers. The Romanianised Roma and Kalderash come often to the local council to claim documents required for social benefit applications. The volume of claims is overwhelming for the local state workers. Even the physical space of the local council seems insufficient to accommodate their attendance. During my visits, I observed many Roma standing in the hallways of the council's building, especially Kalderash families with their children, waiting to get in and ask for information and documents. The atmosphere was always tense and full of anxiety and there were frequent quarrels between Roma and local state employees. I had many informal conversations with social workers in their offices, during opening hours when most of the Roma would come and ask for documents or apply for social benefits. I used to visit two offices: the council's agricultural registry office and the social assistance office where I witnessed informal conversations between local social workers and members of the Roma communities.

I was mainly in the council agricultural registry office of inspector engineer Marius, who, together with his office mate, was responsible for the identification, measurement and registration of all buildings and land properties in the area. He was the local official involved in direct interactions with local Roma, especially with Kalderash. Although he was a supporter of the SDP's political ideology and their local representatives (e.g. Septimiu, mayor Tiberiu and SDP councillors), he disagreed with the local practice of patronage and with Septimiu's strategy of supporting Roma in exchange of votes. As mentioned in the previous chapter, Septimiu is the most important local state and political leader, the local patron of Alexandri, interested in accessing political power through clientelistic relations and direct exchanges with the two Roma communities. Bureaucrats are often unhappy about these clientelistic practices, as they interfere with their capacity to fulfil their responsibilities, overriding the legal procedures they need to follow in their everyday bureaucratic practice.

In the social assistance office, three social workers were responsible for state social benefit applications made by both Romanians and Roma. I should mention here Doru, Roma expert, who was responsible for mediating between Roma communities and local bureaucrats, helping social assistance workers prepare the necessary documentation for Roma social benefit applications. He would also join local officials on their visits to Roma districts. Doru explained that as a Romanianised Roma, he pays attention to Romanianised Roma district and visits the Kalderash's area only when there is an urgent need or local officials need to contact a Kalderash family to resolve legal problems.

All the local council employees emphasised the problematic nature of the local patronage and his supporters, SDP councillors, whose principal aim is to satisfy Roma demands in return for their votes. Generally, the two Roma communities' issues provide a key underpinning for the structure of local patronage politics, which exerts pressure on local council employees to deal with Roma problems. Yet, most of the local officials I talked to considered the Kalderash, who generally lack official papers, to be the most problematic group, as they manage to avoid state control and identification. On the other hand, Romanianised Roma registered with the state institutions are appreciated by the bureaucrats for being easily identifiable.

Other informal conversations I had about the local process of documenting identity were informed by Roma themselves and a local police officer Racov dealing with similar issues. In the next lines, I discuss the importance of documenting identity for maintaining modes of political subjectivity or challenging subjection to state power, which inform the ethnography of this chapter, which seeks to answer the following questions: *Are the Roma communities subjected to state power and local patronage politics? What are the consequences of the clientelistic mediations between Roma and the local state representatives on Roma's political subjectivities?* In the next section, documenting identity is theoretically discussed as a mechanism of state control and subjection, which is further examined in the interactions Roma have with the street-level bureaucracy.

Documenting identity and state subjection: theoretical references

The state categories are not only those of surveillance and control, criminality and illegality, but also those of welfare, which mark out the limits of legibility for applicants. As Caplan and Torpey (2001) argue, the transition from a police state (e.g. Romanian socialism) to a welfare state has entailed the development of new categories of identification and criteria of eligibility for citizens. The 'legibility effect' (Scott 1998) is generated through documentary practices, which indicate "the double sign of the state's distance and its penetration into the life of the everyday" (Das & Poole 2004: 15). In order to be governed, to fall within the scope of the state's welfare net, individuals need to be identified and quantified through documentation procedures (Caplan & Torpey 2001).

In general terms, documenting identity is one of the identification mechanisms that intervenes in any citizen's life. It has both 'repressive' and 'emancipatory' effects, it grants and restricts individual rights and access to benefits (Caplan & Torpey 2001). Individuals seem to be challenged to place themselves either inside or outside the state's sphere of action. Those who accept documenting and identification procedures get permission to use state services and benefits, but become, at the same time, subject to its control and surveillance. Moreover, through the documenting process, individuals can be partly 'expropriated' (Caplan & Torpey 2001: 8) of their own identity and subjected to the state's classificatory categories. They become identifiable governable subjects. Notwithstanding, the performative element of identity challenges the fixed identification categories (Fraenkel 1992; Jeganathan 2004; Poole 2004) proposed by the state and its classificatory procedures. Nelson (2004) argues that the state can have a double face and produce in individuals' reactions of both fear and desire. In relation to this, *membership and belonging* are not individual or institutional choices, but subscribe to the logic of encounters with state actors, who, sometimes, coincide with local patronage ones. Individuals can fear belonging, but desire membership in so far as state laws offer both constraints and opportunities.

In these interactions and encounters, Roma can be subject to state power and local patronage politics. The most significant encounters Kalderash have experienced with the state were those of identification programs carried out by both socialist and post-socialist states with or without their collaboration. The ethnography of this chapter on the Roma encounters with the state goes beyond apparent binary and sharp oppositions between being inside or outside the state mechanisms of control and identification, between the 'repressive' and 'emancipatory' powers of documents. It shows the ways in which relations with the state rules, procedures are performed and negotiated between Roma, bureaucrats and local patronage actors. In this sense, Lipsky's (1971, 1980, 1984) discussion on 'street level bureaucrats' as "ambassadors of government with particularly significant impacts upon the lives of the poor and of relatively powerless minorities" (Lipsky 1971: 392) is relevant. Lipsky (1971) considers that an efficient interaction between bureaucrats and citizens is deterred by a series of factors: "inadequate resources" (e.g. technology, information), "physical and psychological threats", "contradictory or ambiguous role expectations" and "conflicting role expectations" (pp. 393–395). Thereafter, it is useful to explore and understand the barriers of interaction between state bureaucrats and the Roma and what exactly causes inefficiency, dissatisfaction and stress for both parts involved (state bureaucrats vs. Roma). It is also worth mentioning that in the Romanian case, street-level bureaucrats are not simply government ambassadors as Lipsky (1971) defines them in the context of American society, but they are expected to be local patronage followers, too. This overlapping of roles adds another source of conflicting interests, discontent and impediments in the relations between state bureaucrats and citizens. In the next sections, Roma interactions with the local state bureaucrats (e.g. police officers, local council workers) in matters of identification, benefit applications, family and community problems are explored in the light of their performativity and ability to reveal existing modes of subjectification produced by the state and Roma themselves. All these are performed at the state-politics boundary, the local patronage politics, discussed in the next section.

Patronage politics as the state-politics boundary

The local patronage politics which mediates Roma access to state welfare reveals the intersectionality between state and politics as a boundary exploited by both the Roma and patronage actors, which provokes Roma representativeness, caught in between Roma communities, state bureaucracy and patronage politics. As described in the previous chapter, the governmental project for the social integration of the Roma involves monthly meetings at both the regional and local level with Roma experts (e.g. local and regional), informal Roma leaders, Roma experts and mediators, state representatives and public authorities (e.g. police officers, lawyers). During a regional meeting in Derex county, Corina, the regional Roma expert and prefect's councillor on Roma issues, addressed the Roma mediators in the following way:

> Good relationships with the local authorities entail good results. However, there is still a problem with some mayors who do not understand that. "A Roma representative complained that some local authorities would not vote in favour of important council decisions for the benefit of local Roma communities. In this context, Corina made a public statement to all the Roma representatives, participants in the meeting": If I hear that someone from the

Roma community has voted for the mayor's party, I will kill you [irony]. There is nothing more to say on this matter.

(Regional Office Meeting for the Roma, 8 July 2010)

It was an allusion to a specific mayor, present at the meeting, who had refused to release the necessary funding for projects aimed at supporting local Roma communities. Corina also criticised other local mayors, who only seek to please the state employees, part of the mayor's local patronage politics. To her statement, a mayor from a nearby locality replied:

> Thanks so much to Mrs Corina, I have the highest regard for her. However, we have our party bosses who control us, we have party responsibilities, and you all have to try to understand this, because we can't always manage this kind of situations.
> (Regional Office Meeting for the Roma, 8 July 2010)

The vignette suggests the way in which mayors act as local patrons and give the directions of local patronage politics, mediate relationships between Roma communities and local councils. The latter seem to be the most important boundary Roma need to exploit in order to have access to state welfare. Similarly, Roma leaders are the political brokers who mediate between Roma communities and local patronage team and convince the Roma to vote for the local patronage party in exchange for public services.

The politics vs. state accommodations and exploitations constitute the backdoor nature of Roma encounters with the local state and are part of the neopatrimonial context emerged in the transition from a centralised source of power to a decentralised state working through the political field of patronage politics. The boundary state-politics is the locale for the Roma negotiation of membership (access to welfare) or belonging to state structures (subjection to control). In the following sections, Roma interactions with the bureaucratic space are revealed as performative and constitutive to their subjectivities in relation to the signature of the state or, in different terms, state procedures of documenting identity.

Romanianised Roma in interactions with the local patronage actors

During my fieldwork sessions at the local council and in the Romanianised Roma district, I was particularly attentive to the everyday interactions Romanianised Roma have with the local authorities and their accounts of these interactions. In the next two paragraphs I present two vignettes from my field notes, which reflect the way Romanianised Roma interact with the local authorities and the main local SDP patronage actors (e.g. mayor, administrator, deputy-mayor). Marina is a Romanianised Roma who lives on state social benefits. On one occasion, she was asked by the local doctors to pay for the health certificates needed to register her child at school. Marina refused to pay and she went to the local council accompanied by two other women to ask for help. The mayor Tiberiu, SDP representative, offered himself to help her. He called the local surgery, but he was unable to convince the doctors to exempt her from paying for the health certificates for their children. However, the mayor decided to give them the amount of money needed to cover the price of the health certificates.

Adina, another Romanianised Roma woman, had a different experience in her interaction with the local council. She told me a story about how she approached the local council to ask for access to EU benefits (e.g. mainly food products: packs of flour and sugar). Initially, the local mayor repeatedly refused her application and threatened to call the police. Adina did not give up and she continued to pay weekly visits to the local council. One day when a commission from Bucharest was present at the local council, she decided to challenge the mayor's decision by entering the council meeting room unannounced, expressing her discontent with regard to the distribution of EU benefits. At that moment, the mayor, who was alarmed and worried by her unanticipated approach, declared publicly that he would provide the food products to eligible beneficiaries as soon as possible. However, the mayor did not keep his promise and Adina continued to pay visits to the local council for several weeks with no success.

The above accounts offer two different stories about the same mayor, who is sometimes helpful to the Roma, and at other times discriminates against the Roma. An explanation for this behaviour is given by multiple positions that local patronage actors (e.g. mayor, local administrator) occupy across spaces of power (e.g. state and politics) and interest. Both mayor Tiberiu and local administrator Septimiu are state representatives, but, at the same time, they are main SDP patronage actors who are interested in getting Roma's votes. In this context, the mayor does not have a consistent approach in relation to Roma. It is also well known that he is supportive of the Romanian community and less so with his Roma clients. However, in many cases the mayor provides clientelistic support to the Roma as part of the system of local patronage politics. On the other hand, as showed above, actions of local institutions are sometimes discriminatory and work as a deterrent in their everyday life. The Romanianised Roma report they are confused in their relations with the local administration as they are not sure whether they can rely on institutional support or not. Generally, they have expectations of support from the local patronage team interested in solving their problems in exchange for their votes and political support. Their queries are sometimes institutionally rejected, but are most of the times solved through the backdoor of local patronage politics. In this way, Septimiu, the local patron and administrator, is always able to obtain Romanianised Roma's votes and support during electoral campaigns.

Yet, the Romanianised Roma are aware of these differences between local patronage actors and institutional practices and they know that in their everyday issues they need to negotiate with the local SDP party members, rather than with the common state bureaucrats. Nevertheless, compared to the Kalderash's approach, they do that as identifiable governable subjects of the state, from within its identification procedures. The result is the reproduction of the local patronage politics and Roma's subjection to neopatrimonial state power, based on contradictory

138 *A historical political ethnography*

feelings of obligation, appreciation, but also discontent and revealed through the process of documenting identity, which is discussed in the next sections.

The state signature and procedures of identification: Kalderash's interactions with the local state bureaucrats

Generally, documentation of identity is produced through individual-state encounters, negotiable interactions between the Roma and local state workers performed at the intersectionality between state and politics/patronage politics. The state procedures of documenting identity are often domesticated and conducted through unofficial means by local patronage actors. In the following, I provide an analysis of the interactions and debates the Kalderash have with the local state authorities (e.g. local council, police) in matters of welfare distribution, documenting identity and access to state services.

Kalderash are locally known as those who avoid the documentation of their properties. Most of them have neither property papers nor construction certificates for their buildings. Usually, they buy land without papers from the Romanian farmers with the aim of avoiding identification by the local authorities. This lack of property documentation creates many problems regarding tax collection and for these reasons the local council has frequently been fined by the regional and national financial headquarters. There are also many situations in which the Kalderash, who are not eligible for state social benefits[2], insistently visit the local council and ask for housing and child social support. In these instances, the council workers are not usually able to help them, as far as for any kind of support, the Kalderash need to prove that they do not run a firm. Local council workers frequently feel annoyed about the fact that the wealthy Kalderash families always attempt and sometimes succeed in getting state social benefits by avoiding the identification process. They are frequently upset and stressed about the whole situation, as they know that many Kalderash are much wealthier than they are, and yet still manage to obtain social benefits. As Goffman (1956) argues, bureaucrats as 'servers' who experience a lower socio-economic position in relation to their clients engage subtle forms of aggressiveness in their attitudes, which underlies the tense interaction between the parts, which many times erupts in quarrels.

On the other hand, many Kalderash do not understand why some of them are eligible whereas others are not. Few of the cases are clear-cut, which are usually the older people who have received reparations for their deportation, during WWII to Transnistria. Yet, both parts (e.g. Kalderash and bureaucrats) accuse each other of defiance. Whereas the bureaucrats consider that the Kalderash are wealthy and not entitled to claim state benefits, the Kalderash claim they are discriminated by the bureaucrats. Nevertheless, eligibility is the product of communication between state functionaries and Roma applicants. Documents are subject to negotiable meanings by both parties (Das & Poole 2004). In the following paragraphs, I present an account of a quarrel between local council workers and a young Kalderash man who wanted to apply for a certificate to confirm his address

Street level bureaucracy 139

in Alexandri, needed for his ID card renewal. Marius, the local inspector on building issues, advised him to ask the people he lived with and probably had property papers, to help him with this matter. The young man came back with his mother and they told engineer Marius that they could not find the other person they live with, but they really needed the certificate. Marius aggressively refused them.

[The Kalderash man]: What do you want? Money?
[M. smiling nervously]: Yeah, that would probably work.
[The Kalderash man]: We need ID cards to vote for your party [the SDP patronage party].
This was the moment when engineer Marius became annoyed.
[The Kalderash man]: Why are you being so mean?
[M.]: I'm simply telling you how it is. I am sincere. At the same time, he asked his female colleague: Do not give up, do not surrender to them, if you do that I will never help you again. [To the Kalderash] : God will give you justice! Then he asked them loudly to get out. Take your ID cards and get out now!

In addition, the mother of the young Kalderash man told me that several days before, some police officers together with *bulibasa* Victor came to remind them that they would have to renew their ID cards if they wanted to vote for elections. The story reveals some of the common tensions between local bureaucrats and Kalderash who usually have informal claims, which cannot legally be fulfilled. Patronage politics is the main source of confidence for Kalderash, as well as a source of stress and disruption for local bureaucrats who are required and entitled to apply the state laws to solve documentation problems. Local council bureaucrats are also aware that Kalderash's performances are supported by connections they have with main local SDP patronage actors – Septimiu and Tiberiu – and they need to decide whether to follow the law or the local SDP patronage interests. These contradictory directions produce inconsistency in their actions as state bureaucrats, who many times feel overruled by the local patronage politics, which gives access to state welfare to ineligible Roma. In this context, Roma-state interaction, 'situation' in Goffmanian terms, is never clearly defined. It is rather continuously negotiated between Roma, state bureaucrats and local patronage actors. 'The situation' is a space of negotiation between state laws, Roma claims and local patronage interests. The latter can variably support or reject the Roma's state benefit entitlement. Therefore, the source of information needed for a clear definition of 'the situation' of interaction (Goffman 1956) between bureaucrats and the Roma is highly unstable.

With this lack of coordination of the role expectation and performance, interactions between Roma and state bureaucrats remain in a state of "anomie that is generated when the minute social system of face-to-face interaction breaks down" (Goffman 1956: 6). In Goffman's terms, the interactions lack a 'working consensus', which takes place between "participants [who] contribute to a single overall definition of the situation which involves not so much a real agreement as to what exists, but rather a real agreement as to whose issues will be temporarily honoured" (p. 4). Real agreement is also made in order to avoid "an open conflict of definition of situation" (p. 4). In the absence of this kind of tacit agreements over the definition of interaction, the encounters between Roma and local council bureaucrats take, most of the time, the form of intense quarrels. Nonetheless, in the case of local council workers interactions with the Kalderash, there is a generalised lack of agreement, which also includes non-agreement in issues of documenting identity.

Often these claims and queries focus on exchanges between Roma interested in state benefits and the local council interested in tax collection. The mayor and the deputy-mayor decided that before being able to get certificates, ID papers and benefit applications, the Roma must pay their fines and local taxes. However, the exchanges are contextualised and mediated by political interests. The mayor and the administrator, who are local SDP representatives, have a considerable interest in attracting more Roma supporters to their party. They are the ones to establish the rules and they change them to suit their own preferences. Those Roma who promise to vote for SDP are exempted from paying council tax. In this context the exchange, local council documents vs. benefits, is a productive mechanism of control over Roma's voting behaviour.

During the 2009 presidential elections, Kalderash would come in large numbers to renew their ID cards. In order to renew their ID cards, locals need to get a certificate from the local council proving that they live at a certain address within the administrative area of Alexandri. Official proof of an address is given on the basis of the property papers for buildings or land used. However, as already stated, Kalderash do not have any property documents and frequently use the affinities between local patronage politics and the state's administration in order to get new identity papers. As happened frequently during my fieldwork, a Kalderash man, who had no contract for his land and buildings came to the local council to ask to renew his ID card.

M: He has not paid the council tax. Aren't you Romanian? Why don't you pay the council tax? Why do I pay it? They come before elections without ID cards and they say they want to vote and we cannot refuse them.

His office fellow added: We cannot refuse their right to vote. We need to let them vote.

M: Maybe they want to take advantage of the local council's desire to get their votes for the local ruling party in the presidential elections. They are going to see what will happen after these elections!

(Marius, local council official)

Marius's actions seem to be caught somewhere between enforcing the state's rules and protecting local patronage's interests. The latter have, in Goffmanian terms, a disruptive character for the self-conceptions of personality of state bureaucrats, who are overruled by patronage actors' promises and actions. For these reasons, many times, local council workers feel discredited and lack authority as bureaucrats who are entitled to apply the state law. Marius himself frequently mentioned that Septimiu, the local patron, and his followers undermine bureaucratic authority. In his narrative, the difference between local council and local patronage politics is also blurred. His statements are interesting as they show how spaces of power (e.g. state and politics) communicate and overlap to the point where they can get mixed up in the local council workers' experience. When I asked him why they didn't have a system for identifying Kalderash, who do not pay taxes, he replied by saying that he was still waiting for the elections to be over, as before and during the elections Kalderash constantly come to the local council to claim papers, promising to vote for the local ruling party. He then added that in this way the administrator of Alexandri, SDP representative, Septimiu compromises himself. He suggested in this way that Septimiu is the person who asks the local bureaucrats to close their eyes and tolerate the Kalderash's non-payment of council taxes. Thus, Kalderash's clientelistic expectations are raised before and during elections. They define from the beginning their encounters with state workers as connected to local patronage interests. As Goffman (1956) argues, that is a way "the individual starts to define the situation and starts to build up lines of responsive action" (p. 5). Although, as already mentioned, they do follow the game of the local patronage, local council workers do not necessarily agree with this definition which undermines their bureaucratic authority.

As an illustration of this tensioned inconsistency, a Kalderash man explained to me how he succeeded in getting a new birth certificate from the local council. The local council officers asked for the house construction license and the Kalderash man could not provide the document, so he decided instead to threaten them by saying: "I have many friends and during the elections you will need me!" This proved to be a very good strategy as he received the certificate he needed. Another example comes from a Kalderash woman who wanted to renew her ID card:

> Victor [*bulibasa*] told us that we needed to go to the local council and renew our ID cards because we had to vote! And we are afraid of him. We do as all the others do and we vote the same sign [SDP political party logo].

Generally, common Kalderash exploit the interrelatedness between state and party politics, expressed in local patronage politics and are able in this way to threaten the local bureaucrats, when their demands are not met. It also reveals how sometimes Kalderash subordinate their interactions with local council workers to the controllers of these exchanges: political brokers. The latter are, most of the time, their customary leaders who perform the brokerage between different political parties and the Kalderash community, opening the community's doors to the main local authorities and institutions. Therefore, voting is the main mechanism through which Kalderash exploit the boundary of state–politics. The next section explores the way Kalderash, supported by clientelistic relations, create *identity fictions* to get access to state welfare.

Identity fictions and identity recognition: Kalderash's interactions with the local bureaucrats

Many Kalderash who buy houses from farmers demolish the old buildings and construct new larger ones without the necessary authorisation. On the other hand, the local council is pressurised by the regional and central institutions to report the payment of state revenue for the areas built on. This is a reason why the Kalderash frequently find themselves in conflict with the local council. Due to these tensions, the local council resorts to the police force to get the precise size and other measurements of the Kalderash's constructions. Usually, when these inspections occur, the Kalderash shut their doors and refuse to speak to, or even harass the local council representatives, and that is why police are often considered to be more effective in this form of control over Roma's 'identity'. This form of identification, which is enforced by the police, does not require recognition from those identified, rather it is imposed and established along the lines of general identificatory categories, used by the police and state mechanisms of surveillance: residency and official names. Police officers use both formal and informal mechanisms in identifying Kalderash. The former chief officer Racov was able to give me more details about this.

C: Have you ever had problems in identifying the Kalderash?
R: No. I knew them all, their name, nicknames, their parents, relatives. I know their whole family.
C: How did you get to know them?
R: From my direct contact with their district. I used to go there often and try to get a feel for the area.
R: There are 20 people with the name Mateiescu Ion and 30 others called Mateiescu Maria. I had the names and their pictures and so they couldn't hide from me. It was a way to prove that I knew them and that they didn't need to run from me because they couldn't escape.
C: Where did you have their pictures from?
R: Besides the fiscal files, we had lots of other things for which the Roma were investigated, usually minor things (. . .)
C: Who was a good informer for you? A *bulibasa* or an ordinary Roma [Kalderash]?
R: The ordinary Roma. I have never given them [*bulibasi*] any more attention than they deserved.
C: Were they interested in supporting the police or the community?
R: They played a double game. They were supportive when they could see an advantage for themselves.

(Racov, former chief officer, Alexandri)

The officer's confidence in being able to identify those Kalderash who have the same names relies on his close experience with the Kalderash community. The relationship does not always need mediation from a Kalderash customary leader, as this would reduce a police officer's control over the Kalderash's actions. Racov suggests that Kalderash leaders cannot always be trusted as they have multiple interests (e.g. personal, communitarian or political) in different circumstances, supporting either the community or the institutions of the state. On the other hand, the connection between police officers and customary leader is still maintained as it provides fast access to the community in urgent situations. Generally, the local police mechanisms of identification are upheld by a well-developed local relational dynamic between police officers and community members. As Migdal (2004) argues, "people can accommodate multiple boundaries and multiple senses of belonging, even ones with radically different principles underlying their practices" (p. 22). Notwithstanding, this form of identification made by the local police officers has an external character compared with the negotiated and performative character of interactions between Roma and local council bureaucrats. Kalderash's profiles are often obtained through databases, which offer details about criminal convictions. Identification is made in a one-way direction, by a police officer who may work undercover and who gathers information through daily interactions with members of the Kalderash community. Hence, the general features of this form of identification made by the local police are externality, unidirectionality and non-performativity.

The other main mechanisms of identification are those used by the local council. The cadastral campaigns of the local council are part of the local procedures of collecting taxes on land that has been built on, and constitute one of the main mechanisms for the identification of Kalderash's properties. This could clarify the matter of their addresses, which are often not officially known. Yet, Kalderash avoid the official cadastral service and get permission to build their houses through informal negotiations. In addition, the address is a well-known state mechanism for identifying individuals and controlling their social activities: "[I]t does involve the ability to locate and take various forms of action, such as blocking, granting access, delivering or picking up, charging, penalizing, rewarding, or apprehending. It answers a 'where' question rather than 'who' question" (Marx 2001: 312).

For the case of the Kalderash communities, the state considered the 'where' questions to be more important than the 'who' questions. As the Kalderash used to be nomads without a fixed address, the socialist state was always interested in a clear answer to the 'where' question and, therefore, in their identification through settlement. These days the Kalderash have settlements, but they are still mobile, without official proof of their place of residence. They do have ID cards, but they do not have property papers for the buildings and land they own, which are needed for ID renewals. Yet, by asking main local patronage actors – Septimiu and Tiberiu – for help they manage to renew their identification papers without the proof of an official address. This lack of documents creates a lot of problems and annoyance for the local council employees, who need to close their eyes to the informal local patronage arrangements. Additionally, the name and the location[3] are the only identification references mentioned in the ID cards. This weak identification procedure together with local patronage politics assist the Kalderash's avoidance of the mechanisms the state uses for identification. Notwithstanding, all these ambiguities related to their IDs and documents needed for social benefit applications become flexible points of reference in the interactions with local council employees. During my observation trips, at the social work office, a Kalderash woman wanted to apply for child benefit, but she did not have any proof of her husband's income, which is an important criterion for eligibility.

> The Kalderash woman responded to the local council requirements by saying: I do not have kids with him [her partner], I don't have anything, and I am not married. On the other hand, she confirmed that her partner has a business. Doru, the Roma expert at the council, asked her ironically: "But who did you make the kids with?

The Kalderash woman disappeared for a few minutes, then she came back with her partner asking him to declare that he was the father of her child. Her partner replied to the local council employees:

> I have a business, but I do not have any marriage papers; what other papers do I need to bring? [a bit irritated] This is how things work at this local council. I think this law is made only for Gypsies. The social worker replied ironically, for the benefit of myself and her colleagues. So they think that they are the only ones who need to bring papers, that no one else has to do that. Look, showing some papers, she is Romanian and she has all the necessary documents in order to apply for social benefits. Then, the Kalderash man, contradicting his previous statement, replied by saying he had no firm. Another social worker added: So why don't you go to the financial office and bring the certificate? [in order to confirm that he doesn't have a business and that he is eligible for some social benefits].

This short snapshot of the interaction between bureaucrats and the Kalderash couple can be analysed through Goffman's analytical conceptualisations of performance and dramaturgy, engaged more or less successfully by the participants. First, the dialogue between the parts misses what Goffman (1956) calls 'tact': "image of disinterested involvement in the problem of the client while the client responds with a show of respect for the competence and integrity of the specialist" (p. 4). Local council employees know the Kalderash's expectations, which are considered to undermine their authority as state bureaucrats. For these reasons, they reject the Kalderash's 'definition of the situation' by showing their open disavowal from the beginning. On the other hand, with no alterations in the course of interaction, the Kalderash couple continue to play the 'card' of informality and lack of papers, which, if successful, can source their eligibility for the child benefit. In general terms, they were trying to negotiate their eligibility and create an *identity fiction* in order to avoid state restrictions and control (Cave 1988: 489), without success in this case. The two Kalderash partners devised a combination of identity elements in order to fit the state classificatory categories required for an application for social benefits. It is interesting to observe how they performed their relationship in terms of both togetherness and separateness. They were affirming an intimate relationship to prove that they are the parents of the child and, at the same time, they showed the lack of an official connection that represented an advantage in accessing the child benefit.

At the beginning of the interaction, the woman performed separately from her partner, attempting to get access to benefits as a single mother. However, her status was informally connected to her partner's through her child. In this case her partner was required to produce a performance of his legal eligibility (e.g. the lack of firms or additional sources of income) to secure the child benefit. The man confirmed and denied, at the same time, that he runs a commercial company. Although his statement looks like a paradox and untruthful statement, it reveals a multidimensional reality. Kalderash are known to set up and run informal businesses, which are officially non-existent and most of them are not officially married. In general terms, respondents' accounts are evidence of non-formalised relations and practices: a long-term intimate relationship without a marriage certificate, a commercial practice without a legalised status. Additionally, Kalderash are aware that the informal nature of their intimate relationships and economic practices would give them access to social benefits. Knowing this, the couple aimed at performing a disjunction between informal practices or relationships and their legal status. The eligibility was performed through an *identity fiction*, which was not necessarily true or false, but corresponded to the informality of their practices, which can assist them in getting recognition of a legible status. The fictionality of their performances was mainly connected to the absence of documents, rather than to their actual practices or relationship.

The contradiction in statements about the father's child, the sudden appearance of the father and the bureaucrats' impolite reactions generated a 'scene', which arises "when team-mates can no longer countenance each other's inept performances and blurt out immediate public criticism of the very individuals with whom they have to be in dramaturgical cooperation" (Goffman 1956: 133). The scene took the form of an ironic quarrel, which as Goffman (1956) argues has the effect "to provide the audience with a backstage view and another is to leave them with the feeling that something is surely suspicious about a performance" (p. 134). By leaving the room and inviting her partner to come and face the bureaucrats, the woman made available to the local council employees a backstage view of their performance. The couple was pushed to discuss the issue of the firm ownership, an important criterion for the child benefit eligibility.

During the interaction, the local council employees acted from both positions: state workers and residents of the locality, neighbours who are familiar with their informal practices. The state workers, who are locals too, challenged their documented identity and not the one they were familiar with in the local informal everyday life practices. As Das (2004) argues, there is no sharp difference between state functionaries and the community. However, the boundary between the two categories of actors lies with the law and its classificatory categories, which grant or restrict access to welfare and are negotiated and domesticated through performances in daily encounters with the local council workers. Moreover, as Caplan and Torpey (2001) suggest, documents are signs that individuals are not always in the control of their identity. For these reasons, the Kalderash couple negotiated the control over their identities in such a way as to have access to state aid and services, but to escape restrictions of the documenting identity process and, therefore, belonging to the state structures and categories. To sum up, compared to the identification made by the police officers, which is an external, unidirectional performance of law enforcement, identifications made in interactions with street level bureaucracy are performative and reveal *Roma as active actors in the negotiation and domestication of the categories of law and state eligibility*. In their encounters with the local bureaucracy, the Kalderash perform accounts of membership to state institutions, but avoid belonging to state structures. They manage to navigate state rules and classifications and play at its margins and often exploit these new intersectionalities between state administration and local patronage politics.

Conclusions

In post-socialist Romania, the reformation of the state through the political field of patronage politics resumed citizens' interactions with the state bureaucracy at the boundary of the state with the local level politics. The latter became the locale of Roma's power struggles for identification and preservation of political subjectivity in a dialectical interaction with mechanisms of identification employed by the police, the repressive state apparatus. From within this interactionist arena Roma membership to state structures is continuously negotiated through a performative assessment of their abilities to devise and enact *identity fictions*, during the identification and legibility process carried out by the state bureaucracy, which is nonetheless ruled by the local patronage politics. These interactions are a source of subjection of the identifiable Roma's subjectivities to the neopatrimonial state power (e.g. Romanianised Roma) and an escape and preservation of the political subjectivity for the not fully identified subjects of the state (e.g. the Kalderash). The latter are able to claim accounts of membership without belonging, at the boundary of the state with politics, by performing *identity fictions* as disjointedness between informal practices and their legal status. Thus, state bureaucracy entangled with patronage politics is a space of power struggles mainly for its less identifiable subjects (e.g. Kalderash), who look for access to welfare state membership and preservation of their political subjectivities, not yet extraneously constituted. In addition, local development of the patronage politics brought both Roma groups in a direct relation with local patronage state actors and their followers with whom they were able to negotiate their queries. These and transformations of Roma leadership – for both groups – into a state mechanism of expert knowledge production and governance diminished Roma leaders' authority among community members. It produced an individualisation of the Roma encounters with the state, a reduction in the group leaders' control, and a direct engagement of Roma with state bureaucrats and patronage actors.

To conclude, the social change in Roma encounters with the state bureaucracy from socialism to post-socialism was triggered by the development of patronage politics and state mechanisms of capture of Roma leadership. For Kalderash, the new relation with the state revised their forms of self-governance, which, as showed in the last chapter, were enforced more through religious discursive practices. For Romanianised Roma, relations with the state bureaucracy mediated by local patronage and political brokers became a main source of survival, which begot a high-level subjection to state welfare provision and local patronage politics.

Notes

1 Eyal et al (1998), Verdery (1996, 2002).
2 Many Kalderash who claim housing benefits are considered ineligible by local bureaucrats, because they either lack the necessary documentation or they are involved in informal businesses with high returns which are not documented.
3 In the rural areas street name and number are not mentioned on the ID cards.

Bibliography

Caplan, J. And Torpey, J. (2001) *Documenting Individual Identity: The Development of State Practices in the Modernity*. Princeton, NJ: Princeton University Press.
Cave, T. (1988) *Recognitions: A Study in Poetics*. New York: Oxford University Press Inc.
Das, V. (2004) 'The Signature of the State. The Paradox of Illegibility'. In V. Das and D. Poole (Eds.) *Anthropology in the Margins of the State*. Santa Fe: School of American Research Press, pp. 225–253.
Das, V. & Poole, D. (2004) 'State and Its Margins: Comparative Ethnographies'. In V. Das and D. Poole (Eds.) *Anthropology in the Margins of the State*. Santa Fe: School of American Research Press, pp. 3–35.
Eyal, G., Szelenyi, I. & Townsley, E. (1998) *Making Capitalists Without Capitalists: The New Ruling Elites in Eastern Europe*. Verso: New Left Books.
Fraenkel, B. (1992) *La signature: Genese d'un signe*. Paris: Gallimard.
Goffman, E. (1956) *Presentation of Self in Everyday Life*. Social Sciences Research Centre. Monograph No. 2, University of Edinburgh.
Jeganathan, P. (2004) 'Checkpoint: Anthropology, Identity, and the State'. In V. Das and D. Poole (Eds.) *Anthropology in the Margins of the State*. Santa Fe: School of American Research Press, pp. 67–81.
Lipsky, M. (1971) 'Street-Level Bureaucracy and the Analysis of Urban Reform'. *Urban Affairs Review*, 6(4): 391–409.
Lipsky, M. (1980) *Street-Level Bureaucracy: Dilemmas of the Individual in Public Services*. New York: Russell Sage Foundation.
Lipsky, M. (1984) 'Bureaucratic Disentitlement in Social Welfare Programs'. *Social Service Review*, 58(1): 3–27.
Marx, G. T. (2001) 'Identity and Anonymity: Some Conceptual Distinction and Issues for Research'. In J. Caplan and J. Torpey (Eds.) *Documenting Individual Identity: The Development of State Practices in the Modernity*. Princeton, NJ: Princeton University Press, pp. 311–328.
Migdal, J. S. (2004) 'Mental Maps and Virtual Check Points'. In J. S. Migdal (Ed.) *Boundaries and Belonging States and Societies in the Struggle to Shape Identities and Local Practices*. Cambridge: Cambridge University Press, pp. 3–27.

Nelson, D. M. (2004) 'Anthropologist Discovers Legendary Two-Faced Indian! Margins, the State, and Duplicity in Postwar Guatemala'. In V. Das and D. Poole (Eds.) *Anthropology in the Margins of the State*. Santa Fe: School of American Research Press, pp. 117–141.

Poole, D. (2004) 'Between Threat and Guarantee: Justice and Community in the Margins of the Peruvian State'. In V. Das and D. Poole (Eds.) *Anthropology in the Margins of the State*. Santa Fe: School of American Research Press, pp. 35–67.

Scott, J. (1998) *Seeing Like a State: How Certain Schemes to Improve the Human Condition Have Failed*. New Haven: Yale University Press.

Verdery, K. (1996) *What Was Socialism and What Comes Next*. Princeton, NJ: Princeton University Press.

Verdery, K. (2002) 'Whither Postsocialism?' In C. M. Hann (Ed.) *Postsocialism, Ideals, Ideologies and Practices in Eurasia.* New York: Routledge, pp. 15–29.

10 Self-governance and the political subject

Romani Pentecostalism vs. semiological state apparatus of capture

The previous chapter mainly showed documenting identity performed in interactions with street-level bureaucracy as a mechanism of subjection to neopatrimonial state power, which nonetheless constitutes a space of power struggles for identification and preservation of political subjectivity. On the other hand, religion[1] reveals as a similar space of power struggles for authority, self-government and resistance to consecutive and historical mechanisms of capturing Roma leadership and politics engaged by the state and neopatrimonial power, discussed in the previous chapters on Roma leadership and political fields.

Many of the Kalderash who experienced socialist state violence directly, as a form of repression of their nomadic lifestyle and capture of their vernacular form of self-government – customary leadership – into state apparatus, converted to Pentecostalism, looking to restore their political subjectivity through religious reflexivity, dialogues with God and idiosyncratic practice of communion. In addition, as discussed elsewhere (Voiculescu 2012), Roma Pentecostalism[2] seems to be able not only to release alternative forms of agency and empowerment, but also act from grassroots as a form of politics, external and distinct from Romani leadership and existing Romani civil society, constituted by state and neoliberal governmental power (Trehan & Sigona 2009). Its ethics are "addressing local issues in locally comprehensible terms" (Robbins 2004: 129; De Bernardi 1999) promoting an egalitarian doctrine, which offers equal opportunities to believers with different levels of education and financial resources (Noll 2001) to experience God as inspirational authority (Corten 1997; Cucchiari 1990) and religious reflexivity.

Based on two other researches carried out in the UK about Romanian Roma migration and Roma migrants in other European countries (Voiculescu 2012), Romanian Roma Pentecostal unions[3] seem to be organised around extended families, having a volatile, reticulated character within the EU (WSREC 2015). Romanian Roma, who constantly travel, live and work in various EU countries, institute unions they can easily divide or dissolve if necessary (e.g. conflicts between families, migration to a different country), to be recreated in a different city or country, in a different format, with different or more/less Roma members (WSREC 2015). This depicts the image of a rhyzomatic-irregular, dispersed, decentralised – and highly unstable movement of cells of self-government disembodied from central routes of governance. Additionally, other Roma such as Spanish Gitano

(Delgado 2010; Gay y Blasco 2002), Gypsy Travellers from all over Europe build transnational networks through Pentecostal unions and organise annual global conventions (Voiculescu 2012). All these suggest that Global Roma Pentecostalism can act as a form of reticulated self-ministry and decentralised movement, grounded in personalised social 'networks', 'profoundly localised' (De Bernardi 1999; Robbins 2004) and comprehensively idiosyncratic. It can be viewed, in Deleuze and Guattari's (2005) terms, as *a war machine*[4], a relaying force, which constitutes its enactments outside conceptually territorialised spaces of the state and contribute to the renaissance of a new political subject. The latter is the product of a process of political subjectification, which as Ranciere (1999) argues, can be seen as "a disidentification, removal from the naturalness of place" (Ranciere 1999: 36) assigned by *the governors* to *the governed* (e.g. Roma's position as the marginalised assigned by transnational neoliberal government) and a direct engagement of the governed with the governing as an expression of a political will and affirmation.

Conversely, in Deleuze and Guattari's terms, the state acts as a force of internalisation of pre-existing social and political forms, a mechanism of demarcation between subject and law, governed and governor. It is a political entity able to capture or internalise the substance of the external political-social enactments and constitute 'the governed' by striating or regulating its space of political and cultural articulation. Furthermore, neoliberal discourse of social integration, adopted both by transnational polities (e.g. EU, WB, UNDP) and the state (e.g. social integration of Eastern European Roma) can act as a *semiological apparatus of capture*[5] (Deleuze & Guattari 2005), which is able to internalise existing forms of governance and constitute them as subaltern politics through acts of cultural translation[6], performed by state experts or royal scientists, in Deleuze and Guattari's terms.

Additionally, as Trehan and Sigona (2009) duly remarked, religious movements among the Roma, such as Pentecostalism, seem to be an almost unexplored area in terms of political mobilisation, struggles for self-affirmation, empowerment and contestation of externally imposed forms of authority. In this context, the chapter enquires into Roma religious discursive practices as a possible form of political subjectification of the 'governed' and as a counter discourse to the state semiological acts of capturing forms of self-governance through acts of cultural translation performed by expert knowledge. In connection to these theoretical articulations, some important research questions are worth paying attention to: *Can Pentecostal religious practice be seen as a new semiology of power for the Roma, alternatively construed to the semiology of state governance? Can Roma conversion to Pentecostalism be seen as a form of self-government and political re-subjectification?*

In the following, the local religious foundations are revealed in the light of divisions among the two Roma groups as subjects of different ideological discourses of power generated by the state or self-generated. The next sections will concentrate on the pastor's *power to*, believers' struggles for authority, self-government and political subjectification. In the end, the chapter develops a discussion about expert knowledge, the political subject and semiological state apparatus of capture.

Figure 10.1 Kalderash's prayer inside the Pentecostal church.

Local religious foundations and associated attitudes

Under socialism, both Roma communities in Alexandri used to be Orthodox believers. As the priest and many locals suggested, the central church was always overcrowded during the key religious feasts (e.g. Christmas and Easter), when local farmers and Roma used to come in large numbers. However, congestion was not the main reason for setting up a Pentecostal church. Cristian, the first Pentecostal preacher, told me the story of how the Pentecostal church came to be in Alexandri. He is a Romanian Pentecostal believer, who wanted to establish a single church for the Romanianised Roma and started to preach informally at his house. In the beginning, in order to make the Pentecostal gathering more attractive to the Romanianised Roma, at each religious service he used to provide food and packages to poor families. As he complained, the Romanianised Roma were regular attendees as long as food and material help were provided. When he was no longer able to obtain funding for his charitable gifts, he decided to invite, attract and convince Kalderash to convert to Pentecostalism. As he told me, Kalderash were not just interested in conversion, but were also very receptive to the Pentecostal preaching and prayer. He portrayed them as superstitious and worried about the future of their finances and informal businesses. He has been quite happy to give private religious services to Kalderash families experiencing conflicts or just worried about their informal economic activities.

After a while, the Kalderash decided to have their own building for church services and prayer. In the years that followed, they struggled to find the money to buy the land and pay for the construction of the church. In 2008, the building was erected, and the Kalderash believers, as well as some new ones who had joined the congregation, started to attend church services at the new venue. According to the Kalderash preacher Dominic, in 2008 there were only 45 Kalderash converts. By 2010, their number had reached 135, which shows an increased level of conversion among local Kalderash. Yet, at the beginning, Cristian, the founder of the local Pentecostal union, was invited to be the main preacher but, in time, a wealthy Kalderash, Dominic, who had attended some religious training sessions, replaced him and started to preach the gospel in the Romani language to the Kalderash converts. He is one of the few Kalderash with sufficient formal education to enable him to read and interpret the Bible. Nevertheless, since then no Romanianised Roma, who were mainly interested to get material support, have attended church services and the Pentecostal church in Alexandri has become the Kalderash's church. The Kalderash wanted to differentiate themselves from other Roma by building their own cultural environment and a new local congregation: preaching in Romani, having a Kalderash preacher, enjoying a dramatic style of praying on themes of general interest to Kalderash, such as overcoming troubles with their informal economic practices.

Generally, Pentecostalism brought changes in Kalderash's believers' lifestyles. All converts claimed to have renounced bad habits (e.g. alcohol consumption, fighting, partying) and that there was a strengthened sense of cohesion and egalitarian values. Notwithstanding, converts' rhetoric about a new lifestyle is not related to the social integration expected by the state and the local population, but is grounded in the Pentecostal doctrine, which encourages a symbolic detachment from the past and a rebirth into a new life purified of bad habits (e.g. drinking, crime, domestic violence, entertainment and partying) (Brodwin 2003; Wacker 2001). Kalderash's conversion to Pentecostalism did not bring important changes in many other aspects considered wrong by the state. Early marriages and informal economic practices (e.g. the non-payment of state taxes) continue to play an important role in Kalderash's everyday lives, as far as interdictions and changes to ways of living vary from one congregation to another and create the basis for empowerment and cultural revival (Pelkmans et al 2005). Therefore, as Wanner (2007) suggests for the case of Ukrainian believers, Pentecostal conversion does not necessarily bring a complete rupture with the past, but a reformulation of the self in interaction with the Other, a possible transfer from one subjection to another (e.g. from state and customary leaders to religious self). In this context, it is interesting to explore in which ways Kalderash's conversion to Pentecostalism becomes a form of empowerment and political subjectification or rather a new form of subjection to power or submission to religious doctrine. The next sections inquire into the role of the Pentecostal Roma pastor, religious conversion as a new language of power and the way this language of power differs from state projects for social inclusion and challenge the existing forms of authority (e.g. customary leaders, state).

Roma Pentecostal pastors and domains of subjection

The Pentecostal church in Alexandri followed the model of a small congregation that incorporates or negotiates local cultural norms and the believers' experiences and expectations. In general, the atmosphere during the church services is quite different from that in the Romanian non-Roma Pentecostal churches, where believers follow pastor's directions and listen in silence to his prayers, sing in the choir and pray in a moderate voice. In the Kalderash's church, believers pray loudly and speak in tongues in accordance with their cultural expectations and meanings. Furthermore, as believers suggested, the Pentecostal religious performances are different from those permitted within an Orthodox church, which are mainly directed by the priest, who performs ministerial *power over* a community of values, which are taught, not presumably reflected upon. The divine authority is not delegated, but is personified in the image of the priest who rules the believer's religious self in a continuous rhetoric of submission to a transcendent Holy Spirit and disengagement from endeavours of self-government. On the other hand, during Pentecostal sermons, Roma believers are expected to actively and creatively participate to the new architecture of their subjectivities, practise the art of self-dialogue through testimonies and prayers, deterritorialise existing domains of subjection and incorporate the self into a communion with the immanent Divine, appropriated as life partner. Notwithstanding, similar to Pentecostal Gypsy Travellers (Voiculescu 2012), pastors are not identified with customary leaders exercising *power over* believers and are not followed as advisers on self-conduct. They are rather expected to enhance the believers' participation in the religious community (e.g. sermons), to extend and strengthen social bonds and financial support among community members, without interfering in their private lives and sphere of decision-making.

Likewise, there is a practice of ethical communion which promotes equalitarianism and condemns affluence as a source of alienation from an authentic self, construed in a dialogical personalised relationship with God, an immanent authority defiant of alternative forms of subjection. Dominic, the charismatic preacher of the Pentecostal Union, often calls for the dissolution of the differences between wealthy and poor Kalderash. Additionally, believers themselves do not agree with a clear-cut division between rich and poor, which from their viewpoint would generate conflicts between members of the community. For instance, at one sermon, a young woman performed a song, a call for the wealthy Kalderash to offer money to the poorer ones. In exchange for their good actions, the rich would receive rewards from God. Similarly, but in a different day, a Kalderash woman on her way to the church contemplated the affluent Kalderash's 'palaces' and told me that their wealth means nothing in God's eyes. This kind of utterance and performance suggests that wealth is ideologically seen in opposition to the religious community of values and sharing in which all are brothers and sisters. In other terms, Roma believers, who share a socially unbound rhetoric of a dialogical self in relation to God, go beyond a collective ideological communion, and guided by the pastor help each other financially when needed (e.g. illness or death of family members). Additionally, all the concerns related to interactions with the local authorities and life problems (e.g. poverty, sickness) are portrayed in songs or testimonies and discussed collectively inside the church.

These symbolic enactments of local community governance are usually harmonised by a pastor who carries the duties of gathering believers, connecting those in need to those supportive and dealing with administrative issues that can affect religious community unity. Yet, as many Romanian Roma believers in Alexandri stated, the pastors' authority is limited to *power to* administratively build and organise a religious community, occluding control over believers' everyday lives. This kind of community governance is commonly practised in all Romanian Roma Pentecostal unions all over Europe, including those established in Glasgow and those instituted among Pentecostal Gypsy Travellers in the UK (Voiculescu 2012; WSREC 2015). Notwithstanding, these do not indicate an integration into a social and cultural space of the majority, as Podolinska and Hrustic (2014) claim for the case of Slovak Roma. On the contrary, as Delgado (2010) argues in the case of Spanish Gitano, believers are already integrated in social networks and identify with Roma local communities, but they distinguish themselves from the non-Roma (Gay y Blasco 2002). Mainly, Roma Pentecostals are looking to emphasise the idiosyncrasies of a moral self, fed by a religious reflexivity in a seamless dialectical conversation with non-Roma culturally enchanted modern forms of subjection (e.g. state).

It is interesting to notice, in this sense, how speeches about the role of belief and religion vary in relation to the preachers' identities. Irrespective of their cultural or ethnic background, pastors from other Pentecostal Unions are often invited to preach at the Kalderash's church. On one of these occasions, a Romanian non-Roma pastor, Teodosie, from a nearby locality, was invited. His speech was different from Dominic's and followed the logic of controlled governance imposed from above. In his speech he mentioned that believers should avoid doing informal commerce. He gave as an example an illiterate woman who used to cheat at the market and, after she became a Pentecostal believer, without being able to read the Bible, she received the Holy Spirit and gave up cheating. However, Teodosie's speech was not very well received. His preaching was rather didactic, with questions from the Bible to which no one knew the answers. Many of the Kalderash believers either started laughing or left the church. At the end of the service, non-Roma pastor Teodosie informed me about his views on Pentecostal religious practice, which he saw as a form of education, promoting literacy and the reduction of criminality among the Roma in general. He indirectly confirmed that his preaching aimed at producing a contiguous effect. It was an authoritarian way of approaching Pentecostal religious practice, as a form of teaching from above, usually performed ideologically by the state aiming at tracing the border between 'governors' and 'governed' (Deleuze & Guattari 2005). Nonetheless, Kalderash preachers and administrators of the Union follow the local, contextualised, character of Pentecostalism, and predicate a softer version of change, which does not exclude the so-called Roma 'customs' (e.g. early marriages, informal economic practices). Yet, the new local cult is not disconnected from local struggles for

Self-governance and the political subject 155

influence which take place in the sphere of party politics. Although they gain authority over others and locate control in their private relations with God and themselves, Kalderash Pentecostal believers are still influenced in their voting options by the preachers or church administrators who have their own political interests. When asked, many Kalderash Pentecostal believers avoided giving a clear answer whether their voting options are influenced by others or not, and they mainly claimed that they do not 'listen' to others. In an interview I had with Dumitru, a Pentecostal Roma believer, I tried to find out his voting intentions for the presidential elections and his explanation for his choice.

C: If Daniel [administrator of the church] told you who to vote for, would you follow his advice?
D: Yes, we could do that. If they told us good things, that wouldn't be a bad lesson.
C: Did Daniel tell you with whom to vote?
D: It is a secret – I cannot tell you that.

(Dumitru, Pentecostal believer)

Dumitru avoided telling me clearly whether Daniel influenced him in his voting options, but admitted that in certain matters (e.g. party politics) he would follow his advice. Additionally, many Kalderash believers confessed they did not follow church administrators' advice, but did not deny the preacher's and Roma brokers' influence upon their voting choices, which is a common performance in any election process. Hence, it cannot be assumed that Pentecostal conversion brings a total exclusion of external sources of influence, but makes a substantial change in the believer's locus of authority situated in the intimate sphere of private relation with God, which ultimately might hide the influence of others on the decision-making process. Yet, the relation between God and believer's self receives priority compared to other forms of relationality, which are nonetheless not necessarily excluded from being influential in the believers' everyday forms of social existence. This hierarchy of relational significance – religious self-divine authority and then Others – leaves space for individual authority and contestations of *power over*, among believers. In general terms, Pentecostal religious practice cannot be considered to produce an expected state subjection (e.g. disciplined behaviour and integration in institutional structures of the state), but rather a domestication of religious practise, and a reformulation of the subject in relation to an internalised authority – God, which releases and establishes a new sphere of self-ministry and hermeneutics of the self, thoroughly discussed in the next section.

From *Bulibasa* to God: self-ministry and struggles for authority

In many informal conversations about leadership, Kalderash believers claimed that they no longer 'listen' to their customary leaders – *bulibasi* – and that their roles are limited to mediation between the community and the police, when needed.

The presence of God became more important and even replaced the leading role of the customary leader in their everyday lives. In addition, many believers started to claim that their ultimate *bulibasa* is God. In a conversation I had with one of the church administrators, Daniel, the transfer of authority between *bulibasa* and God was clearly stated.

C: Do they [Kalderash] still listen to *bulibasa*?
D: Who listens to *bulibasa* today? He does not matter anymore. We listen to God. Why should I listen to *bulibasa*? Does he give us anything?
C: Who gives you support? *Bulibasa* or God?
D: Long before, *bulibasa* helped us. Now it is finished with *bulibasa* [institution].
C: What does he do now?
D: He handles police claims or intervenes when there are fights among us, and that is all.
C: Do you have other bosses?
D: No. We just listen to God.
C: Why are they *bulibasi* then ?
D: It is just that they consider themselves *bulibasi*.
C: What role do they have in relation to you?
D: They have no role. Instead of helping the poor they tell everything to the police.
(Daniel, Pentecostal Union's administrator)

As with many other Kalderash believers I talked to, Daniel explained that the *bulibasi* are self-appointed and are part of the self-interested affluent community, and lack authority among the poorer Kalderash. Mediation with the police is again mentioned as the single role customary leaders still play. On the other hand, Pentecostalism, as practice and belief, seems to blur the division between rich and poor and generate a transfer of government from *bulibasa* to God and, finally, to the Kalderash themselves. It gives to individuals a sense of empowerment, who are no longer in a relation of dependence on extraneous sources of authority. Dumitru, a believer from a moderate wealthy Kalderash family, seems to confirm this assertion. He is one of the Kalderash Pentecostal believers who claimed that Jesus is the new *bulibasa* and the only leader in his life.

C: But, who is *bulibasa* now?
D: Everyone is her/his own master. *Bulibasa* deals with police issues only. It is just a word: *bulibasa*. They are *bulibasi*, but not our masters – we have Jesus.
C: Do you fear him [*bulibasa*]?
D: We feel fear because he is our *bulibasa*, but we have no issues with him. If they [*bulibasi*] help you, they ask for money. It is better to manage yourself. If you are weak and don't know what to do, you still go to him [*bulibasa*]. He sometimes says come to me, if you do not come, I'll beat you. We have our *bulibasa*, that is, Jesus.
C: Can you still have a *bulibasa* here, or is Jesus the new *bulibasa*?

D: *Bulibasa* is a name, but we are masters of ourselves. If someone comes to me to harm me, I go directly to the police and complain. I'll go to courts and ask for his arrest.

(Dumitru, Pentecostal believer)

Similarly to many other Kalderash, when referring to the roles and importance of *bulibasa* for the Kalderash community, Dumitru's statements are contradictory: "we feel fear because he is our bulibasa" vs. "they are *bulibasi*, but not our masters". The distinction indicates that the customary leader is no longer an authority, but just a source of fear and control for the 'weak' who ask for mediation services in relation with the local authorities. Believers' strength in their relation with external forms of control comes through their private relationship with God. From this viewpoint, Dumitru's statements become relevant and suggest that religious partnership with God is a "process of 'self–mastery' [or 'self-mediation'] through which believers get control over themselves and over relations with Others" (Voiculescu 2012: 6.1): "everyone is her/his own master" and "we are masters for ourselves". As other Roma believers, Dumitru also considers that they do not need mediators or representatives (e.g. *bulibasi* or pastors). The self-governance gained through the new religious Pentecostal experience and partnership with God replaced leaders' mediation of their everyday problems. It introduced believers into a much closer relation with local authorities (e.g. police and local council), and many of them claim they can approach state institutions directly and solve their problems with no help from customary leaders. Hence, on one hand, Roma believers endorsed a domesticated Pentecostal ethic and on the other expanded their private space of decision over the interactions and relations with heteronomous sources of authority (e.g. state, leaders), which ultimately are mediated by the religious self. Additionally, Roma believers claim to be both masters of themselves and have God as master of their private lives and generally tend not to differentiate between divine authority (e.g. God or Jesus) and dialogical religious self (self-God) (Voiculescu 2012). Thereafter, the religious partnership with God is able to internalise the centre of decision-making and control over acts of translation, authorising a new hermeneutics of the self to evolve into a new form of self-ministry.

Notwithstanding, conversion implies both affirmation of self in the process of decision-making and submission to the Pentecostal religious doctrine. The double process of religious experience as empowerment through submission is explored in an interesting ethnographic study concerning the women's mosque movement in Egypt (Mahmood 2001), which emerged as a reaction to the newly secularised understandings of Islam, mainly produced by the liberal state. Mahmood (2001) argues that women, who decided to teach and transmit Islamic doctrine and practice, piety and ethics perform agency and show resistance to state secularisation and objectivation of Islam culture. She considers that significance of religious acts, like piety, should be disconnected from the liberal understandings of subordination and they should be rather explored in their subjective meanings connected to "desires, motivations, commitments, and aspirations of the people to whom these practices are important" (p. 255). Similarly, it can be said that for the Kalderash believers, Pentecostal practice is not an expected form of social integration as the non-Roma pastor suggested, but an exercise of individual authority, able to re-constitute their subjectivities, challenge external forms of authority such as state and customary leadership and their associated modes of subjection. The conversion to Pentecostalism changes Roma's locus of authority from external actors (e.g. customary leaders, state) to the religious self and generates a religious empowerment from within self and community through self-mastery and practice of ethical communion. Generally, Pentecostalism is able to contribute to the constitution of a new subject able to govern herself/himself in a dialectical opposition to 'the governed', a subject construed by the state and transnational polities through programs for social integration, which internalise Roma subjectivities into their language of power and governance.

Discussion: Roma Pentecostalism's political subject and semiological state apparatus of capture

Inspired by this case study and previous research carried out by the author (Voiculescu 2012), Roma Pentecostalism is able to engender an individualisation of the space of decision-making, which is not in any sense a space of responsibilisation associated with a 'reflexive modernisation' (Beck et al 1994) that can easily be translated into the liberal understanding of the 'free will', which stands at the core of projects of human development and social integration for the Roma. Individual decisions are not the expression of a 'free will' but, on the contrary, decisions considered wrong by the state and the proxy Other are transferred to the responsibility of God – 'what God speaks' – the uncontested authority which cannot be challenged from within the religious discourse, pervasive and incorporated into the believers' everyday social lives (Voiculescu 2012). Hereafter, by claiming the supreme authority of God, Roma believers feel more able to manage the relation with external forms of authority and manipulate discourses on right and wrong, good and bad, which are normally structured by state power through institutions, norms and laws. Furthermore, through the new form of religious reflexivity, they became more confident in negotiating relations with state bureaucracy and play at its boundaries, claiming membership and rejecting belonging, a theme discussed in the previous chapter.

In the power triangle, believers, customary leaders and the state, God is the "symbolic interface and signifier who can delegate authority to believers" (Voiculescu 2012), which makes believers more able to struggle for authority, negotiate and contest institutional and leadership power. In other terms, localised Pentecostal practice leaves space for the domestication of religious doctrine, which does not beget the submission expected by the state, but is rather translated into *self-government*, which strengthens and internalises the centre of individual decision-making and underpins the expropriation of other forms of authority (e.g. state institutions, customary leaders) from their everyday life. In this case, the *agential power* is more than *performative* (Butler 1997), it is predominantly relational, sourced by shared, domesticated relations with relevant Others, including the divine authority. The locus of authority and empowerment is *disaffected* into the private space of relations with God and the religious self, and Pentecostal religious semiology acts, in my terms, as *disaffected power*, undoing the subject from the state and other external architectures of power (e.g. neoliberal government). Furthermore, centred on a dialogical religious self (God-self), Pentecostalism deterritorialises domains of subjection for the religious self to be re-territorialised into a dialectical form of governance, construed in relation to the state, featuring the main conceptual characteristics of *self-ministry* or *nomad*[7] *self-governance*, previously defined for the case of Kalderash's pre-socialist form of leadership, which has been captured by the socialist state.

Notwithstanding, Romanianised Roma, who were more subjected to socialist state programs of assimilation and maintained a closer relation to the state institutions were not able to recognise Pentecostalism as a mode of self-reformation and government. There is also a sharp contrast between the statements coming from the two Roma groups about the role of the state in their lives: "The state should help us, we had jobs during socialism" (Romanianised Roma) vs. "The state did not do anything for us, on the contrary they beat us and took our gold, why should we do anything for the state?". In this case, *the differential relation with the state indicates a differential ideological subjection to an external authority, which is strongly challenged by Kalderash and appropriated and incorporated by the Romanianised Roma in their world views and socio-economic existence.* The latter, as ideological subjects[8] of the state, are more inclined to miscognition[9] of state domination and misrecognition of alternative forms of self-governance such as Roma Pentecostalism.

In general terms, Roma Pentecostalism as self-affirmation is a mode of constituting a political subject in relation to extraneous forms of authority such as the Roma state experts, customary leaders and state institutions. It is a way of undoing *the governed* as a subject and reconstructing the one who governs herself/himself without submitting to the language of assertion of other forms of governmental power such as state and neoliberal social integration[10], which assume superiority in relation to its idiosyncratic modes of self-expression. On the other hand, the term of social integration itself suggests a force of internalisation, opposed to *political affirmation*[11] as the modus operandi of a war machine (e.g. Global Roma Pentecostalism), which assumes, as Deleuze and Guattari (2005) suggest, in a reversed Clausewitz-ian formula, "that politics is the continuation of war by other means" (p. 421), contributing to the constitution of a political subject.

Yet, the semiotics of Roma Pentecostalism are not always reflectively problematised by many Romani studies researchers. The latter can act as state experts who aim at incorporating Roma Pentecostalism into semiological content of state governance aiming at their social integration. The Roma pastor is sometimes portrayed as the governor, holding *power over* believers and leading the formation of the local opinion "achieved by silent control over the members of the community" (Slavkova 2003: 10). In this translation, Roma pastors are "desired partners of local governments in solving the accumulated Roma problems" (Todorovic 2004: 1017), state brokers able to discipline the community as promoters of state social integration (e.g. Podolinska & Hrustic 2014). However, Pentecostal Roma pastors have no instituted *power over* the transfer of the community government to the arborescent state power apparatus, but only *power to* locally organise religious community. As my fieldwork data and previous research show (Voiculescu 2012), pastoral *power over* is *disaffected* to believers through self-reflexivity and internal dialogues with God. Contiguous to this, experts and scholars in Roma issues seem to translate the Pentecostal ethics into a form of 'normalisation' and 'education', a successful program of social 'taming', a substitute for state programs for social integration, which helps to produce submissive Roma.

> If we refer to the change of behaviour within these communities and the forms of coexistence with others, then we can say that (. . .) the Neo-protestant church has succeeded in integrating Roma into society (. . .) We cannot compare what the state does with what the church has succeeded in doing for them.
> (Horvath 2009, Adevarul-Cluj)

> The strong emphasis on bible studies, sermons and devotional literature creates a high literacy rate among the Pentecostal converts that in turn leads to a valorisation of education as a way of social achievement (Gog 2009: 106); the internalisation of moral codes and the puritan ideals allows the converted Roma to articulate distinct practices that are totally contrary to the general perception of Roma as vagabonds that steal, cheat and are dirty.
> (p. 108)

The statements and meanings assigned to the Roma Pentecostal conversion show how a genuine form of self-government can be semiologically incorporated into the language of normalisation of a centralised governmental power. They also unmask a thought territorialised by the state that thoroughly makes "the distinction between the legislator and the subject under the formal conditions permitting thought, for its part, to conceptualize their identity" (Deleuze & Guattari 2005: 376). They can generally be considered symbolic procedures of wielding the semiology of the state apparatus of capture.

Following Deleuze and Guattari (2005), it can be further argued that the translation of Roma Pentecostalism reflects two operations constitutive to the semiological apparatus of capture: "direct comparison and monopolistic appropriation" (p. 444), which presuppose each other. In the act of comparison with the state social integration, Roma Pentecostalism is, in Deleuze and Guattari's terms '*overcoded*', reconstituted in the act of translation and incorporated into state technologies of governmental power. Roma new form of self-governance is translated into a sovereign model, a colonising discourse which can ingest creative acts of redefinition of self and community. The latter are reconceptualised into the theorematic apparatus of the state which assumes social integration as a scientific solution and an internalised model of governance. In other words, Roma Pentecostalism that can globally act as a war machine and locally as nomad self-governance can be 'overcoded' by scientific language, the subtle mechanism of subjection to the symbolic power of the state and transnational neoliberal governmental, which classify Roma as *the governed*. Hence, the semiotics of social integration used by scholars and experts in their analyses of Roma Pentecostalism enclose the symbolic power of classification and identification[12], and can be seen, in Dean's (2012) terms, as the signature of governmental power with subtle and secret mechanisms of enactment, which go beyond the language itself. Notwithstanding, any research inquiry (e.g. social sciences) implies an idiomatic mechanism for the cultural translation of the social, which can act as a foundation for semiological apparatuses of capture. In Deleuze and Guattari's terms (2005), they can be 'royal sciences', expert knowledge(s), which can lead to the deterritorialisation of the internal idiosyncrasies of a community of thought and its forms of governance and a reterritorialisation of these into the conceptual apparatus of the state and other polities. To sum up, the chapter brought to light an important problematic of governance and empowerment from within self and community, which needs to be carefully articulated in the context of the current transnational program for social integration for the Roma, which can act as a force of internalisation, semiologically deterritorialising and reterritorialising vernacular models of government and political subjectification into the conceptual apparatus of the state and transnational polities. To conclude, the chapter revealed Roma Pentecostalism as a form of *self-governance* and *disaffected power* that can uphold mechanisms of de-subjectification of *the governed* and re-subjectification of the Roma as political subjects, which involves "a break with the axiom of domination, that is, any sort of correlation between a capacity for ruling and a capacity for being ruled" (Ranciere 2010: 32).

Notes

1 Following political philosophy and an extended definition of government, religion is seen as a form of government and pastoral power (Foucault 2009).
2 Roma Global Pentecostalism emerged in mid-1960 and had as a source of inspiration Methodism, which was an American religious movement founded in eighteenth century.
3 Whereas Pentecostal church is a reference to a site for prayer and sermon, Pentecostal union indicates a mode of association and organisation specific to small Romanian Roma Pentecostal communities, mainly based on agnatic solidarity.
4 According to Deleuze and Guattari (2005), a *war machine* is an affirmative force built and acting creatively against arborescent models of power (e.g. state), manifested and engaged by non-State populations, but also by philosophers, local knowledge(s), forms of art and creative mechanisms which oppose themselves to sovereign reason.
5 Deleuze and Guattari (2005) refer to *state semiological apparatus of capture*, which appropriates resources and stabilises power by the use of language as a mechanism of translation and overcoding of economic practice and labour power. However, in my research I use this terminology to designate the mechanism of capturing the existing forms of governance (e.g. Roma Pentecostalism) into the state language of governance and constituting new forms of governance (e.g. Roma civil society) by the use of cultural translation and discursive language of governmental power (e.g. social inclusion).

6 Social researchers who follow the main paradigm of governance – social integration – are usually involved in acts of translation of existing Roma social and political practices into the main language of state governance.
7 *Nomad* feature is indicated by Deleuze and Guattari (2005) as an expression of a political affirmation in dialectical opposition to the state centralised apparatuses of power.
8 During socialism, most of the Romanianised Roma were sedentary, unskilled workers in state factories and farms. Their lives were mainly organised by the state, which still appears in their language as a paternal figure.
9 In this context, I define *miscognition* as a process of mystification performed ideologically by the state or capital, blurring the boundary between reality of the state or capital domination and illusion of independent thinking subject.
10 As an example, World Bank (2005) opposes Roma culture (e.g. Kalderash's culture) to human development, modernity and progress: "aspects of Roma culture and living conditions have reinforced stereotypes and spurred marginalization. Members of more traditional groups, such as Roma, can benefit from integration if it facilitates individual growth and well being" (p. 12). Please also see the discussion on neoliberalism and subaltern subject in the book discussion.
11 The *program for social integration of the Roma*, as a force of internalisation and depoliticisation of the subject, engaged by the states and transnational polities, can be seen in opposition to *the political affirmation of the Black People*, their social and political movements in the United States, which constituted them as political subjects.
12 Roma Pentecostalism was translated into the state program for social integration of the Roma for the good of the market economy and welfare state reduction.

Bibliography

Beck, U., Giddens, A. & Lash, S. (1994) *Reflexive Modernization: Politics, Tradition and Aesthetics in the Modern Social Order*. Cambridge: Polity Press.
Brodwin, P. (2003) 'Pentecostalism in Translation: Religion and the Production of Community in the Haitian Diaspora.' American Ethnologist, Vol. 30, No1, pp. 85-101.
Butler, J. (1997) *The Psychic Life of Power: Theories of Subjection*. Redwood City, California: Stanford University Press.
'Cluj: VIDEO Minunile din Biserica Tiganilor' [Cluj VIDEO. Wonders from the Gypsy Church]. *Adevarul- News from Cluj-Napoca*, 15 November 2009, www.adevarul.ro/locale/cluj-napoca/VIDEO-Minunile-tiganilor-biserica-din_0_153584987.html
Corten, A. (1997) 'The Growth of the Literature on Afro-American, Latin American and African Pentecostalism'. *Journal of Contemporary Religion*, 12(3): 311–334.
Cucchiari, S. (1990) 'Between Shame and Sanctification: Patriarchy and Its Transformation in Sicilian Pentecostalism'. *American Ethnologist*, 17(4): 687–707.
Dean, M. (2012) 'The Signature of Power'. *The Journal of Political Power*, 5(1): 101–117.
De Bernardi, J. E. (1999) 'Spiritual Warfare and Territorial Spirits: The Globalization and Localization of a "Practical Theology"'. *Religious Studies and Theology*, 18(2): 66–96.
Deleuze, G. And Guattari, F. (2005) *A Thousand Plateaus: Capitalism and Schizophrenia*. Minneapolis: University of Minnesota Press.
Delgado, M. C. (2010) 'Gypsy Pentecostalism, Ethnopolitical Uses and Construction of Belonging in the South of Spain'. *Social Compass*, 57(2): 253–267.
Foucault, M. (2009) *Michel Foucault. Security, Territory, Population: Lectures at the College de France, 1977–78*. (Eds.) M. Senellart, F. Ewald and A. Fontana. London and New York: Palgrave Macmillan.
Gay y Blasco, P. (2002) 'Gypsy/Roma Diaspora. A Comparative Perspective'. *Social Anthropology*, 10(2): 173–188.

Gog, S. (2009) 'Post-Socialist Religious Pluralism. How Do Religious Conversions of Roma Fit into the Wider Landscape? From Global to Local Perspectives'. Transitions, Le volumes la XXXIII ont ete publies sous le nom 'Revue des Pays de L'Est' Nouvelles indentites rom en Europe centrale & orientale. (Eds.) Andrea Boscoboinik & Francois Ruegg. Geneve: Universite de Geneve, Institut Europeen, Vol. XLVIII.2.

Mahmood, S. (2001) 'Feminist Theory, Embodiment, and the Docile Agent: Some Reflections on the Egyptian Islamic Revival'. *Cultural Anthropology*, 16(2): 202–236.

Noll, M. A. (2001) *American Evangelical Christianity: An Introduction.* Oxford: Blackwell.

Pelkmans, M., Vate, V. & Falge, C. (2005) 'Christian Conversion in a Changing World: Confronting Issues of Inequality, Modernity and Morality'. *Max Plank Institute for Social Anthropology Report* 2004–2005, pp. 23–24.

Podolinska, T. & Hrustic, T. (2014) 'Religious Change and Its Effects on Social Change for Roma in Slovakia'. *Acta Ethnographica Hungarica*, 59(1): 235–256.

Ramnicelul, B. J. (2011) 'Religion in Romania. Romania's Evangelical Romanies'. *The Economist*, 17th January 2011.

Ranciere, J. (1999) *Disagreement: Politics and Philosophy*. London, Minneapolis: University of Minnesota.

Ranciere, J. (2010) *Dissensus: On Politics and Aesthetics*. London, New York: Continuum.

Robbins, J. (2004) 'The Globalization of Pentecostal and Charismatic Christianity'. *Annual Review of Anthropology*, 33(1): 117–143.

Slavkova, M. (2003) 'Roma Pastors as Leaders of Roma Protestant Communities'. In Dragoljub B. Dordevic (Ed.) *Roma Religious Culture*. Nis: PUNTA, pp. 168–177.

Todorovic, D. (Ed.) (2004) *Evangelization, Conversion, Proselytism.* Nis: Yougoslav Society for the Scientific Study of Religion Komren Sociological Encounters Punta.

Trehan, N. & Sigona, N. (Eds.) (2009) *Romani Politics in Contemporary Europe Poverty, Ethnic Mobilization and the Neoliberal Order.* London and New York: Palgrave Macmillan.

Voiculescu, C. (2012) 'To Whom God Speaks: Struggles for Authority Through Religious Reflexivity Within a Gypsy Pentecostal Church'. *Sociological Research Online*, 17(2–10).

Wacker, G. (2001) *Heaven Below: Early Pentecostals and American Culture*. Cambridge, Massachusetts and London : Harvard University Press.

Wanner, C. (2007) *Ukrainians and Global Evangelism: Communities of the Converted.* Ithaca and London: Cornell University Press.

West of Scotland Regional Equality Council/WSREC (2015) *Eastern European Roma, Police Engagement & Youth Street Culture in Govanhill*. Unpublished report: Glasgow, UK.

World Bank (2005) *Roma in an Expanding Europe. Breaking The Poverty Cycle*, D. Ringold, M., A. Orenstein, E. Wilkens (Eds.).Washington, D.C.: World Bank.

Part III
The return to the political
Epistemological decolonisation of the subject and historical geographies of power

11 Sedentary vs. mobile interaction with spaces of power

The book's historical ethnography of social power aimed at producing an alternative, critical form of knowledge distinct from that produced by the state and transnational organisations of development (e.g. WB, UNDP, EU), which seem to bring under the same discourse of governance distinct Roma populations who experience different socio-economic conditions, leadership and forms of self-government. Fixed categories (e.g. 'exclusion, 'marginalisation', 'poverty') establish symbolic power, in Bourdieu's (1991) words, relations of subordination in relation to a majority and the state, which are easily transformed into categories of governance of the subaltern, constituting the 'governed'.

The mechanism of knowledge production, used in this book, followed the opposite route of policy research, itself government of the self and Others, grounding governmental discourses, by constituting a critique of the whole problematisation of governance for the Roma – social integration – which generally preserves the *status quo*, discussed in the introduction. Overall, the analysis followed Foucault's (1980) suggestion for the study of social power, which needs to be seen "as something that circulates, or rather as something which only functions in the form of a chain" (p. 98), dislocating and destabilising power from sites or fixed classifications produced by governmental discourses. Throughout the book, the historical relations of power among the two Roma groups – Romanianised Roma, Kalderash – were explored in dialogue with transformations occurring across what I called spaces of power of economy, state, politics and religion with their own temporal dynamic. The analysis did not concentrate on changes in their positions from an economic and political regime to another, but on the relations they developed with relevant Others, which were either constraining or facilitating access to social power. State policies and macro-historical transformations were not necessarily the main sources of changes in their life trajectories. The latter approach generally leads to their victimisation under the influence of omnipotent structures (state, social class, etc.). What was considered the main source and *agent of transformations* in their lives was the *relational dynamic* produced by the interactions Roma had with transformations of spaces of power and with the relevant Others (e.g. state representatives, Roma leaders, political representatives, etc.).

Yet, the state projects of assimilation in socialism, respectively social integration after the 1990s, although inefficient or repressive mechanisms, affected the

168   *The return to the political-thesis*

two Roma groups discussed. Besides being repressive, the socialist state modernisation projects were, in Scott's terms (1998), 'state simplifications'/'state mappings' with a narrow perspective on a complex cultural and social reality of the groups targeted. They excluded the Roma's approach to social existence and generally ignored their individual and group mappings. In socialism, state maps acted as technologies of power, representations of a simplified reality which imposed "a layer of apparent coherence laid over alternative voices by the dominant power" (Massey 2005: 110). Nevertheless, as showed in the chapter on economic practices, the Kalderash developed their own 'tentative mappings' as orientations in an uncertain environment. The latter are different forms of mapping, which do not follow the logic and coherence imposed by the state maps used in the governance of the Roma. They rather follow disruptions and discontinuities, "the unexpected, the other", "crucial to what space gives us" (Massey 2005: 112). The 'practical knowledge' (e.g. trading and manufacturing abilities) was used as a flexible reference that supported the management of a self-transforming environment which, as Massey (2005) suggests, is both the product and the source of ongoing social histories. Furthermore, looking to restore their self-government captured by the state, Kalderash converted to Pentecostalism, which reconstituted them as political subjects able to govern themselves and challenge extraneous forms of power (e.g. Roma leadership, state power and its mechanisms of subjection). On the other hand, Romanianised Roma, being already sedentarised and identifiable by the state institutions, were more subjected to incorporation into state structures. Being settled or mobile made a substantial difference to the way Roma were subjected to the state and interacted with spaces of power in a continuous transformation from socialism to post-socialism. Generally, this distinction can be summarised as two models of interaction with the self- transforming spaces of power (e.g. politics, state, economy, religion).

The mobility approach of interaction with the spaces of power mainly corresponds to mobile Roma groups, especially Kalderash. The latter have always had a mobile understanding of their economic practice which maintained them in a permanent communication with the relational dynamics, opportunities and transformations of the state, politics and economy. On the other hand, the mobility approach was opposed to the sedentarist ideology of the socialist state which imposed itself through repressive mechanisms of control. The relation with the *sedentary space of the state* was always one of avoidance. Acting from inside the state structures and being mobile were fundamentally contradictory. The first approach entails settlement, identification, control and subjection to state forms of power. The second, mobile interaction with the transformation of the spaces of power, refers to a more complex movement within *a nomad space*, in Deleuze and Guattari's terms (2005), which involves both life imaginary as movement and territorial mobility. Although Kalderash as *ambulant smiths of a smooth space* (e.g. informal economy unregulated by the state) did not succeed in acting completely outside the state control and its policies, they continued to have a mobile approach to their economic organisation and forms of self-government. The latter offered them access to *a field of opportunities* opened up the contingency of the relational dynamic of the post-socialist informal economy situated at the intersectionality of others spaces of power – politics and state – in a neopatrimonial context. As a result, their mobility appears as a mode of interaction with the self-transforming spaces of power from socialism to post-socialism, which characterises their existence on the move relatively detached from the fixity of the state institutions and structures.

The sedentarist approach of interaction with spaces of power comes in opposition to mobility and mainly corresponds *to the striated/regulated space of the state*. Romanianised Roma interactions from within the state structures were expressions of a sedentarist approach and subjection to state institutions and social programs developed in different historical regimes. The subjection to the state and its models of conduct (e.g. sedentarism, state employment and education) limited their access to opportunities offered by transformation of economy, state and politics. Notwithstanding, local and sedentarist interaction with the informal economy and patronage politics offer them access to a *locally limited navigation of possibilities*, which are highly dependent on the *field of opportunities* accessed by others (e.g. patronage actors or Kalderash's traders). Fields of opportunities are affected in their turn by large socio-economic processes which trigger either limitation or expansion of the fields of possibility. For the case of the two Roma groups discussed, the field of opportunities was mainly a result of the process of deindustrialisation, which became a source for the Kalderash enrichment and their navigation of a smooth space of informal economy facilitated by patronage politics. At the same time, boundaries between power spaces – state-politics/patronage politics, state-religion, and religion-politics[1] – were explored as either opportunities or possibilities by the two Roma groups in their active interaction with their transformations.

For a comprehensive and complete understanding of power relations, special attention was paid to the *Roma brokers* who bridge local, regional and central levels of power. This new form of Roma leadership was constituted through the post-socialist transformations of the political space built through *political fields* – patronage politics and political patronage – which created opportunities for the new customary leaders to source their power in party politics, convince community members to vote for one party or another, and thus make the transition from *socialist state Roma brokers* to *power brokers*. Power brokers are those Roma leaders who decided to remain informal, able to circulate between different spaces (e.g. politics, state, informal economy) and levels of power and support different political parties. Generally, it can be said that they have access to *circulatory power within loose power webs*, which do not impose strains on their relations and practices. Similarly, all those who are less subjected to state forms of control (e.g. wealthy Kalderash), avoid identification and are successfully involved in informal businesses can be considered to have access to *circulatory power*. It is an intentional form of extended connectivity outside community, an ability to navigate power spaces in their historical transformation. However, *state brokerage* was not completely dissolved, but recreated by post-1989 governments' strategies of Roma inclusion which organised a complex multi-level architecture

170 *The return to the political-thesis*

of governance, which transformed informal Roma leaders into Roma experts and therefore *state and patronage brokers*, mainly under the control of both central and local state governance. They achieved access to *connectivity power* within *tight webs* of multi-level state governance from within which Roma experts face multiple responsibilities in the mediation between local state, community and patronage, and are subjected to state neopatrimonial power more than others.

To sum up, the book's ethnography suggests that the source of complexity and dynamics of social power is generally given by relations and practices at the intersections between spaces of power – state, politics, economy and religion. These boundaries are continuously exploited by the Roma individuals and groups through power struggles in interaction with historical movements as transformations. The overall social dynamic creates the basis for an interactive map or analytics of power which explores the movement of groups and individuals within and across self-transforming spaces of power. In the following section, the summarised ethnographic observations are conceptualised as an analytic of social power – *historical geographies of power* – which can be applied to the study of populations and groups who are excessively subjected to state or neoliberal programs of governance. The frame is discussed in a critical dialogue with Pierre Bourdieu's theory of social space, fields and capitals, as a relevant reference to a theoretical and methodological grounded theory construction.

> One needs to investigate historically, and beginning from the lowest level, how mechanisms of power have been able to function (Foucault 1980: 100). But if power is in reality, an open, more-or-less coordinated cluster of relations, then the only problem is to provide oneself with a grid of analysis which makes possible an analytic of relations of power.
> (Foucault, 1980: 199)

12 Historical geographies of power

A theoretical and methodological framework for the study of social power

As Foucault (1980) suggests power is not an entity, but 'a network-like organisation' placed on a historical continuum of emergent transformations of microsocial relations, which configure both the social and the political, which, at their turn, can translate, capture and alter relational configurations:

> One must rather conduct an *ascending* analysis of power, starting, that is, from its infinitesimal mechanisms, which each have their own history, their own trajectory (. . .) and then see how these mechanisms of power have been – and continue to be – invested, colonised, utilised (. . .) by ever more general mechanisms and by forms of global domination.
> (Foucault 1980: 99)

Furthermore, inspired by Deleuze and Guattari's (2005) vision of society as micro-politics, *mobility* itself is a main feature of social power, a referential for social foundations, or a 'molecular' anatomy built through connections and reconnections between small units by their emergence and transmutation. This capillary processual formation of the social and political is opposed to 'molar' forms of apprehension, capturing fluxes of meaning and relationality into enduring macro substances. Henceforth, the social space with a molecular composition can be seen, in Deleuze in Guattari's terms, as a 'smooth' space, opposed to the 'striated'/regulated and sedentary space of the state. The social space itself should be seen as a 'non-metric' space of boundless 'absolute movement', "filled by events or haecceities, far more than by formed and perceived things" (Deleuze & Guattari 2005: 479), as "all becoming [transformation] occurs in smooth space" (486).

Conversely, in Bourdieu's (1989) understanding, *social space* resembles a 'geographical space' or a metric territorial space with distances between relatively fixed positions individuals have in relation to the capitals they hold. Individuals, by being "assigned to a position or a precise class of neighboring position" (Bourdieu 1985: 724), possess specific resources and capitals and are therefore able to enter "in a game of cards, in the competition for the appropriation of scarce goods" (Bourdieu 1989: 16). As he implies, further interactions and dynamics of relations within the social space do not produce change, but reflect "the objective relations" (Bourdieu 1989: 16) already established between positions individuals occupy in the reproductive game of power. Furthermore, Bourdieu (1985) compares the general picture of a stable social space with a social world of 'being', in which interactions and relations between groups follow the rules of a structure which gives stability to some 'groupings' and instability to others. In general terms, Bourdieu's world of 'being' can be translated into a world of experiencing order, or the phenomenological understanding of dwelling, inhabiting an ordered space.

The main critique of Bourdieu's understanding of *social space* is that it generates a great sense of stability, order and reproduction of existent social structures, a model that might fit stable socio-economic environments, but exclude those affected by fast dramatic changes (Vigh 2009). This critique is grounded in a mobile understanding of space – *space turn studies* – generally inspired by Foucault (1980) and developed by social geographer Massey (1999a,b, 2005):

> 'space' cannot be a closed system: it is not stasis, it is not defined negatively as an absence of temporality, (. . .) would be constantly in the process of being made (. . .). It would be integral to space-time.
> (Massey 1999b: 264–5)

From this perspective, space is not 'dwelling' but, as Massey (1999b, 2005) suggests, it is in permanent connection with the temporality of social relations it is made of. Following this understanding, and the book's historical ethnography, *social space* is not inhabited and has no sites of established power. It is rather relational and temporalised, namely, processual. What I define as spaces of power (e.g. state, politics, informal economy, religion) are processes constructed by the experience of relations of power in their spatial (e.g. local-regional-central) and temporal extensions (e.g. from socialism to post-socialism). I showed how Roma relations with the state have adapted and changed according to a transition from a socialist paternalist centralised state affected by local domestications, to a neopatrimonial state which acted as a space of clientelistic relations. Transformations of the political space were connected to this neopatrimonial context. On the other hand, space of economy was affected by large transformations (e.g. deindustrialisation, privatisation, etc.), which did not have a clear direction and were compounded and experienced through a complex web of clientelistic relations. The dynamics of spaces of power were given by practices and relations which had the force of alteration and change, both in socialism and post-socialism. Thus relations were the agents of transformation, which shaped individuals' existence.

Another question related to the social power dynamic is that of movement within the social space and fields,[2] pictured by Bourdieu as stable and reproductive. Yet, in *Distinction* (1984), Bourdieu mentions two forms of movement:

1 *Vertical movement* upwards and downwards in the same *field*, which entails a decrease or "increase in the volume of the type of capital already dominant in the asset structure" (p. 113). For instance, vertical movement of Kalderash

in the economic space, or what Bourdieu calls *field*, would be their transition from the position of small traders in socialism to big businessmen in post-socialism.

2 *Transversal movement*, which ensures a reproduction of the position produced in the vertical movement through "a shift into another field and the reconversion of one type of capital into another or of one sub-type into another sub-type" (p. 131). For example, Kalderash who used their clientelistic relations to avoid identification, tax payment and became successful in their business illustrate this situation.

Nevertheless, in the Romanian socio-political context, the situation does not look as simple as described by Bourdieu (1984), in so far as these clientelistic relations cannot be classified as social capital or clear possessions or resources. They are part of the dynamics of the neopatrimonial context which mainly gets expression at the intersectionality between spaces of power (e.g. politics, economy and state). This identifies a major difference between Bourdieu's field and my understanding of spaces of power. Bourdieu (1985) claims that the field carries "its own logic and hierarchy" (p. 724) and structure and is relatively independent from other fields. The book's political historical ethnography revealed the opposite *that all spaces of power interrelate* and are mainly connected through neopatrimonial relations expressed in what I called the *field of patronage politics*. The latter is a process that bridges different levels of power (e.g. local, regional, central) and works across and at the intersectionality between relational spaces of the state, politics and informal economy. Furthermore, I considered that *boundaries between these spaces are fields of possibility and opportunity* which are accessed and exploited differently by the two Roma groups. Going back to the movement within and across spaces and fields, Bourdieu's theory of fields can be complemented with three forms of movement which are hereby rendered as new directions that need to be followed in the study of social power. Two of these forms of movement are inspired by Vigh (2009).

1 Movement of the environment, or fields themselves, in Bourdieu's (1984, 1985) terminology.
2 Movement of individuals, their interactions with the continuous transformations of the environment, or what I call throughout the book spaces of power struggle.

The third movement derives from book's historical political ethnography and Foucault's understanding of power as circulation and all of them can be summarised as following:

1 *Movement of the spaces of power* (e.g. transformations of state, politics, economy and religion) or their temporal transformations (Massey 1999),
2 *Individuals' interaction with transformation*, self-transforming spaces of power.
3 *Circulatory movement* – movement of individuals/groups/brokers across and at the intersectionality of spaces of power.

Furthermore, Bourdieu's (1984) understanding of individuals as almost rational actors, who can develop strategies, invest and translate capitals is mainly challenged by the movement and transformation of the social space, which creates uncertainties (Vigh 2009). In the Romanian and Eastern European context, or as acknowledged for the case of African countries with high levels of economic and political instability, individuals and groups do not develop coherent strategies, but follow, in Vigh's terms, 'tentative mappings', across and within spaces of power struggle. Notwithstanding, in Bourdieu's (1984) vision power struggles are the reflection of an already constituted social structure. They are employed and manifested in 'competitive struggles' which take the "form of class struggle (. . .) a reproductive struggle" (Bourdieu 1984: 125), revealing power relations as agents of social reproduction. Conversely, following the book's historical ethnography of social power and Foucault's (1980) understanding of power as circulation, the new analytic approaches power relations as agents of transformation and change and relations as a medium for the circulation of power within spaces, which do not have a pre-established distribution of resources, but are rather characterised by a specific form of relationality (e.g. clientelism).

What is the role of individuals in this context? Taking into consideration Foucault's statement that individuals are at the same time 'effects' and 'vehicles of power' (Foucault 1980: 98), the book's historical political ethnography showed that individuals are not only subject to power, but participate in their constitution and transformation. The most relevant example is perhaps the case of Roma Pentecostal believers. Carriers of a religious doctrine – a form of power – which promotes an internal locus of control, the believers are able to change the language of established power and escape subordination to the state and leaders who act as power or state brokers. On the other hand, *power brokers*, constituted and affected by neopatrimonial relations seem to be the main 'vehicles of power'. They are those who mediate between community, state and political representatives, able to circulate and exploit different levels and spaces of power. In general terms, through a parallel with Bourdieu's theory of social space and fields, the book's study of social power among the Roma brings the power dynamics back and, inspired by the space turn studies (Massey 2005), constitutes a good grounding for a new analytic of power, namely, *historical geographies of power*.

The term *historical geographies* is largely used in social geography, but is mainly substantiated by David Harvey (2008) who criticises a Kantian understanding of 'absolute space', which is "marked by contingency, fragmentation and uniqueness [and] contrasts radically with the universality that attaches to the concept of unidirectional time that points us teleologically towards some destiny" (p. 44). Harvey (2008) argues that these two perspectives – history and geography – should not be perceived as opposite, but as a compound for the understanding of social worlds in transformation. Additionally, as Foucault (1980) argues, space is "fundamental in any exercise of power" and "a whole history remains to be written of spaces – which would at the same time be a history of powers" (p. 252), an "ongoing history" (Massey 2005) of a relational dynamic space-time. Following Foucault (1980), Harvey (2008), and Massey (2005), as well as the book's historical political ethnography, a *historical geography of power* should take account of the following methodological and theoretical statements:

1 Social space is the expression of a temporal relational dynamic continuously transforming its composition (Massey 2005), rather than an expression of a fixed structure of positionalities (Bourdieu 1984, 1985, 1989) which reproduces the power relations.
2 Suggested by the book's historical ethnography, spaces of power (e.g. politics, economy, state and religion) are disclosed in a dynamic of relations across their boundaries.
3 Informed by the book's historical ethnography, special attention is paid to the intersectionality and overlapping(s) between spaces of power and the way they create in their temporal transformation fields of possibility and opportunity for individuals and groups to explore and exploit.
4 The framework focuses on the movement or transformation of spaces of power, individuals' interaction with transformations and movement across these spaces.
5 Throughout the book, brokerage practices, which connect different levels of power and make the power dispersed and effective in its capillarities, are inquired into. The brokers' actions and involvement in steering relations constitute a map of the power webs, which expands beyond the local level of practice. They are those who connect (e.g. *state brokers*) and circulate (e.g. *power brokers*) different levels and power spaces. Therefore, a specific attention to *brokers'* actions can offer a comprehensive picture of a dynamics of social power, which rather than triggering social reproduction, is frequently played at the boundaries between spaces in their temporal transformations, generally silenced in Bourdieu's model.

Throughout the book's historical political ethnography, the capacity of the temporal dynamic of individual and group power relations and discursive practices to produce transformations in the life trajectories of the Roma groups is explored. Generally, the study is concentrated on both power relations and discursive practices within and across different spaces of power struggle which are inter-related (e.g. state-politics-informal economy, or politics-religion). The focus on local level power struggles within and across different spaces resembles what Foucault (1980) proposed as an "ascending analysis of power" (p. 99). In general terms, the overall analysis is concentrated on *two movements or transformations*. First, there are the transformations of what I call *spaces of power struggle*, including state, politics, economy and religion, from socialism to post-socialism. Second, there is the individual and group movement and interaction with the macro-transformations. These larger transformations created both constraints and opportunities for the two Roma groups, which interacted differently with the socialist and post-socialist transformations. The temporal dynamic of social power within and across spaces of contest ultimately creates the transformative tendencies of what I called throughout the book *power relations*.

All these are part of a new analytic of power – *historical geography of power* – which follows an epistemological direction contrary to that of neoliberal government aimed at conducting the Other as a subaltern subject. The book's historical political ethnography does not start from the categories used by governance to define a problem (e.g. marginalisation, exclusion, poverty) down to the 'reality' of those governed, but it rather offers a bottom-up relational understanding of social power, following individuals' practices into large transformations. It has the capacity to analyse social dynamics without reproducing the language of neoliberal governance which carries the characteristics of 'symbolic violence' described by Bourdieu (1991). It enables the dislocation of power from sites where it can be reproduced, and deconstructs a polarised manufactured reality of a struggle between an invincible omnipotence (e.g. majorities, governing bodies) and the defeated powerless (e.g. 'the poor', 'the marginalised', 'the excluded'). By avoiding these sites, it makes available a comprehensive view of power performed through social relations and discursive practices. It is a reflective research act which steps outside the governmentalised field of knowledge within which categories of governance or identification are used extensively – ''vulnerable', 'marginalised', 'poor', 'excluded'. The latter contribute to the constitution of what Foucault (1980) called 'regimes of truth', in a logic of governmentality which becomes barely contested. As a methodological and theoretical frame for the study of social power, it also opens up the opportunity of comparative research into different populations, who are subject to social integration programs devised by the neoliberal government (e.g. New Zealand's Maori, Australia's Aboriginals, Canadian and American Indians, Indigenous Populations in South America, etc.). Thereafter, a *historical geography of power* should be able to unpack the hermetic pre-existing subject (e.g. subject of social integration as neoliberal governmentality), explore its constituencies and, therefore, contribute to its epistemological decolonisation and ongoing political subjectivity in the making. The latter as a process is theoretically explored, in the next section, in relation to Jacques Ranciere's discussion of politics vs. police, heralding a new epistemological thesis, able to question the neoliberal subject and resurrect the political.

13 The return to the political-thesis

As Ranciere (1999) suggests, whereas the undoing of the subject and its subsequent re-subjectification are political questions, the pre-existing subject reveals power in its exercise, articulating the subject's regime of acting and enunciation. The latter engages a mechanism of identification by an already constituted subject with a population subject to government power, which can only be released through the political action that "shifts a body from the place assigned to it or changes a place's destination" (p. 30). In other terms, from within the neoliberal discourse, a political act would involve a disentanglement of the subject from architectural power, which allocates its capabilities and functionalities within a general regime of signification and commandment by the market and capital. Yet, epistemological depoliticisation performed by the neoliberal discourse through expert knowledge – social integration as neoliberal governmentality – discussed in the introduction of this book, is thoroughly involved in the constitution of Roma as subaltern subjects, ungoverned labour power not yet integrated into the rationality of the market and moral economic ordering of neoliberalism. The latter is configuring *mechanisms of subjectification of labour power* based on an epistemological assessment of a presumed 'vulnerability' of the Roma as insecurity or risk of unemployment, through which entrepreneurial models of the self, sustaining and preserving market moral reasoning (e.g. self-reliance, profit expansion, state welfare reduction) are projected onto their subjectivities.

From the perspective of the political action, *subjectification*, as Ranciere (1999) defines it, opposes *police*. The latter is "first an order of the bodies that defines the allocation of ways of doing, ways of being, and ways of saying, and sees that those bodies are assigned by name to a particular place and task [regime of signification]" (p. 29).

> By subjectification I mean the production through a series of actions of a body and a capacity for enunciation not previously identifiable within a given field of experience, whose identification is thus part of the reconfiguration of the field of experience.
>
> (Ranciere 1999: 35)

Although his definition seems to concern political subjectification only, a process of constituting the political subject, subjectification can also refer to a depoliticising mechanism of incorporating neoliberal forms of self-government into models of subjectivity shaped by instrumental rationalities of the market. A distinction between depoliticised neoliberal subjectification and political subjectification makes sense as far as the political subject finds itself in a dialectical movement between modes of policing self and behaviour engendered under epistemic regimes yielded by the capital's commandment, and vernacular forms of knowledge and self-government. This dialectic can be seen, as Ranciere (2010) inspires, as the main characteristic of politics as "a paradoxical form of action", which authorises "the existence of a subject defined by its participation in the contraries" (p. 29) (e.g. the ruler and the ruled). Similarly, the epistemological awareness of both and dialectical tension they engender increase the chances for a political re-subjectification "by questioning the relationship between a who and a what in the apparent redundancy of the positing of an existence" (Ranciere 1999: 36). The book's ethnography questioned this relation, the epistemological apparatus that colonises Roma subjectivities. Identifying Roma as 'the vulnerable', 'the marginalised' and 'the poor' of Europe, as previously discussed in the introduction, is a depoliticised mode of subjectification, constituting the subaltern subject through identification categories corresponding, in Bourdieu's (1991) terms, to the 'symbolic power' of language. These mechanisms of identification and, therefore, subjectification are epistemological apparatuses of a governmentality/ problematisation (Rose 1999) which sets the frame of governance that seeks the solution to an already defined problem (van Baar 2011). Following this, *European social integration can be seen as a neoliberal problematisation of governance which acts as a 'regime of truth', a force of internalisation of the Roma subjectivities into the regime of signification of capital and the market and their instrumentalities ('the governed'), opposed to the political affirmation of the subject as 'the governor', able to expand its idiosyncratic modes of self-government into the territorialised spaces of neoliberalism.* It brings into being a relation of subordination and 'suspension' in which Roma are left waiting, in an endless process of integration as the unready subjects of neoliberal government. The latter seamlessly authorises through programs of human security or development, the liberal policing of the self (e.g. actions and behaviour), which aims to incorporate ungoverned labour power into entrepreneurial models of realisation of the market, which stand at the core of neoliberal governmentality.

In this context, *politics builds itself as a deterritorialising force in opposition to the neoliberal moral order and capital's commandment.* The latter acts as a territorialising force and follows, in Ranciere's terms, the 'logic of police', which "is characterised by the absence of void and of supplement: society here is made up of groups tied to specific modes of doing, to places in which these occupations are exercised, and to modes of being corresponding to these occupations and these places" (Ranciere 2010: 36). "In this matching of functions, places and ways of being, there is no place for any void" (Ranciere 2010: 36), for enacting alternative forms of subjectivity and self-government, making the invisible visible, undoing and disclosing the subject of neoliberal government as a speaking, political subject.

Although for Foucault (2008) *police* is a form of government and knowledge production directed from above as domination by the state, aimed at strengthening its administrative power and wealth, for Ranciere (1999) *police* is not necessarily repressive, but productive of "an order of the visible and sayable that sees that a particular activity is visible and another is not" (p. 29). Extensively, it is generative of entrepreneurial forms of self-mastery, which impose themselves as authoritarian models of liberal self-policing, invalidating 'the void'/public sphere "constitutive of the very nature of political space" (Ranciere 2010: 34) and emergent political subjectivities in 'dissensus' with the logic of capital and the market. Constituting self and institutions as enterprises, as small units of capital's commandment operating throughout the social, *liberal police* is a mechanism of governing society through society, opposed to the logic of politics. Henceforth, *the return to the political* can be envisaged as a process of exposing the speaking subject, the political subject, "the bearer of signs of politicity" (Ranciere 2010: 38), an epistemological liberation of a 'void' territorialised or conceptualised by neoliberal governmental power. Detaching the subject from its subalternity, constituted through the epistemological apparatus of the market realisation and capital's commandment, can be achieved through a process of knowledge production portraying its belonging to a logic of contradictions, prompted by a dialectical power movement of individuals continuously shaping their governance by being governed by the social, economic and political power. A *historical geography of power* is this kind of unbounded mode of knowledge production, emancipated from the exercise of neoliberal governmental power, revealing the Roma as speaking subjects, ruling and being ruled, seamlessly engaged in the constitution of their political subjectivities.

A renaissance of the political subject would also entail "a break with the axiom of domination, that is, any sort of correlation between a capacity for ruling and a capacity for being ruled" (Ranciere 2010: 32), able to release its political affirmation as potentiality in a dialectical conversation with state and neoliberal government's force of internalisation of pre-existing social and political forms (see chapter on Roma Pentecostalism and political subject). Hence, the book's historical political ethnography, epistemologically exposed a dialectical movement between macro- and micro-transformations of social power, central and local group forms of government, eluding "the 'normal' distribution of positions that defines who exercises power and who is subject to it (. . .)" (p. 37). In this case, the break with the *logic of police*, opposed to the *logic of politics*, can also be performed through a break with categories of knowledge and self-government (e.g. enterprise) produced, in Deleuze and Guattari's (2005) terms, around axiomatics of the market.

Notwithstanding, self-government and engagement of the ruled with the ruling has been appropriated by "neoliberalism [which] (mis)recognises such features of subjectivity as consistent with its own framework" (Bondi and Laurie 2005: 399). Generally, neoliberalism engages two intertwined mechanisms – *subjectification and semiological capture* – through which governing at distance is exercised. One conceives entrepreneurial behaviour and consumption as models of subjectification, self-ruling and realisation of the market. The other one aims at incorporating idiosyncratic forms of self-government and resistance into neoliberal programs of government through translation. However, in a liberal version resistance "may be constitutive of the rule" (O'Malley 1996: 322), "an integral part of and contributor to programmes regarded as successful, and be incorporated into programmes rather than merely acting as an external source of programme failure" (p. 312). Although during this process the Other's self-government (e.g. Roma Pentecostalism as self-government vs. social integration) might be translated, adjusted and altered to match neoliberal 'governing mentalities', the opposite is supposed to be involved as well: "rule is at least potentially destabilized and subjected to a transformational politics" (p. 312). Yet, the question that remains is whether this 'transformational politics', which blurs the boundary between the governor-ruler and the governed-ruled from the perspective of the governor, aims to contribute to the success of the ruling or the politics of the ruled. From the perspective of the neoliberal moral economic order and the marketisation of freedom, it would contribute to both. Nevertheless, as far as the reformative aim is that of adjusting neoliberal governance through translation, capture and incorporation of the Other's idiosyncrasies, the so called 'transformational politics' betrays itself as an instrumental strategy of the ruler which deters the undoing of 'the governed' and constitution of the political subject.

Social integration as neoliberal governmentality and force of internalisation of existing Roma subjectivities and associated forms of self-government[3] was considered to be this kind of transformational politics, a program of empowerment and development aiming at 'repoliticisation' and 'citizenship partnership' engaging the struggle of Roma activists to challenge its modes of subjectification associated with subalternity (Van Baar 2011: 18). Nonetheless, the problematisation itself is not necessarily a base for 'citizenship participation', but it seems to be, in Bourdieu's (1984) terms, "a reproductive struggle, since those who enter this chase (. . .) are beaten before they start" (Bourdieu 1984: 125). The distinction between governed and governor, ruled and the ruler is emphasised through categories of knowledge associated with subalternity as a mode of subjectification, the incorporation of the non-integrated subjects into the logic of the market and capital. On this ground, the return to the political subject would imply, in Ranciere's (2010) terms, a break with the "logic of arkhe [which] thus presupposes that a determinate superiority is exercised over an equally determinate inferiority" (p. 30). In an extended view, it would designate a break with the categories of knowledge (e.g. poverty, marginality, vulnerability) produced around an axiomatic of the market or 'axiom of domination' and a 'logic of commandment' or capital's commandment, which territorialise existing political subjectivities. In addition, neoliberal programs of governance and vernacular models of government would need to be kept in dissensus, dialectical movement, as manifestations of contradictory processes of constituting the political subject. These foundations of the political were followed throughout the book's historical ethnography of power, as a critical mode of knowledge production *questioning social integration as neoliberal governmentality*. The latter process followed the main methodological principle discussed by Foucault (2009) himself as a disentanglement of the object of study (e.g. the Roma as the 'vulnerable') from the structures of governmental power, which constituted its existence and associated modes of objectification and subjectification: "refusing to give oneself a ready-made object, be it mental illness, delinquency, or sexuality (. . .) [and] grasping the movement by which a field of truth with objects of knowledge was constituted" (p. 163). Notwithstanding, the authority of instrumentalised knowledge is able to establish the truth and configure the object of knowledge, and, therefore, the subject of governance by carrying depoliticising effects that do not challenge the neoliberal problematisation of governance (e.g. social integration). The latter, through pretences of reflexivity – researching the governed – "continually seeks to give itself a form of truth" (Rose 1999: 7), "structure the possible fields of others" (Foucault 2000: 341) and apply categories of knowledge (e.g. 'exclusion', 'poverty', 'marginalisation') to complex conditions of existence. Yet, as Ranciere (2010) argues, the political subject is both a speaking subject and a "particular *dispositif* of subjectivation[4] and litigation through which politics comes into existence" (Ranciere 2010: 39). Henceforth, whereas the question of governmentality is one of identification of the subject of governance, the object of politics is political subjectification, "a disidentification, removal from the naturalness of place" (Ranciere 1999: 36) that denaturalises the order of the liberal police, its disciplinatory modes of subjection, and deconstructs the subaltern subject (e.g. 'the poor', 'the vulnerable') of neoliberal government. On these grounds, inquiring into the constituting power of the social, historical geographies of power amongst the Roma and Roma's 'politicity' as speaking subjects, can contribute to this political subjectification and epistemological decolonisation of the subaltern subject of neoliberal governmentality. Thus, a return to the political cannot be seen as 'the return to the politics', which Ranciere (2010) classifies as a mode of distinguishing and tracing borders between the social and the political. *The return to the political* represents a return to a critical knowledge undoing the pre-existing subjects, taking consideration of the movement or interactions of individuals with the social transformations/movement of spaces of power, revealing alternative modalities of self-government and affirmation as manifestations of a political subject in its constitution.

In other words, studying from the perspective of fixed positionalities and following theoretical models of social reproduction can give way to nonreflective reproductive knowledge and preservation of an existent neoliberal mentality of governance (e.g. social integration) and its associated subaltern subject. Yet, a challenge to the latter cannot come from within the dynamics of governmentality itself, but from the exploration of historical manifestations of social power within which political subjectivities are enmeshed in an ongoing process of constitution. A study about Roma and other populations excessively targeted by neoliberal government should not be concentrated on the side effects of governance, but on the exploration of their *historical geographies of power*, which can bring contestation of the existing reproductive discourses of governance. The latter are often approached as omnipotent powers, absolute knowledge(s) and sometimes uncontested truths for social sciences, which are heavily governmentalised. In these terms, following Foucault's (1991) analysis of governmentality as both institutional and discursive practices, with the power to constitute 'regimes of truth', *governmentalised knowledge* can be seen as the product of a process through which categories of governance are translated uncritically into academic knowledge and expert social research. The field of Romani studies seems to carry along these categories of knowledge defined by a pre-existent problematisation of governance (e.g. marginalisation-vulnerability-exclusion-social integration), and thus it is governmentalised on general lines. Categories of subalternity (e.g. 'vulnerable' and 'poor'), commanded by the liberal policing of the non-integrated labour power into the logic of the market and constructed around entrepreneurial models of subjectification, are taken for granted and considered realities, problems which need to be researched and solved. The latter are not necessarily reflected upon and examined as 'regimes of enunciations' (Rose 1999), part of a neoliberal governmentality which can be questioned for a consideration of the Roma's political subjectivities, constantly evolving from a dialectical movement between neoliberal and vernacular models of self-government. *Thereafter, a return to the political subject would institute a break with the logic of the police, which constitutes 'the governed' and internalises previous subjectivities, or in other terms, an epistemological break with the logic of capital and its commandment.*

Notwithstanding, as Ranciere (2010) argues, sociology and social sciences herald the 'end of politics' suggesting "that the logical *telos* of capitalism entails the extinction of politics" by focusing on the loss of sovereignty and expansion of networks globally and "other forms that match those of the social pertaining to the highest stage of capitalism" (p. 43). On the other hand, Burawoy (2007) considers that society itself is colonised by market fundamentalism, or in other terms by neoliberalism, and thus sociology needs to politicise its aims through social intervention, cease "to collaborate with market and state" and "engage directly with society before it disappears altogether" (p. 357). Nevertheless, before starting any form of activism, social researchers should reflect on the *problematisation of governance* from within which they act and produce knowledge, on the dominant discourses of governance which might reproduce the power structures, relations of force and preserve the status quo. In these terms, neoliberal governmentality is not only an effect of the governance-oriented research, but the product of discourses produced by multiple and different institutions and actors involved in the government of the social, among which social researchers have access to the mechanisms of 'symbolic power' to participate in the conquest of truth (Bourdieu & Wacquant 1992). They have the capacity to categorise and speak on behalf of others, "power to produce, to impose, and to inculcate the legitimate representation of the social world" (Bourdieu & Wacquant 1992: 51).

Furthermore, sociological knowledge can shape modes of subjectification, which can support or deconstruct self-policing models produced by the logic of the market – logic of police – which authorises its moral economic order and the constitution of a subaltern subject. A political subjectification would imply the disentanglement of the subject from the existent order – neoliberal moral order – affirming its existent capacities and producing "a multiple [a heterogeneity] that was not given in the police constitution of community [e.g. the poor, the marginal – the subaltern subject], a multiple whose count poses itself as contradictory in terms of police logic" (Ranciere 1999: 36). The latter homogenises, and subsumes

Roma's heterogeneity to a fixed classification and mode of identification associated with the needs of the market, through which they are governed as subaltern subjects or non-integrated subjects of the neoliberal moral economic order. Defying this logic and exposing *the multiple* would involve a political affirmation of the subject in its manifold modes of identification and constitution of the self, shaped through a social power dynamic equally, engaged with micro- and macro-historical transformations, which this book realises.

Thereafter, the study of social and neoliberal governmental power in a dialectical movement with alternative forms of government, able to contribute to the constitution of a political subject in dissensus with the logic of capital and the market, should be a strong fundamental for a critical sociology, which needs to be prioritised in relation to other forms of sociology (e.g. professional, policy-oriented, public sociology, etc.)[5]. In other words, in so far as "[t]he truth always defines itself as a limit – an end in itself" (Jabes 1991: 39) and expert knowledge "professes to be a knowledge of the truth" (Foucault 1997: 14), a rehearsal for a crime committed in the name of order, the task of the critical scholars is to question and deconstruct the truth, its mechanisms of emergence and consolidation, pursue an endless genealogy of existing order and sense and contribute to the epistemological decolonialisation of the subaltern subject. Critical knowledge, productive of political subjectivities should seize the "emission of the despotic signifier [neoliberalism] (. . .), which fixes the signified", revitalise the multiple "from sign to sign, (. . .) from one territory to another, [its] circulation assuring a certain speed of deterritorialization" (Deleuze & Guattari 2005: 126) of the neoliberal subject, a release from its commandment constitutive structures of power, enacted by relations between answers and questions, which seamlessly need to be questioned for the affirmation of the political.

Notes

1 For instance, through privatisation of the relation with God, the Kalderash Pentecostal believers became disengaged from external sources of authority. Roma experts and power brokers no longer impose their voting options.
2 The *field* is defined by Bourdieu (1985) as a "multi-dimensional space of positions such that (. . .) agents are distributed within it (. . .) according to the overall volume of the capital they possess and (. . .) composition of their capital" (p. 724).
3 Please see the chapter on Roma Pentecostalism and semiological state apparatus of capture.
4 Ranciere (1999, 2010) uses *subjectivation* and *subjectification* alternatively.
5 A typology of forms of sociology is extensively discussed by Burawoy (2007).

Bibliography

Bondi, L. & Laurie, N. (Eds.) (2005) *Working the Spaces of Neoliberalism: Activism, Professionalisation and Incorporation*. Malden, Oxford: Blackwell Publishing.

Bourdieu, P. (1984) *Distinction: A Social Critique of the Judgement of Taste*. Cambridge, MA: Harvard University Press.

Bourdieu, P. (1985) 'The Social Space and the Genesis of Groups'. *Theory and Society*, 14(6): 723–744.

Bourdieu, P. (1989) 'Social Space and Symbolic Power'. *Sociological Theory*, 7(1): 14–25.
Bourdieu, P. (1991) *Language and Symbolic Power*. Cambridge, Malden: Polity Press.
Bourdieu, P. & Wacquant, L.J.D. (1992) *An Invitation to Reflexive Sociology*. Cambridge: Polity Press.
Burawoy, M. (2007) Public Sociology vs. the Market. *Socio-Economic Review*, 5: 319–367.
Deleuze, G. & Guattari, F. (2005)[1987] *A Thousand Plateaus: Capitalism and Schizophrenia*. Minneapolis: University of Minnesota Press.
Foucault, M. (1980) *Power/Knowledge: Selected Interviews and Other Writings, 1972–1977*. (Ed.) C. Gordon. New York: Pantheon Books.
Foucault, M. (1991) 'Governmentality'. In G. Buchell, C. Gordon and P. Miller (Eds.) *The Foucault Effect: Studies in Governmentality*. Chicago: University of Chicago Press, pp. 87–104.
Foucault, M. (1997) *Ethics: Subjectivity and Truth. Essential Works of Foucault (1954–1984)*. (Ed.) P. Rabinow. New York: The New Press.
Foucault, M. (2000) 'The Subject and Power'. In J. Faubion (Ed.) *Power Essential Works of Foucault 1954–1984*. New York: The New Press, pp. 326–348.
Foucault, M. (2008) *The Birth of Biopolitics: Lectures at the College de France, 1978–79. Michel Foucault*. (Ed.) M. Senellart. London and New York: Palgrave Macmillan.
Foucault, M. (2009) *Michel Foucault. Security, Territory, Population: Lectures at the College de France, 1977–78*. (Eds.) M. Senellart, F. Ewald and A. Fontana. London and New York: Palgrave Macmillan.
Harvey, D. (2007) 'The Kantian Roots of Foucault's Dilemma'. In J. W. Crampton and S. Elden (Eds.) *Space, Knowledge and Power: Foucault and Geography*. Aldershot: Ashgate, pp. 41–48.
Jabes, E. (1991) *The Book of Resemblances: Intimations the Desert*. Hanover and London: Wesleyan University Press.
Massey, D. (1999a) 'Entanglements of Power: Reflections'. In J. P. Sharp, P. Routledge, C. Philo and R. Paddison (Eds.) *Entanglements of Power: Geographies of Domination/Resistance*. London, New York: Routledge, pp. 279–285.
Massey, D. (1999b) *Space-time, 'science' and the relationship between physical geography and human geography*. Transactions of the Institute of British Geographers (N.S) 24. 261–76.
Massey, D. (2005) *For Space*. Los Angeles, London, New Delhi, Singapore, Washington, DC: Sage.
O'Malley, P. (1996) 'Indigenous Governance'. *Economy and Society*, 25(3): 310–326.
Ranciere, J. (1999) *Disagreement: Politics and Philosophy*. London, Minneapolis: University of Minnesota.
Ranciere, J. (2010) *Dissensus: On Politics and Aesthetics*. London, New York: Continuum.
Rose, N. (1999) *The Power of Freedoms: Reframing Political Thought*. Cambridge: Cambridge University Press.
Scott, J. (1998) *Seeing Like a State: How Certain Schemes to Improve the Human Condition Have Failed*. New Haven: Yale University Press.
Van Baar, H. (2011) *The European Roma: Minority Representation, Memory and the Limits of Transnational Governmentality*. Amsterdam: Geboren te's Gravenhage.
Vigh, H. (2009) 'Motion Squared: A Second Look at the Concept of Social Navigation'. *Anthropological Theory*, 9(4): 419–438.

Index

agential power 159
agential self-materialising 26
art of government 12–13
ataxic democracy, emergence 9
authoritarianism 6, 16, 19–21, 113, 119, 154; authoritarian models of self-conduct, despotism 16, 19; neoliberalism (comparison) 20
axiomatics of the market 14, 16, 18, 22, 28, 179; instrumental rationality of the market 7, 15–16, 25

Bourdieu, Pierre 55, 167, 170–6, 178, 180, 182; capitals 170–4, 178, 180, 182; fields 169; power struggles 30–1, 38–9, 55; space 167, 170–5, 178
brokerage: organised forms 108; practices 175
brokers: actions 175; impact 98–102; power brokers 175; state brokers 175
bureaucratic space 136

capital augmentation 17
capital commandment 18–20, 22, 25, 27–8, 55, 178–80; apparatus of commandment and moral economic ordering 16, 18, 20, 22, 28, 177–8
capital's commandment and logic of the market 177–83
capitalism 10, 13, 16, 18, 20, 32, 48, 52; new forms 52
capture, semiological apparatus 150, 160
capture, semiological state apparatus 158–61; Pentecostalism, contrast 149
CEE economies 26
Central and Eastern European (CEE) countries, informal economy 67
circulatory movement 173
circulatory power, access 169–70

circulatory power *vs.* connectivity power 169–70
citizen 16, 72, 79; subject of rights 16
clientelism 32, 47, 51, 53–4, 77, 79, 86, 108, 113–14, 118–19, 128, 133–4, 137, 141, 172–4; politics 32
clientelistic relations 128
client-patron relationship 120–1
collaborators networks, *Securitate* 50
colonial chiefs 93, 95, 109; and customary leaders (contrast) 93
colonialism, post-colonialism (parallel) 108–9
colonial state vs. socialist state 93, 109
commandment: logic 180; ontology 21
communist ideology 48–9
Communist Party 48–50, 92, 113, 121; control strategy 50
community of values, ministerial power 153
conduct 6, 12–13, 16–19
connectivity power, access 170
control, socialist apparatuses 92
critical sociology 183; knowledge 182–3; political subjectification 182–3; social sciences 182–3
cultural translation 150, 161
customary law 93, 109
customary leaders 92–4, 96–8, 100–1, 104, 107, 109

decentralised despotism 109
de-collectivisation 52
deindustrialisation 52
Deleuze, Gilles 10, 12, 15, 25, 55, 75, 81, 86–8, 101, 109, 150, 154, 159–61, 168, 171, 179, 183
Deleuze, Gilles and Guattari, Felix 75, 81, 86–8, 101, 109, 150, 154, 159–61, 168,

186 *Index*

171, 179, 183; ambulant artisans 87–8; axiomatics of the market 179; expert knowledge(s) 150, 161; micropolitics 171; molecular vs. molar 171; nomad 101, 109; nomad vs. sedentary space 75–6, 87–8; royal sciences 150, 161; sedentary space of the state 101; semiological capture 179; semiological state apparatus of capture 150, 158–61; smooth vs. striated space 67–88; striated vs. smooth space 169, 171; territorialisation vs. deterritorialisation 150, 153, 159–61; Tradition vs. Custom 109; war machine 109, 150, 159, 161
depoliticisation 177–8, 181; marketisation of freedom 22, 26, 31, 180
depoliticising, action 31–2
destructive empowerment 101, 103; contradictions 103
development programs, design 31–2
development, security (relationship) 5
disaffected power 159, 161
disciplinary neoliberalism, poor (subjects) 18–19
dislocated spatialisation 4
dislocated spatialised intercession 9
dispositif 21
dissent, expressions (shaping) 31
Distinction (Bourdieu) 172
documenting identity 132–47; repressive vs. emancipatory effects 134–5
documenting identity-state signature 136, 138–41
domestication of law 146
dominance and resistance 37–8
domination, axiom 180
dwelling, space (contrast) 172

Eastern Europe 3–7, 9, 13–17, 19–21, 24, 28, 30, 32–4, 38–40, 42, 49, 51, 61, 67, 68, 69, 71. 73, 74, 77, 88, 98, 100, 101, 140, 150, 157, 160, 173, 174, 184; development 3–5, 9, 11–14, 17–21; economic development/democratisation (infrastructural device) 13–14; neoliberalism 3–4, 6, 9–11, 14, 18, 23–4, 28, 32; poverty 4–6, 14, 17–18, 23–5, 28–9, 32–3; sovereignty 9–13, 15, 19
economic development 9, 11, 13, 18, 20, 24, 48
economic survival 75
economic transformations 39
economy: informal economy, nomad-smooth economy, interactions 87–8; sedentary-striated spaces, interactions 87–8; smooth/striated spaces (contrast), Roma interactions 67
emergent void, policing (role) 10–11
empowerment 149–50, 152, 156–9, 161
entanglements of power 38, 48–55
enterprise, behaviour 18
entity-approach 97–8
entrepreneurial field, instantiation 16; space, environment, movement 173
epistemological apparatuses 178–9
epistemological colonisation 22
epistemological decolonisation 165–83
epistemological individualisation and totalisation 12
epistemological mobility 12
epistemological state apparatus 13
epistemological supervision 17
European governance, neoliberal conception 3
European social integration, neoliberal governmentality 22
European transnational government, other role 3
European Union (EU) 167; exclusion 167, 181, 182; economic consequences 7; social exclusion 23
expert knowledge 11–18, 22, 28, 31
external authority, differential ideological subjection 159
external policing, self-policing (nexus) 20

field: movement 173; vertical movement 172–3
field of opportunities, access 168–9
field of opportunities vs. field of possibilities 168–9
field of others, structuring 181
field of possibilities 87; spaces, boundaries 173
formal education, usefulness 80
Foucault, Michel 8, 11–13, 15–16, 18–19, 22–3, 29–31, 37–9, 167, 170–6, 179, 181–3; governmentality 176, 181–2; government liberal 8, 12–13, 15; and neoliberal governmentality 11–12, 15–16; power 167, 170–6, 179–83; regimes of truth 176, 182
free will, liberal understanding 158

generalised reciprocity 86
global governance, neo/liberal system 18–19
global neoliberal governmental power, ataxic democracy (emergence) 9

Global Roma Pentecostalism 150, 159
God: internalised authority 155–8; responsibility 158; self-God 157; symbolic interface 158–9
God-authority 149, 155–8
Goffman, Ervin 138–41, 144–5; audience 145; backstage view 145; definition of the situation 139–41, 144; dramaturgical cooperation 144–5; working consensus 139
Goffmanian dramaturgical perspective, usage 55
governance 14; categories, usage 176; dislocated spatialisation 4; global governance, neo/liberal system 18–19; good governance 5, 19; exercise 6–7; liberal governance, impact 17; neoliberal problematisation 178; nomad governance 98–102; population governance, paternalist model 49–50; post-socialist state structures, impact 108; power, exercise 14; problematisation 182
governed, political resubjectification 55
governmentalised knowledge 181–2
government of the self 12, 22, 26
Guattari, Felix 10, 12, 15, 25, 55, 75, 81, 86–8, 101, 109, 150, 154, 159–61, 168, 171, 179, 183

Harvey, David 174–5; historical geographies 171–6; space-time 172, 174
historical ethnography, usage 175
historical geographies of power 170–6, 181; analytics of power 170, 174, 176
history, contingency approach 38
Holy Spirit, receiving 154
Human Development 5–6, 9, 14, 18–19, 21, 23–5, 31; concept 25; programs 6–7
Human Development Report (UNDP) 24–5
human rights 4, 6, 9, 14, 17–18, 24; morality, perspective 6; promoters 14; realisation 9
human security 25, 178

identification: categories 32; categories, usage 176; local police mechanisms 143; mechanisms 143; state signature/ procedures 138–41
identity: documentation 132; theoretical references 134–5; fictions/recognition 142–6
identity fictions and identity recognition 142–6

ideological subjects of the state vs. nomadic subjectivities 87–8
incomplete field of action 116
informal economic practices 104
informal economy 67, 78, 80, 83–7, 97; informality, symbol 119; locally restrictive labyrinth, social navigation 86–7; moving/self-transforming space 78; nomad/smooth space, navigation 88; second economy 67, 84, 87
informal leadership, strengthening 106
informal salary arrangements 67
informal sector, income generation opportunities 26
internalisation, force 178, 180
internal Orientalism 3
internal Other 3
intuition in action 81–2
invention, activity 81
Iron Curtain, fall 51

Juridical Theory of the Sovereign Technologies of Governance 12

knowledge 3, 5, 7–8, 11–19, 22–3, 26, 28–31, 44, 52; expert knowledge 11–18, 22, 28, 31; social sciences 12, 14, 16, 19, 28, 55

labour market, Roma integration/ participation 7
labour power 10, 17–18, 23, 25, 27, 177–8, 182; capital accumulation 17, 39; poverty 17–18, 23; ungoverned labour power 25, 27, 177–8
labour power, subjectification: axiomatic apparatus 10; neoliberal ontogenetic mechanisms 25
laissez-faire 15; neoliberalism, relationship 16
law and order, establishment 9
leadership: actions, subordination 127; change 96; forms 94–7; liberalised economies, populations (existence) 7–8
leadership as power relation and government 101, 110
legibility effect 134
liberal governmentality 8, 9–21, 22–8
liberal police 177–9, 181; enterprise 179; entrepreneurial models of subjectification 182; self-government 178–81; subaltern subject 179, 181–3
Life Imaginary, movement 168
local barons, local patrons (comparison) 53
local bosses, reaction 53

local community governance, symbolic enactments 154
local histories and cultures 22–3, 25, 31
local labyrinth, field of possibilities 87
local level politics 114–17
locally limited navigation of possibilities, access 169
locally restrictive labyrinth, social navigation 86–7
local patronage: actors, party, support 121–2; team, support 137
local patronage politics: commonness 125–6; dynamic 108
local patrons 32, 53–4, 113, 136; and local barons (comparison) 53–4
logic of commandment 180
loose and tight power webs 169–70
loose power webs, circulatory power (access) 169–70

macro-movement, power manifestation 47
macro-social transformations 39
market: axiomatics 14; contiguous economic rationalities 21; rationality, rule of law (interdependence/entanglement) 20; realisation, subject-entrepreneurs (production) 16
market economy: failure, poverty (result) 23; micro-power 39
migration: management, impact 6; securitisation 18
minorities, governing 19
miscognition and misrecognition 159
mobility approach 168–9
moral economic order 18
moral economic ordering, apparatus (engagement) 18–19
movement: circulatory movement 173; focus 175; transversal movement 173; vertical movement 172–3
movement within movement 88
multiplicity 102–4

neoliberal government 23
neoliberal governmentality 176–8, 180–2; neoliberal governmental power 179, 183; neoliberalism 177–9, 182–3; problem 15
neoliberal interventionism 9–10, 16–17, 182
neoliberalised economy, uncertainty/instability 86
neoliberalism 8, 9–21, 22–8, 29, 32–3, 55; authoritarianism, comparison 20; economic moral order 17–19;
laissez-faire, identification 16; moral economic order 9; territorialised spaces 178
neoliberal moral economic order 20, 25
neoliberal moral order 178, 182
neoliberal political rationality 18
neoliberal social integration 159
neoliberal subjectification models 27
neopatrimonialism 113, 116–20
neopatrimonial state power, Roma subjection (documentation) 132
new order, establishment (sovereign power role) 10
Nietzsche, Friedrich 22
nomad governance 98–102
nomadic space 87
nomadic subjectivities 70–6, 93, 109; preservation 88
nomad self-governance 98, 101, 109; nomad-smooth economy, interactions 87–8
nomad/smooth space, navigation 88
non-metric space 171
normalisation 160

ongoing history 174–5
ontology of commandment 21
opportunities: field of opportunities, access 168–9; navigated fields of opportunities 88; Organization for Security and Cooperation in Europe (OSCE) 4, 7; securitisation programs 20
Orientalism 3, 28
Other: development/governance 7; enterprise, governing 23; European transnational government role 3; internal Other 3
overcoded, term (usage) 160–1

party politics, local public administration (interdependence) 117
patronage 45, 47, 53–5, 87, 92, 102, 108, 110, 113–30, 132–41, 143, 146–7, 169–70
patronage politics 113–30, 132–41, 143, 146; expression 116; local dynamics 117–20; restitution politics, transition 122; state-politics boundary 135–6; state-politics boundary and political brokers 135–6, 141, 147
Pentecostal ethics, translation 160
Pentecostalism: conversion 150, 152, 158; impact 152; Roma conversion 150; semiological state capture apparatus, contrast 149

Pentecostal religious practice 154–5
logic of police, governance 177
police 12, 15, 19–20, 40, 49–50, 55; government 12, 15, 20, 55; policing the poor 17
policing of the self 178–9, 182
political affirmation 178–9, 181–3; the political 178–83
political brokerage 124–5
political fields 113–20, 169; entanglement 127; usage 113
political parties 114–16, 120, 122–5, 128–9
political patronage 113–30
political patronage orientation 124
political re-subjectification 150
political space 113, 116–20, 130
political subject: Roma Pentecostalism 158–61; self-governance, relationship 149
political subjectivity 133, 146, 149, 153, 158
political subjectivity, securitisation 4–6, 8–9, 16–17, 18, 20–4, 27–8, 29–47; migration 4–6, 18, 22, 28; poverty 4–6, 14, 17–18, 23–5, 28–9, 32–3; subjection/submission regime, questioning 29
political transformations 39
political voting options, monopoly (creation) 128
politicisation 117–18
politics: construction, deterritorialising force 178; importance 127; informality, combination 118–19; local level politics 114–17; patronage politics 113, 120–3; restitution politics 120–3; Romani politics 113, 123–9; state accommodations/exploitations, contrast 136; transformational politics 180
population 4–7, 13, 17, 21–22, 24, 29, 32–3, 38, 40, 42, 48–54
population governance, paternalist model 49–50
positions, redistribution 53–4
post-developmental studies 31
post-1989 neopatrimonial system 119
post-socialism 32; mediator networks 97; socio-economic changes 33
post-socialism leadership: change 96; restoration 109–10
post-socialist economic uncertainty, social navigation 77–82
post-socialist patronage politics 116
post-socialist political space 113

post-socialist state 104–8
post-socialist transformations 88
poverty 167, 181; Eastern European occurrence 24; market economy failure 23; securitisation 18
power 29–47, 48–55; ascending analysis 171, 175; axiomatic apparatus 15–16; circulatory power, access 169–70; connectivity power, access 170; dynamics 37; entanglements 38; historical entanglements 48; historical geographies 170, 171, 174–6, 179, 181; loose power webs, circulatory power (access) 169–70; loose webs 123; macro-micro social histories 28; manifestation 47; micro and macro power 30, 37–9, 47; micro-power 39; network-like character 37; privatisation 113; self-transforming spaces 29; social body, co-extensiveness 39; social power, study (theoretical/ethnographical considerations) 37–9; stabilisation 119; state assemblages 78; study, reasons 29; symbolic power, mechanisms 182; violence, relation 22
power brokers 101, 123–4, 129–30, 169, 175; actions 123
power dynamics 32, 37, 174; empowerment and subjection to power 32–3, 54
power relations 30–3, 37–9, 48, 51–4, 88, 113–31, 169, 174–5; constraint 127–8; mapping, political fields (usage) 113; power struggles 170, 173–5
power spaces 175; dynamics 172; interaction, mobility approach 168–9; interaction, sedentarist approach 169; interrelation 173; intersectionality 52–3; movement 173; sedentary/mobile interaction, contrast 167
power struggle 101–2, 116; dynamic 54; spaces, transformation 39, 175
power to *vs.* power over 153–5, 159–60
practical knowledge 168
"Prince, The" (Machiavelli) 12
privatisation of power 54, 113; parcelisation of sovereignty 54
problematization, object 18
problem-space, shaping 13
proletarianisation 48; socialist programs 37
pure power 120–1

qualitative state intercession 10–11
quantitative state intercession 10–11

Index

Ranciere, Jacques 55, 176–83; dissensus 179–80, 183; logic of politics vs. logic of police 176–7, 178–9; the multiple 182–3; political subject 176–83; ruled-ruling 179–80; speaking subject 179, 181
reflexive modernisation 158
regimes of enunciations 182
regimes of truth 176, 182
relational dynamic space-time 174–5
relationality, forms (comparison) 155
relations, informal patterns 67
religious reflexivity 149, 154, 158
reproductive struggle 180
resistance, theorisation (criticism) 38
restitution politics 120–3, 125, 129–30; transition 122
reticulated movements, impact 101
reversal of values 119
role expectation/performance, coordination (absence) 139–40
Roma: allegiances 120–3; civil society, NGOisation 32; conditions 6; customs 154–5; entrepreneurship 26–7; experts, state broker role 104–8; formal employment 26–7; identity, control 142; inclusion 24; interactions 67; issues 105; labour market integration 7; leaders, transformations (interactions) 97; life, politics (importance) 127; local voting behaviour, transformations 124–5; marginalization 24, 26; measurement problems 24; mobile groups, protection 99; partnerships, requirement 6; pastors, partner status 159–60; Pentecostal pastors, subjection domains (relationship) 153–5; political voting options, monopoly (creation) 128; poverty, increase 23; regional offices 114–15; regular jobs, absence 25; slavery, abolishment 42; social integration 5; state, transformations 92, 97–8; subgroups 24; subjectivities, colonisation 178; unemployment/under-employment 26; voting behaviour, responsibility 123; vulnerability 25–7
Roma brokers 92–110, 123–4, 126, 129
Roma communities: empowerment 31–2; monitorisation, hierarchical bureaucratic apparatus 114
Roma Decade Program 28
Roma experts 93, 104–8, 110
Roma groups: diversity 24; interaction 39; socio-economic transformations 70
Roma integration: business engagement 27; government strategy 104
Roma leadership 92; discussion 108–10; local/regional political organisation 114–17; questions/references 97–8; state manoeuvre/capture mechanism 101; transformations 55
Romanian neopatrimonial political space (development), patronage politics (local dynamics) 117–20
Romania, socialism/post-socialism (shift) 48
Romani politics 113–30; independent political field 116–17
Roma Party: activist network development 96–7; councillor, election 106; national SDP political patronage 124; Sotu support 126; support, change 126
Roma Pentecostalism: conversion 150; political subject 158–61; self-affirmation 159; semiological state apparatus of capture 149, 158–61
Roma state and power brokers 169, 174–5
rule of law 9, 13–14, 19–20; market rationality, interdependence/ entanglement 20
rule of the market 20

SDP political ideology 133
second economy 49, 52, 69, 70–7, 84, 87–8
Securitate 92, 94–100, 109; collaboration 94; collaborators, impact 49–50, 94–5; co-optation 92–3; monitoring actions 73; relation 100
security 3–7, 18–19, 21, 24–8; development (relationship) 5; human security and development 5, 24–5
security risk 25
sedentary space of the state vs. nomad space 168
sedentary-striated spaces, interactions 87–8
self: affirmation 157–8, 159; pedagogies, promotion 16; redefinition 160–1
self-conduct, authoritarian depoliticised models (authorisation) 16–17
self-God 157
self-governance 92, 101; form 55; nomad self-governance 101; political subject, relationship 149; self-reliant, inter-modes 27
self-government 15, 22, 25–8, 33; associated forms 180; cells, movement (instability) 149–50; idiosyncratic

modes 178; model 33; neoliberal forms, architecture 22–23; neoliberal forms, incorporation 178; neoliberal models 28; techniques of the self 15
self-mastery, process 157–8
self-mediation 157
self-ministry 150, 155–8, 159; conceptual characteristics 159; dialogical self 153
self-policing, external policing (nexus) 20
self-reliance, cultivation 80
semiological apparatuses 7–8
semiological capture 179–80
semiological state apparatus of capture, Pentecostalism (contrast) 149
semiotics of social integration 150, 152, 154–5, 158–61; signature of governmental power 161
smooth space 171
social behaviour, management 14
Social Democrat Party (SDP) patronage 118; actors, impact 139
social government, impact 22
social inclusion local plan, implementation/incorporation 115
social integration 4–8, 18, 21, 22–8, 29–31, 33, 37, 55, 92, 167, 176–8, 180–2; marginalisation 6, 23, 25–6, 28–9, 32; neoliberal governmentality 180; questioning 180–1; social exclusion 23, 25, 28; vulnerability 24–5, 27–8, 32
social invention: Field of possibilities vs. Field of opportunities 88; use 88
socialism 97; assimilation, state project 167–8; continuity 51–2; post-socialism, parallel 108–9; second economy 70–6; shift 48, 67; socio-economic changes 33; state repression 70–6
socialist state violence, 149
socialist vs. post-socialist economy 70, 77
social lifestyles, emergence 48
social navigation 77–82
social power 167, 170–6, 179, 181, 183; complexity/dynamics, source 170; perspective (Foucault) 37–8; study 167
social power, study: contributions 33; theoretical/ethnographical considerations 37–9; theoretical/methodological framework 171
social relations, horizontality image (creation) 31–2
social space 170–2, 174–5; becoming vs. dwelling 171–2; expression 175; theory 170; understanding (Bourdieu), criticism 172

social structure 172, 174; social reproduction 172–5, 181
social taming, program 160
social welfare: recipients, governing 19; systems, asymmetrical Roma participation 26
society 5–6, 11–17, 19, 22, 24, 27, 29–30, 32, 37, 50, 113, 120, 135, 149, 160, 171, 178–9, 182; governing 15, 31, 179
socio-economic existence 159
socio-economic-political environment 39
socio-political organisation, forms 94
sovereign: judicial power 13; juridical theory 12
sovereign neoliberal power, usage 11
sovereign power 9–10, 12–13; increase 12; new order role 10
sovereignty, parcelisation 54
sovereign wealth, increase 12
space: boundaries 173; closed system, impossibility 172; dwelling, contrast 172; interaction, mobility approach 168–9; interaction, sedentarist approach 169; mobile understanding 172; navigation 101; nomadic space 87; non-metric space 171; perspective (Foucault) 37–8; power spaces 167; self-transforming spaces 29; smooth space 171; social space, expression 175
spaces of power struggles 35, 39, 113, 116
space-time- movement 172, 174
space turn studies 172, 174
state 4–5, 7, 9–16, 19, 24–7, 29–30, 32–3, 37–9, 42, 44–5, 47–55; accommodations/exploitations, politics (contrast) 136; apparatus, repression 101; brokerage, incomplete dissolution 169–70; capture 92, 98–104; centralisation 50; classificatory categories 134; economy, sedentary/striated space (interactions) 87; institutional structures, disciplined behaviour/integration 155; mappings 168; repression 70–6; rule of law 9, 13, 19–20; simplifications 168; striated/regulated space, correspondence 169; subjection, theoretical references 134–5; transformations 92; welfare, local distribution 128–9
state brokers 101, 175; Roma expert role 104–8
state bureaucrats: authority, undermining 144–5; personality, self-conceptions 140–1

state governance: alternative 13; semiology 150
state-led intervention, impact 11
statelessness 53
state membership and belonging 132, 134, 136, 146
State Neopatrimonial Power 170
state-patronage politics brokers, impact 122, 129
state-politics boundary 135–6
state power: sources 92; space, Roma leaders/transformations (interactions) 97
state social integration 159; apparatuses 92
state subjection 134–5
status quo: preservation 167; reproduction 33
street level bureaucracy 132; street level bureaucrats 135
subaltern (the) 167, 176–83; the governed 167, 178, 180–2; Political Subject and Subjectivity 168, 176–83; Sedentarist vs. Mobile Approach 167–70; Spaces of Power 167, 181; State Mappings vs. Tentative Mappings 168, 174
subalternity, categories 182
subject 3, 8, 9–21, 22–8, 29–47, 50, 54–5, 149–61; epistemological colonisation of the subject 22–8; epistemological decolonisation 28, 55; existence 178; neoliberalism, moral economic order 9; neoliberal subject subaltern subject 9–21; political subjectification 149–50, 152, 158–61; political will and affirmation vs. the governed 150; subjection 149, 152, 153–5, 158–9, 161
subject and knowledge 3, 22–3
subjectification 3, 10, 13, 16, 18, 22–5, 27–9, 32, 55, 177, 179–83; category (vulnerability) 24; labour power 177–8, 182; neoliberalism 177–8, 180–3; the political 177, 180–3; political re-subjectification 150; state mechanism 55; subjectification of labour power by the capital 10, 25, 27
subjection domains, Roma Pentecostal pastors (relationship) 153–5
subjection to state power 92, 110
subjectivity, types 75
subordination, liberal understandings 157–8
surveillance 19, 47–9, 75–6, 87, 92, 96, 132, 134, 142; securitate 49–50, 92, 94–6; spying infrastructure 50; state centralisation 50

survival: economic survival 75; possibilities, stability 83–7
symbolic patronage 120–1
symbolic power 101; mechanisms 182; and violence 167, 176, 178, 182

targeted populations, identification apparatuses/mechanisms 7–8
techniques of government 13, 15
technologies of power 168
temporal relational dynamic, social space expression 175
tentative mappings 39, 81, 88, 168, 174
territorialisation *vs.* deterritorialisation 178, 183
territorial sedentarisation 33
transformation 98; agent 167; economic transformations 39; focus 175; forms 39; individuals, interaction 173; macro-social transformations 39; mechanisms 38–9; political transformations 39; post-socialist transformations 88; power manifestation 47
transformational politics 180; citizenship 180
transition 4, 6, 9, 10, 16, 23–4, 26, 32, 51–2, 78, 119, 122–3, 130, 134, 136, 169, 172–3; de-collectivisation 51–2; de-industrialisation 51–3; informal economy 26, 35, 47
trans-local authorities, relations 74
transnational government power/enactments 7–8
transnational neoliberal governmentality 9–21; neoliberal governmental power 9–10, 15, 22, 24
transversal movement 173
truth: regimes 182; self-definition 183

uncertainty 81
United Nations 7
United Nations Development Program (UNDP) 4, 167; human rights, realisation 9

values: community of values, ministerial power 153; reversal 119
vernacular forms of knowledge and self-government 168, 178–82
vernacular self-government 149, 161
vertical movement 172–3; position, reproduction 173
violence, power (relation) 22
void, epistemological liberation 179

votes: buying, susceptibility 125; local distribution, control 108
voting: intentions 155; mechanism 141; option, influences 155
vulnerability 182; analysis 25; concept 24–5; epistemological category 27; ethnicity, association (absence) 27; group affiliation, association (absence) 27; Roma vulnerability, displacement 25; security risk 25; subjectification category 24
vulnerable: category 29–30; social integration 6–7

war machine, expression 109, 150
wealth: accumulation 75; production 80
welfare: local distribution 127; spending, requirements (reduction) 28
welfare state 15–16, 134, 146; governmentality 15–16
West, Orientalism 3
World Bank (WB) 167; agenda, setting 10–11; assistance 20; best practice 11; country assistance 10; international actor 4